AI-Driven Inno
in Healthca

The integration of artificial intelligence (AI) in healthcare organizations is no longer a futuristic concept—it's here, reshaping patient care, optimizing operational efficiency, and enhancing diagnostic accuracy. While AI offers immense potential, finding its practical applications and scaling its implementation are fraught with both technical and practical challenges, including data security, ethical concerns, regulatory practices, and workforce adaptation. For digital health leaders, adopting AI successfully requires a deep understanding of not only the technology itself but also the organizational and human factors that can make or break its success. *AI-Driven Innovations in Healthcare* is a practical guide designed to help digital health and IT professionals, chief medical information officers, administrators, and policymakers navigate these complexities and leverage AI to achieve sustainable improvements in care delivery.

This book is not a technical manual on AI algorithms, but rather a guide to show how leaders are adopting AI within their own healthcare organization or practice. The book includes contributions from multiple executives and academics, with chapters focused around AI's place in helping to create innovations in healthcare operations, design, and delivery.

This book draws on real-world case studies, spotlighting successful attempts to implement AI in a range of healthcare environments, from small clinics to major hospital systems. The book begins with an overview of AI's role in healthcare and its key applications, such as predictive analytics, personalized treatment planning, robotic surgery, and administrative automation. Each chapter also features case studies and expert insights from leading healthcare organizations that have successfully navigated the AI adoption process. These examples will provide practical lessons and real-life scenarios to help readers anticipate challenges and proactively design solutions. Each chapter is organized into similar sections for each organization's case study: strategy and vision for AI, implementation best practices, initial results, challenges, and future opportunities.

AI-Driven Innovations in Healthcare

Best Practices and Case Studies

Edited by
James R. Langabeer, PhD and Karima Lalani, PhD

Routledge
Taylor & Francis Group
A PRODUCTIVITY PRESS BOOK

Designed cover image: Shutterstock

First published 2026
by Routledge
605 Third Avenue, New York, NY 10158

and by Routledge
4 Park Square, Milton Park, Abingdon, Oxon, OX14 4RN

Routledge is an imprint of the Taylor & Francis Group, an informa business

ISBN: 978-1-041-02889-5 (hbk)
ISBN: 978-1-041-02888-8 (pbk)
ISBN: 978-1-003-62129-4 (ebk)

DOI: 10.4324/9781003621294

Typeset in Garamond
by Deanta Global Publishing Services, Chennai, India

To all the healthcare information innovators around the world who dare to challenge the status quo—may your vision and determination drive the exponential advancements that will reshape the future of health. This book is for you.

Contents

PART 3 AI FOR SMARTER HEALTHCARE OPERATIONS

Preface

The past few years have marked a turning point in how artificial intelligence is shaping the future of healthcare. Across clinical, operational, and administrative domains, AI is no longer a distant promise—it is an active force driving change, delivering tangible improvements in quality, efficiency, and patient safety. From predictive analytics that reduce hospital readmissions to natural language processing tools that ease documentation burdens, we are witnessing an extraordinary wave of innovation. Healthcare systems, insurers, and technology vendors are all starting to embrace AI in multiple ways.

This book was conceived by the editors in response to the magnitude of discussions and presentations we have seen at conferences and meetings throughout the country that focus on the intersection of AI and healthcare. We were struck by the volume and depth of real-world applications being presented; solutions not just in pilot stages, but in some cases embedded within systems of care that deliver measurable outcomes. We wanted these stories needed to be shared more broadly.

In this edited volume, we bring together some of the leading voices from across the healthcare ecosystem—clinicians, data scientists, health IT professionals, policy experts, and innovators—each offering a perspective on how AI is transforming their corner of the system. The chapters span a diverse range of use cases, from diagnostic support in radiology to AI-powered dentistry, from workforce optimization to fraud detection.

Together, these contributions offer more than just a snapshot of progress—they illuminate a roadmap for responsibly scaling AI in ways that align with the core mission of healthcare: to deliver high-quality, equitable, and safe care to all. We are grateful to the many contributors who shared their insights, and to the broader technology community for recognizing the importance of fostering collaboration and dialogue in this rapidly evolving space.

We hope this book serves as both inspiration and a guide, showing what's possible when technology is harnessed with intention, care, and a commitment to better health outcomes.

— James R. Langabeer, PhD and Karima Lalani, PhD
Editors

About the Editors

James R. Langabeer, PhD, MBA, FHIMSS, is an Executive Director and tenured full professor of Biomedical Informatics at the University of Texas Health Science Center, a major academic medical center in the Texas Medical Center. He has led numerous large-scale data-driven projects focused on behavioral, cardiovascular, and addiction medicine. He is a trusted advisor to policymakers and firms around technology, operations, finance, and strategy and the author of more than 150 scientific publications and 7 books including *Essentials of Healthcare Strategy and Performance Management* (2024). Prior to this, Dr Langabeer served as the founder and CEO of a large health information exchange company and was the Executive Vice President of a mid-sized global software and consulting firm. James graduated with a PhD in Operations Research from the University of Lancaster (England) and has deep expertise in data science and decision-making. He also has an MBA from Baylor University and received additional training from the University of Chicago Booth School of Business in behavioral economics and decision-making. He is Fellow of HIMSS and a former national committee chair. His insights have been featured in *Oprah*, *Forbes*, *Success Magazine*, and he has made live appearances on all of the major news networks.

Karima Lalani, PhD, MBA, RHIA, FACHE, is Director of the Health Informatics and Health Information Management (HIHIM) programs and Assistant Teaching Professor at the University of Washington School of Public Health in Seattle. She holds a PhD in Health Policy and Management from The University of Texas Health Science Center School of Public Health and brings over 15 years of experience in healthcare workforce development, strategic planning, and digital health. A Fellow of the American College of Healthcare Executives (FACHE) and a Registered Health Information Administrator (RHIA), Dr Lalani is a recognized leader at the intersection of healthcare, education, and technology. She has authored more than 20 peer-reviewed publications and is a sought-after collaborator on interdisciplinary initiatives. Through her leadership, teaching, and research, she continues to shape the future of health informatics, championing innovation and collaboration in healthcare systems worldwide.

List of Contributors

Eric Alper, MD, is SVP, Chief Quality Officer, and Chief Clinical Informatics Officer at UMass Memorial Health Care and Professor of Medicine at UMass Chan Medical School. In addition to his clinical work in Hospital Medicine for the last 25 years, Dr Alper is a seasoned physician executive, having served as the primary physician champion for two large Epic implementations. He has led many clinical and operational improvements. He has served as executive sponsor for UMass Memorial's digital health strategy, Hospital at Home, and other care-at-home strategies. Dr Alper received his medical degree at UMass Medical School and is board-certified in Internal Medicine and Clinical Informatics.

Jan Beger is the Global Head of AI Advocacy at GE HealthCare and a certified medical radiology technologist trained in Germany. With over 20 years of experience in healthcare informatics, medical imaging, and AI, he works to bridge the gap between cutting-edge technology and clinical practice. He is the Executive Director of HelloAI, a global AI education program for healthcare professionals, and the founder of GR4AI.Academy, a nonprofit promoting early AI literacy among children. Jan previously launched and led GE HealthCare's startup and healthcare provider collaboration program, which fostered co-development of AI-enabled digital health solutions. His work focuses on equipping clinicians with the tools and understanding to confidently adopt AI and improve patient care.

Parminder Bhatia, MS. Parry Bhatia is Chief AI Officer at GE HealthCare, where he focuses on integrating AI across medical devices, hospital operations, and the patient journey. He serves on GE HealthCare's internal committee for responsible AI and has been recognized by Modern Healthcare's 40 Under 40, AIM AI 100, and Constellation Research's AI 150. Previously, he was Head of Applied Science at Amazon, developing healthcare machine learning products like Amazon Comprehend Medical and generative AI products like Amazon Q. He has also held research roles at Microsoft and Georgia Tech. Parry holds degrees from the Indian Institute of Technology and Georgia Tech.

Crystal Broj, CPDHTS, is the Enterprise Chief Digital Transformation Officer at the Medical University of South Carolina, where she leads innovative initiatives to improve healthcare through technology. With a background spanning healthcare, insurance, nonprofit, and tech sectors, she brings a fresh, cross-industry perspective to digital strategy. Her work focuses on AI integration, automation, and patient-centered design. Crystal is a national speaker and award-winning leader in digital transformation.

Kerryn Butler-Henderson, PhD, FAIDH, is Head, School of Nursing, Paramedicine and Healthcare Sciences at Charles Sturt University. She is a well-respected digital health academic, with more than 20 years of experience working in health and higher education. She is known for her expertise in digital health, particularly in workforce and digital health implementation science research. Kerryn is an inaugural executive leader of the Australian Council of Senior Academic Leaders in Digital Health and Fellow of the Australasian Institute of Digital Health (AIDH). She was recognized for her expertise in 2021 as a Future50 Health IT Leader by HIMSS and in 2022 as a Telstra Health Brilliant Women of Digital Health Award recipient.

Tiffany Champagne-Langabeer, PhD, MBA, RD, is Associate Professor at the UTHealth McWilliams School of Biomedical Informatics. Her research on the use of telemedicine, health information exchanges, public health, and substance use has been published in over 70 journals and multiple books, including *Essentials of Healthcare Strategy and Performance Management* (2024). Dr Champagne-Langabeer is the Director of Research and Co-Investigator of the Houston Emergency Opioid Engagement System (HEROES), a national clinical trial providing comprehensive treatment for individuals suffering from opioid use disorder. Previously, she was the founding Vice President of the largest health information exchange in Texas. Dr Champagne-Langabeer is also a registered and licensed dietitian. She is Fellow of the Healthcare Information and Management Systems Society.

Elisabeth R. Garwood, MD, serves as the Associate Chief Medical Informatics Officer of AI for UMass Memorial Health and Vice Chair of AI for the Department of Radiology. She co-chairs the UMass Responsible AI committee, leading the effort to operationalize governance and evaluation processes for health AI tools at UMass. She contributed writing and expertise to the development of the 2024 assurance standards guide for the Coalition for Health AI (CHAI), a coalition establishing the guidelines and guardrails for health AI technologies. Dr Garwood is a practicing musculoskeletal radiologist and completed her radiology residency training at the University of California, San Francisco, and her fellowship at New York University.

Kathleen Gray, PhD, FAIDH, OAM, is Professor of Health Informatics at The University of Melbourne. She has worked across health science and information science disciplines for three decades to improve the quality of digital health education and research. She has collaborated on numerous projects to design, implement, and evaluate patient- and citizen-centered digital health innovations. Her interests also include digital health workforce development and digital contributions to health system sustainability. She publishes extensively and is active in national and international forums, such as the Australian Council of Senior Academic Leaders in Digital Health and the *International Journal of Medical Informatics*.

Archita Jain, BSc, DDS, was raised in Toronto, Ontario, Canada, where she earned her undergraduate degree in Biomedical Sciences from York University. She went on to receive her Doctor of Dental Surgery from the University of Minnesota School of Dentistry. During dental school, she held several leadership roles, including Student Ambassador, Academic Tutor, and Teaching Assistant, reflecting her dedication to dental education. Her passion for working with special needs children, developed through roles as a leisure buddy and integration counselor for the City of Vaughan, led her to complete the MNLEND fellowship. This experience deepened her commitment to inclusive care and interdisciplinary collaboration. Dr Jain aspires to contribute to evidence-based research that enhances patient outcomes and advances clinical practice in dentistry.

Lisa Lucadamo Jarrett, MBA, MIS, is a product executive with over 20 years of experience in software, SaaS, cloud, data, analytics, and AI. Her work has spanned strategy, software, and services in multiple industries for Fortune 500 companies at IBM. Lisa's work over the past ten years has focused on healthcare data platforms and AI solutions, beginning with Watson Health, with ongoing efforts for acute care and provider identity management, and for payers focused on healthcare credentialing and network builds. Lisa's passion lies in leveraging health data, analytics, and AI to improve patient outcomes and accelerate healthcare efficiency, evidenced by work across most healthcare segments. She is an energetic advocate for Responsible AI (RAI), establishing cross-functional frameworks and delivering AI capabilities that are fair, transparent, ethical, and impactful to health organizations. Currently leading the AI and Data platform product team at PointClickCare, she is dedicated to transforming care in post-acute settings and for vulnerable populations.

Taha Kass-Hout, MD, MS, is the Global Chief Science and Technology Officer at GE HealthCare, where he leads innovation at the intersection of healthcare, AI, and machine learning. A trained interventional cardiologist, Dr Kass-Hout is advancing AI-enabled medical imaging, diagnostics, and health system efficiency. He chairs the AdvaMed Digital Health Tech Division Board of Directors. Previously, he held executive roles at Amazon, including Chief Medical Officer and VP of Machine Learning, where he led key health AI initiatives and COVID-19 diagnostics. Dr Kass-Hout was also the first Chief Health Informatics Officer at the FDA and formerly led informatics at the CDC. He holds an MD and an MS in Biostatistics from the University of Texas Health Science Center.

David Kim, MBA, is the Founder and Chief Executive Officer of Compass Health Advisors. He has over 25 years of experience as a trusted IT strategic advisor to executives at leading healthcare organizations seeking to navigate the short- and long-term impacts of alternative payment methodologies and value-based care delivery. Before founding Compass Health Advisors, Mr Kim served in numerous leadership roles at other healthcare consulting firms, where he led practice and services development related to digital health enablement. He is a frequent speaker at industry forums, board retreats, and conferences and has been published on numerous topics related to Digital Health, Value-Cased Care, and Population Health Management. Mr Kim holds an MBA from Columbia University Graduate School of Business. He received his BA in Government from Cornell University.

Sarah Lalani is a medical student at the Perelman School of Medicine at the University of Pennsylvania and an honors graduate of the Canfield Business Honors Program at the McCombs School of Business, University of Texas at Austin. Her interdisciplinary education in business and medicine uniquely positions her to analyze healthcare trends and policies through a financial lens. Currently, Ms Lalani is involved in three research teams focusing on hospital mergers and acquisitions as well as safety-net pharmacy policy. She has presented her research at numerous conferences, including the 2023 American College of Cardiology Annual Meeting and the 2025 Society of General Internal Medicine Annual Meeting. Ms Lalani is dedicated to leveraging her medical education to influence healthcare policy and advocate for patients in need.

Zahid Lalani, BDS, MDS, MBA, PhD, FDSRCS, FFDRCSI, FACHE, is Assistant Professor of Oral & Maxillofacial Surgery at the University of Washington School of Dentistry and an Attending Surgeon at the University of Washington Medical Center, Harborview Hospital, and

Seattle Children's Hospital. His research explores the role of growth factors and cytokines in jawbone healing as well as the use of biomaterials to enhance tissue regeneration. Dr Lalani's research work has been funded by AO North America and the Walter Lorenz Corporation, and he was Co-Investigator on an NIH R01 grant in collaboration with the UT School of Dentistry and Rice University. Prior to transitioning to academia, Dr Lalani spent 18 years in private practice in Houston, Texas. He has an Executive MBA in Healthcare Leadership from Yale University School of Management and is Fellow of the American College of Healthcare Executives.

David T. Marc, PhD, is Associate Professor, Department Chair, and Health Informatics Graduate Program Director in the Health Informatics and Information Management department at The College of St. Scholastica. Currently, Dr Marc teaches courses on healthcare data analytics and research. Dr Marc has a master's degree in biological sciences from the University of Minnesota and a PhD in health informatics from the University of Minnesota. He also holds a certification as a health data analyst (CHDA). Dr Marc has extensive experience working with large healthcare datasets and analytical procedures. Dr Marc is an active member of AMIA, AHIMA, and HIMSS and serves on various committees within these professional organizations. Prior to working for The College of St. Scholastica, Dr Marc was employed at a biotech company where he applied a variety of analytic approaches to investigate the predictive value of biomarkers for psychiatric diseases.

Max P. Rosen, MD, MPH, is the UMass Memorial Chair in Radiology at UMass Memorial Medical Center and Professor of Radiology at UMass Chan Medical School, both in Worcester, Massachusetts. A graduate of Brown University, Tufts Medical School, and the Harvard School of Public Health, he completed his Diagnostic Radiology residency in 1991 at Boston City Hospital, followed by a fellowship in Vascular and Interventional Radiology at Massachusetts General Hospital. Prior to joining UMass, Dr Rosen held a variety of clinical and leadership roles at Beth Israel Deaconess Medical Center in Boston, MA. His research interests include studying the clinical effectiveness of a wide variety of imaging and interventional procedures, and the use of eye tracking to better understand how radiologists interpret images.

Rita Suhuyini Salifu, PhD, is a highly experienced public health specialist with over 18 years of experience in public health, education programs, and community-based interventions. Her research focuses on critical areas such as nutrition, HIV/AIDS, maternal and child health, malaria, neglected tropical diseases, and health systems strengthening. She is widely recognized for her ability to connect public health research with practical implementation, working across academic institutions, policy think tanks, and community initiatives. Dr Salifu holds a PhD in Public Health from the University of KwaZulu-Natal (South Africa), an MA in International Health from the University of Copenhagen (Denmark), and a BSc in Community Nutrition from the University for Development Studies (Ghana).

David A. Shoultz, PhD, MBA, is the inaugural Chief Scientific Officer (CSO) at the Myeloproliferative Neoplasm (MPN) Research Foundation. He was appointed to this role in January 2025. He is also Affiliate Professor in the Department of Epidemiology at the University of Washington and is also on the Board of Directors at Proteotype Diagnostics. Dr Shoultz earned his bachelor's degree, MS, and PhD from the University of Washington in Seattle. His MBA is from the Albers School of Business & Economics at Seattle University, where he was previously a faculty member in the Executive MBA Program. Beyond MPN, he has a special interest in other hematologic malignancies and cancers as well as infectious diseases—including those of importance in low- and middle-income countries (LMIC). Dr Shoultz currently teaches courses on epidemiology in the Master of Health Informatics and Health Information Management (MHIHIM) program and the Master of Health Administration (MHA) program at the University of Washington.

John R. Williford is a transformational senior healthcare executive with over two decades of leadership in complex, multi-site healthcare operations. Currently Vice President of Population Health at Montefiore Health System and the Chief Operating Officer of its Care Management Organization, he has led large-scale operational turnarounds, value-based care initiatives, and integrated delivery systems across Medicare, Medicaid, and commercial populations. His expertise spans strategic planning, P&L management, data-driven care transformation, and executive coaching. John's prior leadership roles include executive positions at ArchCare, Sandata Technologies, iHealth Technologies, and global consultancies such as Deloitte and Capgemini. A frequent speaker at international health summits, he holds a BA in International Studies from the University of North Carolina and has completed executive training at the Harvard Law School.

Acknowledgments

Bringing this book to life has been a deeply collaborative effort, and it is with heartfelt gratitude that we acknowledge the many people who contributed to its development. First and foremost, we extend our sincere thanks to our co-authors. Each of you brought unique insights, dedication, and expertise that enriched every chapter. Collaborating across disciplines, time zones, and schedules is no small feat, and your commitment to quality and collegiality made this project not only possible but truly rewarding.

We are also grateful to our families, friends, and colleagues for their patience and encouragement throughout the long hours of writing, editing, and revision. Your support sustained us through deadlines and revisions.

A special thanks goes to Kris Mednansky at Routledge Publishing and JoAnn Klinedinst at Informa Connect, whose passion and guidance for this subject helped shape this book into its final form. Your professionalism and vision were invaluable. Finally, we acknowledge the broader community of researchers, practitioners, and readers whose work and engagement continue to inspire us. It is our hope that this book contributes meaningfully to the ongoing conversations in our field.

Thank you all.

TRANSFORMING THE CONTINUUM OF CARE

1

We are entering a world where we will learn to coexist with AI, not as its masters, but as its collaborators.

Mark Zuckerberg, CEO of Meta

DOI: 10.4324/9781003621294-1

Chapter 1

Towards AI and Human Collaboration

James R. Langabeer, PhD and Karima Lalani, PhD

Artificial intelligence (AI) has emerged as a transformative force in healthcare, promising to revolutionize how we diagnose, treat, and manage diseases. From predictive analytics that forecast patient outcomes to machine learning algorithms that assist in medical imaging, AI has the potential to reshape the healthcare landscape. In the subsequent chapters, we aim to provide a comprehensive overview of real-world evidence and best practices for implementing AI in healthcare.

1.1 Big Data and the Emergence of AI

We should start this book with a baseline definition for artificial intelligence. It has advanced through many names over the years—expert systems, deep learning, intelligent decision support systems, neural networks, machine learning, and cognitive computing, to name a few. We will define AI here as: *any application, machine, or system that can perform human-like intelligence, in terms of behaving, sensing, learning, reasoning, and decision-making.* More specifically, AI brings together computers and humans to collaborate to improve functions and outcomes, and most applications focus on *automation, data processing, personalization, and analytics.* Most importantly, AI learns from human interactions, adapting and improving performance.

AI can trace its origin to a summer conference at Dartmouth College in the 1950s (Dartmouth, 2025). Researchers were just beginning to hypothesize that computers could eventually have the power of "human intelligence" by becoming more cognizant "thinking machines" (Copeland, 2024). This idea stemmed from harnessing the fields of mathematics and computer science to allow computers to support human decision-making more naturally. Since that time, there has been significant progress, but only recently, in the last decade, have we seen an explosion in the development of AI tools that can truly automate and predict both basic and advanced processes. This technology has moved into many industries, including technology and retail. However, one of the most significant opportunities lies in the healthcare industry.

DOI: 10.4324/9781003621294-2

Remember, the conceptualization of AI came decades before the invention of a cellular phone that could receive digital and voice signals. This was decades before an iPhone or a BlackBerry. At that time, computers were the size of giant rooms and were primarily used for functions like bank record keeping or space flights. Before technology became democratized or ubiquitous, with over 70% of the world's population having a small computer in their pocket, it was virtually inconceivable to imagine computers assisting with all sorts of daily actions. Science fiction movies like Star Trek imagined a handheld device that allowed people to communicate, which inspired the original cellular phone, developed in the 1970s by Motorola (Sloane, 2016). Artificial intelligence is no longer the subject of science fiction—it is here now, and a practical, increasingly indispensable tool that is reshaping industries across the globe. Among these, healthcare stands as perhaps the most consequential.

As most consumers know, AI can be highly transactional, using *agents* to answer questions (e.g., a chatbot). But AI is much more than that. From diagnostic imaging to personalized medicine, from streamlining hospital operations to predicting disease outbreaks, the applications of AI in healthcare are numerous.

This book is about these transformations. It is not a hypothetical inquiry into what artificial intelligence *might* mean for future care delivery. Instead, it is a grounded exploration of how AI is *currently* being applied to solve real problems in healthcare—and what this means for patients, providers, researchers, and the broader systems in which they operate.

1.2 Built on Data: Enter AI

We are living through a time when data are redefining medicine. Estimates suggest that there are several billion *zettabytes* worth of electronic health data. A zettabyte equals one sextillion bytes, or 10^{21} (Gregersen, 2025). That is a lot of data, and it has become virtually impossible to use it without computer support. With the proliferation of electronic health records, wearable sensors, labs, medical imaging technologies, genomic sequencing, and mobile health apps, modern healthcare generates an overwhelming volume of information. Clinicians and administrators face a flood of data, often too vast and complex to process unaided. Traditional analysis methods struggle to keep up with the velocity and variability of health-related data.

Artificial intelligence offers tools to sift through this data, identify patterns, make predictions, and suggest probable interventions. Machine learning *algorithms*—rules or procedural calculations—help detect early signs of disease, flag anomalies, and recommend treatment pathways. Sometimes the accuracy of AI rivals or exceeds that of experienced professionals (e.g., consider electrocardiogram (EKG) machines that read electrical patterns and detect heart attacks). Natural language processing (NLP) can extract relevant insights from unstructured text like clinical notes, research articles, and patient queries. AI-powered robots can assist in surgeries, automate administrative tasks, and even offer empathetic responses in mental health settings. The range of possibilities is staggering.

Yet, for all the promise AI holds, deployment presents unique challenges. Clinical environments are complex, and safety and quality are vital. It also tends to rely on human contact. We will need to consider ethical standards, maintain transparency, earn the trust of clinicians and patients, and deliver accurate outcomes. A misdiagnosis from an AI system isn't just a simple mistake; it could be a matter of life and death. Even more importantly, decisions are rarely binary. They often require nuance, empathy, and a deep understanding of patient context, culture, and values. These are all areas where human judgment still prevails. This tension between AI's power and medicine's complexity sets the stage for the chapters ahead.

1.3 Guiding Principles

In this book, we will read real-world evidence to show the successes and challenges of AI implementation across the healthcare system. You'll hear from clinicians and administrators using AI tools daily and researchers developing tomorrow's models. You'll gain insight into regulatory hurdles, policy discussions, and the evolving standards that aim to make AI safe, equitable, and scalable. As you read these chapters, we offer some guidance about AI overall.

Collaboration over replacement. We suggest you consider AI an adjunct to achieving your goals and work processes. AI is not here to replace providers or technicians, but rather to augment our abilities, serve as an extension of the employee, and relieve people of routine tasks. This should allow for better focus on the quality of care and human interactions.

Data is foundational to AI. We have all heard the adage "garbage in, garbage out". Data cleansing and transformation remain essential steps, as they are with any electronic health record system. The quality, diversity, and integrity of data determine the effectiveness of any AI system. Addressing issues of data bias and representativeness is crucial to building trustworthy tools.

Ethics and change management remain vital. Deploying AI in healthcare without rigorous attention to ethical standards harms patients and erodes public trust. Mechanisms for accountability, fairness, and explainability must accompany every application. In addition, successful deployment will take change management, training, and the development of internal trust.

As we proceed, this book will explore these concepts through multiple lenses. We will examine clinical applications such as diagnostic imaging and behavioral health. We will look at operational applications for the workforce, finance, and fraud. We will delve into the underlying technologies—machine learning, deep learning, NLP, reinforcement learning—and hopefully explain them in accessible terms for readers who may not have a technical background. We'll also discuss aspects of regulations and ethical challenges surrounding usage.

1.4 Subsequent Chapters

These chapters are organized into three parts:

1. **Transforming the Continuum of Care.** In Chapters 2–5, we will highlight various use cases in which AI is shaping the future of medicine, innovating staff engagement, and enhancing patient access to care.
2. **AI Across the Healthcare Ecosystem.** Chapters 6–9 glimpse AI's breadth of impact within the healthcare ecosystem—from dentistry and oral health to addressing public health challenges, defining the future of radiology, and providing tools for life sciences innovation.
3. **AI for Smarter Healthcare Operations.** Chapters 10–13 allow readers to discover AI's impact on healthcare finance, operations, fraud mitigation, and workforce development.

The intelligent transformation of healthcare has begun. Let's explore it together.

References

Copeland, B. J. (2024). History of artificial intelligence (AI). Britannica. Retrieved May 1, 2025, from https://www.britannica.com/technology/artificial-intelligence/History-of-artificial-intelligence

Dartmouth. (2025). *Artificial intelligence coined at Dartmouth.* https://home.dartmouth.edu/about/artificial-intelligence-ai-coined-dartmouth.

Gregersen, E. (2025). Big data: Computer science. Britannica. Retrieved May 10, 2025, from https://www.britannica.com/technology/big-data

Sloane, P. (2016). Think like an innovator: 76 inspiring business lessons from the world's greatest thinkers and innovators. Pearson Education Ltd.

Chapter 2

AI in Healthcare and Medicine: Shaping the Future

Parminder Bhatia, MS, Jan Beger, and
Taha Kass-Hout, MD, MS

2.1 Strategy and Vision for AI in Healthcare

The exponential growth of healthcare data presents both a significant challenge and an unprecedented opportunity. Medical knowledge now doubles every 72 days (Lawry, 2023), with over 3,500 medical articles published daily (PubMed, 2024). Radiologists analyze up to 50,000 images per shift—a tenfold increase over the past 15 years. Yet, despite this surge in data, only 3% of healthcare information is actively utilized, leaving the remaining 97% untapped (Dutta et al., 2019). This underutilization underscores the need for advanced AI technologies capable of unlocking the latent value embedded in these vast datasets to transform care pathways.

Simultaneously, global healthcare systems face acute workforce shortages. The Association of American Medical Colleges (AAMC) projects a shortfall of nearly 42,000 radiologists in the U.S. alone (Stempniak, 2020). This projection is part of a broader anticipated shortfall of up to 124,000 physicians across various specialties. Burnout is pervasive among clinicians, with 49% of radiologists reporting it. According to Medscape's 2022 Physician Burnout & Depression Report, radiology was tied for the eighth position among medical specialties with the highest degrees of physician burnout, with 49% of radiologists reporting burnout (Bailey et al., 2022). Inefficiencies in healthcare workflows, among other factors, only serve to intensify these pressures.

Inefficiencies in the UK's National Health Service result in 13.5 million lost working hours annually due to inadequate IT systems, equivalent to the work of 8,000 doctors (Gokal et al., 2022). Clinicians face growing administrative demands, particularly time spent on electronic health records (EHRs), which detracts from patient care. In the U.S., physicians dedicate 49% of office time to EHRs and only 27% to direct patient interactions, often adding hours of personal data entry at night (Sinsky et al., 2016).

It is possible to address these systemic inefficiencies by strategically utilizing artificial intelligence to streamline workflows, automate routine tasks, and deliver insights from complex data. AI is not a single technology but rather a collection of diverse technologies, each with specific

DOI: 10.4324/9781003621294-3

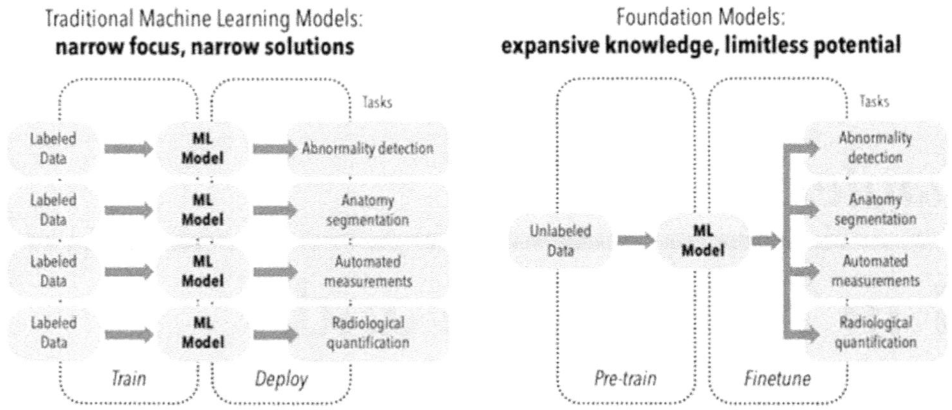

Figure 2.1 A new era of AI—Foundation models create more flexibility and faster scalability to unleash unprecedented efficiencies.

capabilities. Most of these are highly relevant to healthcare, streamlining processes and supporting various tasks while simultaneously alleviating the burden on healthcare providers and enhancing patient care. Traditional machine learning techniques often fall short when faced with the vast complexity of modern healthcare, as they are typically designed to solve specific, narrow problems.

To overcome the limitations of traditional machine learning techniques and narrow AI systems, a new paradigm has emerged: foundation models (Zhou et al., 2024). These represent a groundbreaking evolution in AI, offering unprecedented scalability and adaptability. Unlike other machine learning approaches, foundation models are pre-trained on massive and diverse datasets, enabling them to generalize across multiple challenges, often with minimal retraining. Their scalability and adaptability empower them to integrate disparate data types—imaging, genomics, and electronic health records—offering a comprehensive approach to complex medical problems (Mahesh et al., 2024). This scalability not only enhances operational efficiency but also allows healthcare organizations to address diverse clinical needs. It also ensures that healthcare providers can deploy AI solutions efficiently across varied settings, from large urban hospitals to remote clinics, fostering equity in healthcare delivery. By fine-tuning foundation models to align with specific workflows or specialties, these systems ensure that AI solutions are precisely tailored to healthcare's unique needs. By moving beyond task-specific AI, these models unlock the potential to address healthcare's complex challenges in a more holistic and integrated manner.

One of the notable features of foundation models is their ability to process multimodal data, integrating information from imaging, genomics, histology, and electronic health record (EHR) into cohesive insights. This integration supports a holistic understanding of patient health, paving the way for more accurate diagnoses and personalized treatments. For instance, studies have demonstrated the potential of foundation models to unify disparate healthcare data, enhancing both diagnostic accuracy and clinical decision-making (Li et al., 2024).

By transitioning from a "1-to-1" paradigm, where individual AI systems are developed for each task, to a "1-to-many" framework, foundation models simplify development and scaling. They function as universal backbones for healthcare applications, streamlining processes and enabling efficient deployment across diverse clinical scenarios (Bommasani et al., 2021).

Foundation models are already driving innovation in healthcare. Their capacity to generalize across tasks with minimal fine-tuning makes them particularly valuable for applications ranging from disease diagnosis and drug discovery to personalized treatment planning. For example, in diagnostic imaging, foundation models trained on multimodal datasets have demonstrated superior performance in detecting diseases, such as cancers, across different imaging modalities (Pai et al., 2023; Wilson et al., 2024). Similarly, their ability to integrate EHRs with genomic data is enhancing the predictive power of precision medicine tools, enabling tailored interventions for complex conditions (Robertson et al., 2024).

To take advantage of these advancements and transform healthcare with AI, collaboration with vendors is critical. By customizing foundation models for seamless integration into clinical environments, vendors help healthcare providers focus on deployment and adoption, alleviating technical complexities. Through collaboration, vendors offer expertise in optimizing models for seamless deployment, integrating them into clinical workflows while addressing technical and organizational challenges. With input from clinicians and administrators, vendors are able to ensure that these models are practical, user-friendly, and aligned with real-world clinical needs.

A key advantage of foundation models lies in their ability to bridge the gaps between siloed data sources, heterogeneous data formats, and modalities, thereby enhancing interoperability. By providing clinicians with a comprehensive view of patient health, these models enable more informed decision-making and improved outcomes in complex cases. For instance, integrating imaging data with EHRs has been shown to improve the identification of risk factors for chronic diseases and streamline treatment pathways (Najjar, 2023).

Fully realizing their potential requires scalable infrastructure that supports seamless data exchange and interoperability, accommodating complex workflows and diverse data types. Strategically deploying these technologies can unlock underutilized healthcare data, supporting a more patient-centered approach with real-time, evidence-based insights. The strategic value of AI, particularly foundation models, lies not only in addressing current inefficiencies but also in shaping the future of healthcare. They are driving a transition from reactive, fragmented healthcare systems to cohesive, predictive ecosystems. By transforming these systems, foundation models enable healthcare to proactively manage patient needs, improve outcomes, and reduce costs.

Their versatility and scalability empower clinicians by delivering real-time, evidence-based insights, optimizing workflows, and reducing administrative burdens. For example, by automating routine tasks like medical coding and report generation, foundation models allow clinicians to focus on high-value activities such as personalized treatment planning and patient interaction. Furthermore, their adaptability ensures that even under-resourced settings benefit from state-of-the-art diagnostic tools, fostering equity and accessibility in healthcare.

2.2 AI in Healthcare Today

AI is not just a tool; it is a transformational catalyst for reimagining healthcare at every level. But how will this transformation manifest itself? Imagine a future where a junior doctor in a rural clinic diagnoses with the same precision as a specialist in a major hospital. Trained on expansive, diverse, and responsibly curated datasets, AI can analyze imaging, lab results, and patient histories with remarkable accuracy, detecting subtle patterns that could be hard to capture even for experienced eyes. By democratizing expertise globally, AI ensures that patients everywhere—regardless of their location or provider's experience level—receive high-quality, consistent care. In this future, AI will become an unobtrusive yet indispensable force, enabling smarter, faster, and more human-centered healthcare. The promise of AI lies in its ability to bridge gaps in care quality, diagnostic accuracy, and resource allocation, ultimately creating a healthcare system that is truly equitable.

AI's integration into healthcare is driving a tangible shift in how medicine is practiced and how patients are cared for. From the precision of managing critical physiological parameters to the acceleration of drug discovery and the streamlining of hospital operations, AI's impact is increasingly evident. The following sections highlight specific examples of these breakthroughs, showcasing the diverse ways AI is transforming healthcare and improving patient outcomes.

2.2.1 Precision Medication and Patient Outcomes

Several studies highlight AI's ability to improve patient outcomes through precision management. For example, trials evaluating AI-driven insulin dosing systems have shown significant improvements in maintaining patients within optimal glucose ranges (Han et al., 2024). Similarly, AI-powered intraoperative hypotension monitoring has led to better blood pressure control during surgery (Mohammadi et al., 2024). These advancements underscore AI's capacity to positively provide precise, real-time management of critical physiological parameters, potentially reducing complications and improving patient safety.

Beyond managing physiological parameters, AI is also making strides in disease management. For instance, in diabetic retinopathy, one trial revealed that providing AI-generated risk predictions directly to patients significantly increased adherence to ophthalmology referrals compared to traditional clinician-based grading (Mathenge et al., 2022). This suggests that AI can empower patients to take a more active role in their care. Furthermore, the use of AI-guided nociception monitoring systems during surgery has been linked to reduced postoperative pain scores, demonstrating AI's potential to improve patient comfort and recovery (van der Wal et al., 2023). Similar improvements in insulin dosing and hypotension monitoring have also been found (Nimri et al., 2020; Wijnberge et al., 2020).

AI's impact also extends to proactive risk assessment and preventative care. AI algorithms can analyze patient data to identify individuals at high risk for developing certain conditions, allowing for earlier interventions and lifestyle modifications. For example, AI models can predict the likelihood of a patient developing heart failure based on personal aspects such as their medical history or genetic predispositions (Chu et al., 2020; Zhou et al., 2021). This allows clinicians to implement preventative measures, such as medication adjustments or lifestyle counseling, potentially delaying or even preventing the onset of heart failure. Similar progress has been made in predicting strokes, Alzheimer's disease, and different cancers, to name a few (Teoh, 2018; Joshi, 2025; Wang et al., 2015). Significant advancements have also been made toward leveraging foundation models and external knowledge bases to facilitate interpretable health outcome predictions (Jiang et al., 2024). This proactive approach to healthcare, enabled by AI, has the potential to significantly improve long-term health outcomes and reduce the burden on the healthcare system.

2.2.2 Revolutionizing Medical Imaging and Diagnostics

AI is revolutionizing medical imaging, leading to earlier and more accurate diagnoses. In cancer care, AI models that integrate data from magnetic resonance imaging (MRI), ultrasound images, positron emission tomography (PET) scans, and pathology reports are providing clinicians with more comprehensive insights, leading to various benefits such as improved detection and personalized treatment strategies (Qian et al., 2021; Le et al., 2017; Lipková et al., 2019). This data integration bridges data silos across diagnostic and treatment pathways, enhancing both clinical efficiency and patient outcomes. AI-enhanced imaging technologies are now providing valuable molecular and prognostic data, further refining cancer management. Moreover, AI is contributing to safer imaging practices by reducing radiation exposure by up to 75% without compromising image quality (Omega Medical Imaging, 2021). These models are also improving the detection of early stage tumors with greater precision, leading to better detection rates and improved patient survival (Lipkova et al., 2022).

Recent breakthroughs in AI foundation models are particularly exciting. SonoSAMTrack, for example, combines a promptable foundation model (SonoSAM) with advanced contour tracking, revolutionizing ultrasound imaging (Ravishankar et al., 2023). With just a few clicks, SonoSAM can accurately segment anatomies and lesions in ultrasound images. By integrating with a contour tracking model, SonoSAMTrack enables real-time segmentation and tracking of objects across 2D+t and 3D ultrasound settings, transforming how clinicians interact with ultrasound data. Its efficient and precise segmentation capabilities require minimal user intervention. Interestingly, this model was able to generalize and perform strongly even on anatomies that were not used for training, such as fetal head, breast lesions, and several other anatomies. Another groundbreaking development is a new full-body 3D MRI foundation model (GE HealthCare, 2024). Trained on a massive dataset of MRI images, this model significantly improves image retrieval, classification, segmentation, and even report generation. Its ability to generate detailed 3D representations from 2D MRI slices enhances the analysis of complex anatomical structures and has shown remarkable improvements in disease detection and classification, particularly in areas like prostate cancer and Alzheimer's disease. Other noteworthy mentions include a new full-body multimodal X-ray foundation model trained on over a million anonymized X-ray images, which is poised to enhance image segmentation and classification, providing healthcare professionals with more efficient and reliable diagnostic tools (Valeriano, 2024). This model's ability to integrate and interpret unstructured data from medical images, notes, and device readings holds immense potential for improving the accuracy of radiological diagnoses.

2.2.3 Accelerating Clinical Trials and Research

AI is playing a crucial role in clinical trials and research, accelerating the discovery and development of new treatments. AI algorithms can analyze vast datasets of clinical trial data, identifying patterns and insights that would be nearly impossible for humans to detect. This helps researchers design more effective trials and identify promising drug candidates. Furthermore, AI is being used to automate many tasks involved in clinical trials, such as patient recruitment, data collection, and data analysis, making the process more efficient and less costly.

AI is transforming trial design. By optimizing trial protocols, identifying the most appropriat patient populations, and predicting the likelihood of success, AI algorithms can analyze historic clinical trial data to identify factors that influence trial outcomes. This allows researchers to des' trials that are more likely to succeed. For example, AI can analyze multimodal data to predict events in clinical trials, such as trial duration, patient dropout rate, adverse events, and mor rate. This information can be used to optimize trial design and minimize risks (Chen et al., 2

Patient recruitment, often a bottleneck, is being revolutionized by AI. AI can identi recruit patients who are most likely to benefit from a particular treatment. By analyzing data, AI algorithms can identify individuals who meet the eligibility criteria, making the ment process faster and more targeted. One approach uses deep reinforcement learning trial sites that optimize both enrollment and diversity, addressing the underreprese minorities (Theodorou et al., 2024). AI models can also match patients with trials bas health records and eligibility criteria (Theodorou et al., 2023). Predicting clinical trial success before the trial even begins is another area where AI is valuable. Deep lear

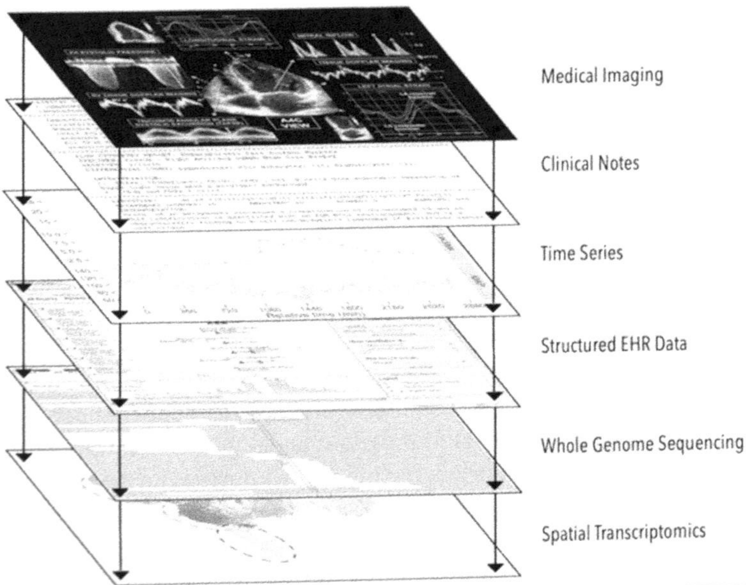

Figure 2.2 Multimodal data integration in healthcare.

Source: Adapted from Luo fet al, 2024.

augmented with large language models, can analyze trial eligibility criteria to predict enrollment success (Yue, Xing, Chen, & Fu, Trialenroll: Predicting clinical trial enrollment success with deep … and cross network and large language models, 2024).

The analysis of clinical trial data is significantly enhanced by AI. AI can analyze these vast …ts to identify patterns and insights that would be difficult for humans to detect. This helps …ers identify promising drug candidates, understand how treatments work, and identify … of patients who are most likely to benefit. Large language models, integrated with … systems, are being developed to perform complex reasoning tasks related to clinical …ng outcome prediction, demonstrating the potential of AI to enhance clinical trial …ing, Chen, & Fu, Clinical agent: Clinical trial multi-agent system with large lan- …d reasoning, 2024).

…ng Operations and Improving Efficiency

…, AI streamlines hospital operations, leading to increased efficiency and …s. Personalized knowledge graphs integrated with EHRs are helping …charge times and bed utilization, enhancing efficiency and improv- …ng et al., 2023). These AI-driven operational improvements free up …hcare professionals to focus on what matters most: patient care. …nalytics in hospital management to predict hospital readmis- …nage resources more effectively. AI algorithms can analyze … demographics, and social determinants of health, to pre- …admission, allowing hospitals to intervene and prevent … et al., 2020). Furthermore, AI is being used to forecast … levels, ensuring that hospitals have the resources they need to meet patient needs (Feng et al., 2021). AI can also predict patient length of stay, assisting healthcare professionals in resource planning and scheduling decisions (Alnsour et al., 2023). Predicting hospital bed demand, particularly from the emergency department, is another area where AI can contribute to better resource allocation (Lucini et al., 2020).

Workflow automation is another area where AI is making a difference. AI is being used to streamline routine administrative tasks—such as scheduling appointments, managing electronic health records, and processing insurance claims—which traditionally consume valuable time and are prone to human error. By automating these processes, hospitals not only reduce administrative burdens and improve accuracy but also free up healthcare professionals to focus on more complex clinical decisions and direct patient care. Research demonstrates that AI-based systems can optimize resource allocation and enhance workflow efficiency, ultimately contributing to improved patient outcomes (Maleki Varnosfaderani & Forouzanfar, 2024).

Finally, AI is also being applied to supply chain management in hospitals. It can be used to optimize hospital supply chains, ensuring that hospitals have the supplies they need when they need them. AI algorithms can predict demand for medical supplies and optimize inventory levels, reducing waste and saving money (Kumar et al., 2023; Jebbor et al., 2022).

2.3 Implementation Best Practices

The adoption of AI foundation models is revolutionizing healthcare, unlocking unprecedented opportunities to improve diagnostics, personalize care, and enhance operational efficiency. These advanced models, with their capacity to generalize across tasks and integrate diverse data modalities, have the potential to fundamentally reshape clinical workflows and deliver transformative outcomes for patients and providers alike. However, realizing this potential requires a thoughtful and strategic approach.

Successful implementation depends on addressing key areas such as stakeholder engagement, responsible development, regulatory alignment, technical readiness, and seamless integration into clinical environments. From defining clear objectives and selecting appropriate model architectures to managing data effectively and ensuring continuous evaluation, each step plays a vital role in building trusted and impactful AI systems.

By focusing on these interconnected best practices, healthcare organizations can navigate the complexities of AI adoption while aligning technology with the unique demands of healthcare systems. This structured approach ensures that foundation models are scalable, adaptable, and capable of addressing real-world challenges, ultimately advancing equitable and high-quality care.

2.3.1 Defining Clear Objectives and Clinical Focus

The foundation of any successful AI initiative lies in identifying specific, high-priority problems that AI can address. Without clear objectives, efforts may drift away from clinical needs or organizational goals, leading to misalignment and inefficiency. Key steps to setting objectives are outlined below.

- **Identifying Target Areas**: Pinpoint areas where AI can make the most significant impact, such as enhancing diagnostic accuracy, streamlining administrative tasks, or optimizing workflows in specific areas like radiology, oncology, or surgery. As Bhatt and Bae (2023) point out, successful digital transformation in healthcare focuses on specific problem-solving rather than technology-driven approaches.

- **Aligning with Stakeholders**: Engage clinicians, administrators, and patients to ensure that selected objectives reflect real-world needs and priorities. Collaboration across these groups ensures that AI initiatives are relevant, practical, and widely adopted. Active clinician engagement, while incorporating the concept of "collaborative intelligence," builds trust. This trust stems from a shared understanding of how the technology produces insights, its limitations, and bias mitigation strategies. Clinicians can then critically assess AI outputs within the clinical context, ensuring practical and effective adoption.
- **Defining Measurable Goals**: Establish clear success criteria, such as improved patient outcomes, reduced wait times, or increased workflow efficiency, to track progress effectively.

AI projects often fail when they begin with the technology, not the clinical or business problems. Active clinician engagement builds trust and drives meaningful outcomes by fostering a deeper understanding of the technology's capabilities, limitations, and alignment with clinical objectives. Clear objectives provide a strategic roadmap for AI adoption, focusing resources on initiatives that deliver meaningful and measurable results.

2.3.2 Stakeholder Engagement and Trust Building

Successful AI deployment in healthcare depends on trust and collaboration among all stakeholders, including healthcare professionals, administrators, patients, and underrepresented groups. Early and consistent engagement ensures AI solutions address practical needs, align with societal values, and gain widespread acceptance. Different aspects of this include:

- **Collaboration with Healthcare Professionals**: Engage clinicians, nurses, and allied health professionals early and consistently in AI development and deployment. This builds trust, aligns AI with clinical workflows and organizational goals, and fosters co-ownership—avoiding late-stage adjustments that erode confidence (Kaye et al., 2024). Early involvement also ensures intuitive solutions, reduces the learning curve, and enhances real-world applicability by accommodating clinical nuances, leading to faster adoption. Studies show late-stage involvement undermines confidence and reduces AI effectiveness in clinical settings.
- **Engaging Underrepresented Groups**: Proactively include diverse populations to address systemic inequities in AI outcomes. Research highlights the need for proportional and context-specific engagement to ensure marginalized groups have a voice in decision-making, reducing disparities in healthcare access (Kaye et al., 2024).
- **Promoting AI Literacy**: Structured AI education tailored to clinicians is crucial. Foundational training builds basic AI understanding and trust, proficient training integrates AI into clinical workflows, and expert-level training fosters collaboration with data scientists. Programs like HelloAI Professional* bridge AI competency gaps, equipping clinicians to interpret and trust AI outputs for safe and ethical patient care (Schubert et al., 2025).
- **Ensuring Transparency and Explainability**: Advanced AI models, especially deep learning, excel in tasks like image recognition and predictive analytics but often lack transparency. Trust in AI requires openly sharing system design, data sources, and decision-making logic to identify biases and assess reliability. Explainability clarifies how models justify

* https://www.helloaiprofessional.com/

decisions—critical in healthcare, where outcomes impact patient care. To maximize AI's potential, developers, clinicians, and legislators must address the limitations of opaque algorithms and collaborate across disciplines (Amann et al., 2020; Beger, 2024).

To achieve this, healthcare organizations must implement structured platforms for feedback, adapt engagement intensity to the specific context, and foster collaborative decision-making to align AI systems with broader social and clinical goals.

2.3.3 Responsible AI and Regulatory Alignment

Adhering to ethical principles and regulatory standards is crucial to ensuring that AI systems are developed and deployed responsibly. Responsible AI alignment not only protects patient rights but also builds trust and fosters sustainable AI adoption in healthcare. Key considerations include:

- **Ensuring Compliance with Regulations**: Align AI initiatives with data protection frameworks such as Health Insurance Portability and Accountability Act (HIPAA), General Data Protection Regulation (GDPR), and region-specific healthcare laws to safeguard patient privacy. Compliance ensures that patient data is handled securely, fostering trust among stakeholders.
- **Mitigating Bias and Ensuring Fairness**: Address potential biases in training data and model outputs to avoid perpetuating healthcare disparities. Bias in AI systems often arises from homogeneous training datasets that don't represent diverse patient populations. Mitigation strategies include using balanced datasets to ensure adequate representation and implementing fairness-aware algorithms to identify and correct biases, promoting equitable performance across diverse groups.
- **Establishing Governance Frameworks**: Implement accountability structures, including interdisciplinary committees, to oversee AI development and deployment, ensuring alignment with clinical values and ethical standards. Governance frameworks, such as the AI Ethics Impact Assessment, provide guidelines to evaluate the ethical and societal implications of AI adoption.

These measures not only protect patient rights but also enhance trust in AI systems, ensuring they are reliable and equitable tools for healthcare innovation.

2.3.4 Model Selection and Pre-Training

Selecting the appropriate foundation model architecture and pre-training approach is fundamental to optimizing performance, ensuring both accuracy and efficient use of computational resources. The choice of model architecture depends on the specific task. For instance, transformer-based models excel at natural language processing, while multimodal architectures are better suited for integrated diagnostics. The specific needs of each healthcare application, such as real-time analysis (requiring efficient models), cost, or complex data integration (benefiting from multimodal architectures), should guide the architecture choice. Moreover, leveraging pre-trained models addresses critical challenges in healthcare AI, including data scarcity and domain specificity. By providing a starting point, these models accelerate development, reduce training time, and ultimately improve outcomes. Foundation models offer the adaptability needed to create tailored AI solutions, critical for addressing highly specialized use cases. This allows for seamless integration with existing clinical workflows, leading to improved efficiency and more effective patient care.

2.3.4.1 Selecting the Right Architecture for Foundation Models

Choosing the right foundation model architecture is crucial, as each type is suitable for its own specific healthcare tasks. Selecting the correct architecture ensures compatibility with the data and aligns with available computational resources. Here's a breakdown of their applications:

- **Textual Data Analysis**: Transformer-based models, such as Generative Pre-trained Transformers (GPT) or Bidirectional Encoder Representations from Transformers (BERT), have become a mainstay for natural language understanding and generation (Lin et al., 2022). They are well-suited for tasks like analyzing electronic health records (EHRs), summarizing patient histories, or generating clinical notes, all of which either enable faster access to critical information or improve efficiency and reduce physician workload (Nerella et al., 2024). To accommodate long-range information, such as the entirety of a patient's medical history, either architectural changes (Dao et al., 2022) or the use of a different model entirely (Yang et al., 2024) are required due to computational limitations.
- **Image-Based Diagnostics**: Convolutional neural networks (CNNs), vision transformers, and hybrid architectures are better suited for analyzing radiological images, pathology slides, and other medical imaging data (Sarvamangala & Kulkarni, 2022).
- **Multimodal Applications**: Emerging transformer architectures designed for handling multimodal inputs—such as text, images, and structured data—are increasingly popular for integrated diagnostics and treatment planning, promising more holistic and personalized care (AlSaad et al., 2024).
- **Segmentation and Annotation**: Innovative foundation models like Meta's Segment Anything Model (SAM) provide advanced solutions for image segmentation, crucial for identifying regions of interest in medical imaging, such as tumors or lesions, enabling more accurate diagnoses and treatment planning (Kirillov et al., 2023).

By selecting the appropriate architecture, researchers and clinicians can unlock the full potential of foundation models for a wide range of healthcare applications.

2.3.4.2 Leveraging Pre-Trained Models

Pre-trained models offer a powerful starting point, reducing the need for extensive domain-specific training and accelerating development while improving performance. However, healthcare presents unique challenges, including sensitive data, strict regulations, and domain-specific requirements. Here are three approaches to leveraging pre-trained models effectively:

- **General-Purpose LLMs**: Models like BERT provide broad capabilities, which can be fine-tuned for healthcare-specific tasks by training on labeled datasets of medical text, such as clinical notes or research articles (Li et al., 2019). Their extensive pre-training on diverse datasets enables them to understand complex language patterns.
- **Domain-Specific Pre-Trained Models**: While general-purpose models can be adapted, their lack of exposure to specialized medical terminology can limit their effectiveness. Therefore, domain-specific models, such as BioBERT or ClinicalBERT, pre-trained on

biomedical corpora, are better suited to healthcare terminology and contexts. These models help bridge the gap between general-purpose training data and healthcare-specific needs (Lee et al., 2020; Huang et al., 2019).

- **Fine-Tuning for Specialization**: Fine-tuning involves retraining a pre-trained model on smaller, domain-specific datasets. For example, fine-tuning a language model on radiology reports can enhance its ability to generate accurate diagnostic summaries (Yan et al., 2022). While this approach allows for specialization, it requires careful curation of the fine-tuning dataset to avoid overfitting and ensure generalizability.

These three approaches offer a spectrum of options for leveraging pre-trained models, allowing researchers and developers to balance the benefits of transfer learning with the unique demands of healthcare data and applications.

2.3.4.3 The Role of Pre-Training in Healthcare

Pre-training foundation models on healthcare data offers immense potential, but successful implementation relies on addressing several critical factors:

- **Data Availability**: Healthcare datasets are often fragmented and sensitive. Incorporating anonymized and representative datasets, reflecting the diversity of patient populations, ensures model generalizability and reduces the risk of bias (Arora et al., 2023).
- **Regulatory Compliance**: Adherence to regulations like HIPAA and GDPR is essential, necessitating robust anonymization and secure handling of training data to protect patient privacy and avoid legal penalties.
- **Bias Mitigation**: Pre-training must proactively address potential biases in data, such as those related to demographic or socioeconomic status, to prevent perpetuating or even amplifying existing disparities in healthcare delivery. Techniques like data augmentation and adversarial training can be employed to mitigate these biases (Sharma et al., 2020; Yang et al., 2023).
- **Computational Efficiency**: Pre-training healthcare models demands significant resources. Cloud-based training, distributed computing, and the use of specialized hardware like Graphical Processing Unit (GPUs) and Tensor Processing Unit (TPUs) can help meet these requirements efficiently.

Addressing these challenges is essential for developing and deploying effective and ethical foundation models in healthcare.

2.3.4.4 Balancing Pre-Trained and Custom Models

Pre-trained models provide a valuable starting point, but the unique demands of some healthcare applications require the development of custom models. This is typically the case when facing the following situations:

- **Highly Specialized Use Cases**: Applications like rare disease diagnostics may require bespoke models trained on unique datasets, enabling more accurate diagnoses and personalized treatment plans for rare diseases (Wojtara et al., 2023).

- **Integration Challenges**: Pre-trained models might not seamlessly integrate into proprietary workflows or legacy systems, necessitating tailored solutions, which can be crucial for maintaining data integrity and operational efficiency.

The selection and pre-training of foundation models are pivotal steps in unlocking AI's potential in healthcare. As the field evolves, a strategic approach to foundation model development, encompassing careful architecture selection, domain-specific pre-training, and addressing unique challenges, will ensure that AI remains a transformative force in healthcare, driving innovation and improving patient care.

2.3.5 Data Management for Foundation Models in Healthcare

The effectiveness of foundation models in healthcare hinges on the quality, diversity, and governance of the training data. High-quality, representative datasets are essential. These can be further enhanced through advanced data augmentation techniques and strategies like federated learning, leading to more robust and equitable AI solutions. Implementing best practices in data management, including rigorous data validation and quality control, ensures these models can generalize effectively across varied healthcare contexts while adhering to ethical and regulatory standards.

2.3.5.1 Ensuring Data Quality

Robust foundation models require high-quality data. Poor data quality not only undermines the reliability of AI predictions and erodes trust in these systems, but can also lead to misdiagnoses, ineffective treatments, and even patient harm. Key aspects of ensuring data quality include:

- **Accuracy and Completeness**: Training data must be accurate, free of errors, and complete. Missing or incorrect information, such as incomplete medical histories or mislabeled imaging data, can skew model training and lead to unreliable predictions. This can be mitigated through rigorous data validation procedures and by utilizing expert review for data labeling (Fredriksson et al., 2020).
- **Consistency**: Data formatting and labeling should be standardized to avoid confusion during model training. For example, inconsistencies in measurement units, terminology, or labeling conventions can hinder the model's ability to learn effectively. Standardization has the added benefit of improving model training efficiency and ensuring consistent interpretation of data (Zhang et al., 2022).
- **Noise Reduction**: Eliminating irrelevant or redundant information improves the model's focus on meaningful patterns. For instance, removing corrupted imaging files or duplicate records enhances the quality of training datasets. Data cleaning methods and outlier detection are often leveraged for this purpose (Miao et al., 2023).

These data quality considerations must be addressed proactively to build trust in and maximize the effectiveness of AI-driven healthcare solutions.

2.3.5.2 Emphasizing Data Diversity

To ensure foundation models support equitable healthcare across diverse populations and clinical settings, diverse datasets are crucial. Without them, models risk reinforcing biases that worsen existing healthcare disparities. Expanding public datasets with varied, real-world clinical cases will enhance benchmarking and help mitigate these biases (Johri et al., 2025). Considerations for diversity include:

- **Population Representation**: Training data should reflect the diversity of real-world patient populations, including factors like age, gender, ethnicity, and geographic location. This ensures equitable model performance across demographic groups. Without it, models may underperform for certain populations, leading to disparities in care (Celi et al., 2022).
- **Clinical Variability**: Incorporating data from various healthcare settings, such as urban hospitals, rural clinics, and outpatient facilities, helps models adapt to different clinical workflows and practices, improving their generalizability and real-world effectiveness (Chen et al., 2023).
- **Rare Conditions**: Including data on rare diseases and atypical presentations equips models to handle edge cases effectively, expanding their utility in specialized scenarios and improving diagnosis and treatment for even the rarest conditions (Wojtara et al., 2023).

Prioritizing data diversity is not just a best practice; it's an ethical imperative for responsible AI development in healthcare.

2.3.5.3 Leveraging Data Augmentation

Data augmentation techniques play a crucial role in maximizing the potential of foundation models, significantly enhancing the robustness and generalization power by artificially increasing the size and variability of training datasets. Key methods include:

- **Synthetic Data Generation**: Using tools like generative adversarial networks (GANs) or diffusion models, which are capable of learning the underlying data distribution and generating realistic samples, synthetic data can mimic real-world variations (Bengesi et al., 2024). For example, generating variations of chest X-rays can help models identify subtle abnormalities more effectively, especially in cases where real-world data is limited (Islam et al., 2024).
- **Transformations and Variations**: Applying transformations such as rotations, scaling, cropping, or adding noise (including Gaussian noise or salt-and-pepper noise) to imaging data improves the model's ability to recognize patterns under diverse conditions (Kumar et al., 2024).
- **Domain-Specific Augmentation**: In text-based healthcare data, techniques like paraphrasing, synonym replacements (e.g., "myocardial infarction" to "heart attack"), or rearranging sentence structures enhance the diversity of language patterns, improving model performance on natural language tasks (Xiao et al., 2018).

By strategically applying these data augmentation techniques, researchers can significantly improve the performance and generalizability of foundation models in healthcare, even with scarce real-world data.

2.3.5.4 Strategies for Generalization

Generalizing foundation models to diverse healthcare scenarios requires targeted data management strategies, extending data beyond augmentation and ensuring diversity:

- **Cross-Domain Training**: Combining data from multiple domains, such as EHRs, imaging, and wearable device data, enables models to handle multimodal inputs and adapt to complex healthcare tasks by exposing them to a wider range of data patterns and relationships (Acosta et al., 2022).
- **Federated Learning**: This approach trains models on decentralized data across multiple institutions without transferring raw data, preserving privacy while improving generalizability across diverse patient populations and institutional settings (Nguyen et al., 2022).
- **Bias Mitigation**: Identifying and addressing biases in training datasets, often through careful analysis of data distributions and model outputs, ensures that model predictions are fair and unbiased across different patient populations, helping prevent disparities in care (Sasseville et al., 2025).

Effective data management is essential for building powerful and generalizable foundation models in healthcare. By prioritizing data quality, fostering diversity, and adopting advanced augmentation and generalization strategies, healthcare organizations can unlock the transformative potential of AI. As research and development in foundation models for healthcare accelerate, addressing challenges such as data accessibility, annotation, and scalability will remain critical to delivering equitable, impactful solutions across the healthcare ecosystem.

2.3.6 Evaluation and Monitoring

The safe and successful implementation of AI foundation models in healthcare depends on robust evaluation and monitoring frameworks. These frameworks ensure models meet clinical standards, perform reliably over time, and comply with ethical and regulatory requirements. Continuous monitoring of new versions is crucial to track performance shifts and drive improvements. Effective evaluation combines automated and expert assessments to balance efficiency with clinical reliability (Johri et al., 2025). Key components of effective evaluation include setting clear quality metrics, enhancing interpretability, integrating feedback loops, and safeguarding data and model privacy.

2.3.6.1 Evaluation Metrics for Model Quality

Evaluation metrics are crucial for assessing the performance and reliability of AI foundation models in clinical settings. These metrics should reflect both technical performance and real-world impact. Key considerations include:

- **Accuracy and Sensitivity**: Metrics such as precision, recall, and F1 score measure the model's ability to identify true positives and minimize false negatives, which is critical in diagnostic applications. For example, in breast cancer screening, sensitivity ensures early detection, while precision reduces unnecessary follow-ups.
- **Generalizability**: Models must perform consistently across diverse patient populations and healthcare settings. Validation on external datasets that include varying demographics, clinical workflows, and equipment ensures robustness and avoids the risk of deploying models that perform well during development but fail in diverse clinical environments.
- **Calibration and Uncertainty Quantification**: Effective models not only make predictions but also provide confidence scores, enabling clinicians to gauge the reliability of outputs.

Calibration techniques, such as Platt scaling or isotonic regression, improve the interpretability of these scores, allowing clinicians to make more informed decisions (Seoni et al., 2023).

- **Operational Metrics**: Turnaround time, computational efficiency, and integration into existing clinical workflows measure the practical viability of AI systems in high-pressure environments like emergency departments. Successful integration might involve direct access to the AI's output within the EHR system or the ability to easily incorporate the AI's insights into clinical decision-making tools.

A comprehensive evaluation of AI foundation models in healthcare must consider all of these factors to ensure both technical validity and real-world clinical utility.

2.3.6.2 Interpretability

Interpretability is essential to building trust in AI systems, particularly in high-stakes scenarios such as surgery or oncology, where a lack of transparency can not only hinder adoption but also pose a direct risk to patient safety. Transparent models allow clinicians to understand and validate predictions, fostering confidence and acceptance. Several strategies can be employed to enhance AI interpretability. These include:

- **Feature Attribution**: Techniques like SHAP (Shapley Additive Explanations) or LIME (Local Interpretable Model-Agnostic Explanations) identify which input features influenced a model's prediction, making outputs more comprehensible and enabling clinicians to identify potential biases in the data (Lundberg & Lee, 2017; Ribeiro et al., 2016).
- **Visualization Tools**: Heatmaps in radiology or annotated genomic pathways in precision medicine provide visual aids that bridge the gap between data-driven insights and clinical understanding, facilitating more informed diagnoses and treatment plans.
- **Simplified Outputs**: Presenting predictions in actionable formats, such as probability-based risk scores or color-coded alerts, improves usability for non-technical stakeholders, empowering them to effectively integrate AI insights into their practice.

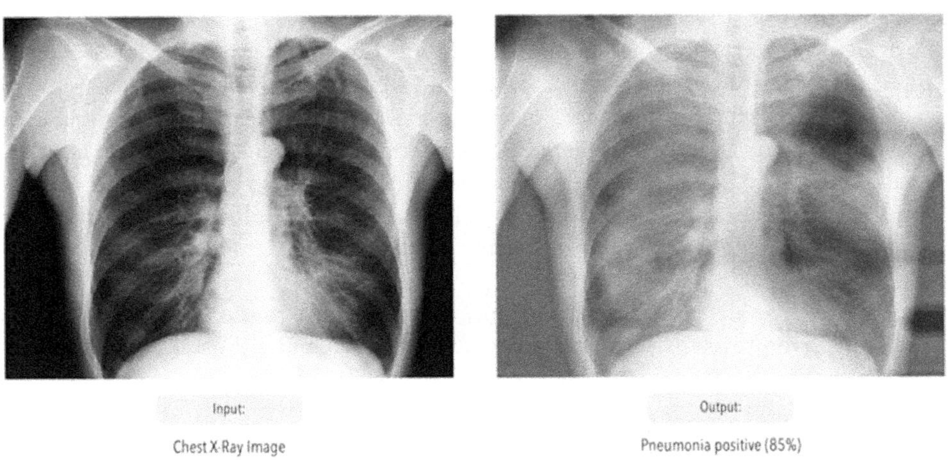

Figure 2.3 Heatmap example.

By employing these interpretability techniques, researchers can develop AI systems that are not only powerful but also trustworthy and therefore readily integrated into clinical workflows. Ultimately, increasing transparency fosters greater acceptance of AI in healthcare and maximizes its potential to improve patient care.

2.3.6.3 Rigorous Testing and Validation

Robust testing and validation are essential for ensuring that AI systems perform reliably and safely in real-world clinical environments. Key approaches include:

- **Shadow Mode Testing**: AI systems operate in the background, generating recommendations without influencing clinical decisions (Halliday et al., 2024). This allows organizations to identify gaps in performance, validate model outputs, and refine systems, allowing for iterative improvement without impacting patient care.
- **Pilot Testing**: Active integration of AI systems into specific workflows enables healthcare organizations to assess their practical value and operational fit before scaling to broader deployment. Pilot testing helps ensure solutions align with the unique requirements of clinical practice, such as integration with existing systems and workflows, and acceptance by clinical staff.

These complementary testing strategies, shadow mode and pilot testing, provide a comprehensive approach to validating AI systems before widespread deployment in healthcare settings.

2.3.6.4 Feedback Loops

Continuous feedback from end users is vital to refining foundation models and maintaining their relevance in dynamic healthcare environments. A structured feedback mechanism enables iterative improvement and adapts models to changing clinical needs. Key components include:

- **User-Centric Evaluation**: Clinicians provide qualitative feedback on model usability, integration ease, and output relevance, informing targeted refinements. This feedback can be gathered through surveys, interviews, or direct observation of model use in clinical settings.
- **Post-Deployment Monitoring**: Automated tools track model performance in real-world applications, flagging issues such as data drift, accuracy degradation, or emerging biases, enabling timely intervention and model updates. Online learning techniques can be employed to continuously integrate new information as it is generated (Hoi et al., 2021).
- **Real-Time Error Logging**: Systems that record discrepancies between model outputs and actual clinician decisions can identify gaps in performance and guide retraining efforts by pinpointing specific areas for improvement.

By incorporating these diverse feedback streams, developers can continuously refine foundation models, leading to improved performance, increased user trust, and ultimately, better patient care.

2.3.6.5 Secure Data and Model Privacy

Protecting sensitive patient information is crucial for maintaining trust in AI systems. Robust privacy and security measures are the foundation of ethical AI deployment and are critical for gaining stakeholder confidence. Best practices include:

- **Compliance with Regulations**: Adhering to frameworks such as HIPAA, GDPR, and other region-specific privacy laws fosters trust and confidence in AI systems and ensures ethical data management practices.
- **Federated Learning**: By training models on decentralized data without transferring raw patient information, federated learning preserves privacy while enhancing model generalizability (Nguyen et al., 2022). This approach minimizes data exposure risks and can facilitate compliance with regulations like HIPAA and GDPR, which emphasize data minimization and control.
- **Anonymization Techniques**: Advanced de-identification methods ensure that patient data used in model training cannot be traced back to individuals. This includes pseudonymization, differential privacy, and other cutting-edge techniques that protect patient identities while preserving data utility (Olatunji et al., 2024). It is important to recognize that while these techniques significantly reduce risk, they do not guarantee absolute anonymity.
- **Robust Cybersecurity Measures**: Encryption, secure access protocols, and regular audits safeguard sensitive data and prevent breaches. Proactive threat detection systems, secure data-sharing protocols, and compliance monitoring further enhance data security.
- **Trust and Adoption**: Privacy and security measures are critical for maintaining trust among stakeholders. A single breach or failure to comply with regulations can erode confidence, slow adoption, and lead to significant ethical, financial, and reputational consequences, as demonstrated by recent high-profile data breaches in the healthcare sector (Alder, 2025).

Prioritizing data privacy and security is not only an ethical imperative but also a key factor in the successful and sustainable implementation of AI in healthcare.

2.3.6.6 Modality Alignment and Cross-Modality Fine-Tuning

To unlock the full potential of healthcare AI, integrating diverse data types—such as imaging, clinical notes, and genomic data—is essential for creating robust and accurate models. Modality alignment and cross-modality fine-tuning are two critical techniques that enable seamless integration and adaptation of multimodal data, addressing key challenges such as data heterogeneity and the need for robust models in the face of limited labeled data in medical AI applications.

- **Modality Alignment** involves harmonizing different data modalities to create a unified representation. This process addresses challenges like inconsistent data structures and varying granularities across modalities. For instance, aligning features from MRI and computerized tomography (CT) scans can improve segmentation tasks, leading to more accurate diagnoses and treatment planning by leveraging complementary information from both imaging types. Recent studies have proposed methods like cross-modality feature alignment subnetworks, which learn to map features from different modalities into a shared latent space to bridge domain discrepancies effectively (Yang et al., 2024).
- **Cross-Modality Fine-Tuning** refers to adapting pre-trained models to new, often scarce, data modalities. This is often necessary because training models from scratch on limited medical datasets is challenging. This approach leverages knowledge from data-rich modalities to improve performance in data-scarce ones. For example, fine-tuning a model trained on natural images to interpret medical images like X-rays or MRIs. Frameworks such as Simple Cross-modal Fine-tuning (SimCMF) have been developed to facilitate this transfer, addressing challenges like modality misalignment and fine-tuning costs (Lei et al., 2024).

These techniques pave the way for more comprehensive and integrated AI solutions in healthcare, leveraging the rich information contained within diverse data modalities.

2.3.6.7 Interoperability and Seamless Integration

Integrating AI systems seamlessly with existing healthcare IT infrastructure, such as EHRs, presents a significant challenge but is crucial for maximizing their impact. Ensuring interoperability and smooth integration into clinical workflows is critical for the success of AI adoption. Key considerations include:

- **Interoperable Platforms**: Systems should enable smooth data exchange between AI tools and clinical workflows, facilitating real-time insights without creating data silos. This interoperability also ensures compliance with data-sharing regulations and supports future scalability. Common standards such as Fast Healthcare Interoperability (FHIR) are adopted and implemented to facilitate this (Vorisek et al., 2022).
- **Minimizing Disruptions**: AI solutions should integrate seamlessly without requiring significant changes to existing workflows or information technology (IT) infrastructure. Simplifying integration reduces adoption resistance, minimizes training demands, and ensures clinicians can focus on patient care rather than technology challenges, ultimately fostering long-term success and widespread adoption.

Prioritizing interoperability and seamless integration is therefore paramount for the successful and widespread adoption of AI in healthcare, ensuring that these powerful tools enhance, rather than hinder, clinical workflows.

2.3.6.8 Ensuring Continuous Improvement

To sustain the impact of foundation models, organizations should establish a culture of continuous monitoring and evaluation. This includes:

- **Adaptive Updates**: Models should be retrained periodically, using robust data pipelines and validation techniques, to incorporate new clinical knowledge, guidelines, and data sources.
- **Ethical Oversight**: Committees comprising clinicians, data scientists, and ethicists should regularly review model outputs, assess potential biases and ensure that models align with clinical values and avoid perpetuating existing disparities (Sasseville et al., 2025).
- **Benchmarking**: Comparing model performance against industry standards, peer-reviewed research, or established clinical benchmarks provides a clear measure of progress and highlights areas for enhancement. This should involve using standardized datasets and evaluation metrics to ensure objective comparisons.

The adoption of AI in healthcare demands a thoughtful, multidisciplinary approach that prioritizes patient safety, clinician trust, operational efficiency, and quality of care. By focusing on clear objectives, engaging stakeholders, and adhering to best practices for implementation, healthcare organizations can harness the transformative potential of AI. When deployed responsibly and transparently, AI becomes not just a tool but a powerful ally in advancing equitable, high-quality care.

2.4 Challenges

2.4.1 Data-Related Challenges

Data-related challenges are among the most significant barriers to successful AI implementation in healthcare. These challenges encompass issues of data quality, diversity, availability, privacy, and security, all of which directly influence the development, validation, and real-world performance of AI systems.

- **Data Quality**: Healthcare data often suffers from errors, missing values, and inconsistencies due to several factors. Manual entry of clinical data by healthcare professionals increases the likelihood of typographical errors or incorrect entries. Data collected from different institutions or devices often lacks standardization, leading to inconsistent formats and measurements. Additionally, many patient records have gaps caused by missed follow-up visits, incomplete diagnostic reports, or unavailable historical data. Poor data quality can negatively impact AI, resulting in unreliable predictions and reduced model accuracy, particularly in critical areas such as diagnostics or treatment recommendations. Inconsistent or noisy data can also lead to overfitting, making AI models less generalizable to new datasets. For example, in radiology, incomplete metadata for imaging studies, such as missing annotations on scans, can significantly hinder the training of AI models aimed at automated disease detection.
- **Bias in Datasets**: Training datasets often fail to capture the diversity of the populations they aim to serve, resulting in bias. This bias can occur due to several factors. Datasets frequently overrepresent individuals from urban, high-income, or majority populations, while data from rural, low-income, or minority groups is often sparse. Rare conditions or those specific to certain demographics may also be inadequately captured in training datasets. Additionally, data collected in academic medical centers may not reflect the broader population seen in community healthcare settings. Bias in datasets can lead AI systems to exhibit systematic disparities in performance, resulting in poorer outcomes for underrepresented groups. For example, in dermatology, insufficient representation of dark skin tones in academic materials and clinical care contributes to disparities in patient outcomes (Montoya et al., 2024). AI machine learning algorithms trained on imbalanced datasets, primarily consisting of light skin tones, exacerbate this issue, leading to missed or inaccurate diagnoses for patients with darker skin.
- **Data Silos**: Healthcare data is often fragmented across multiple systems and institutions for several reasons. Hospitals and clinics frequently maintain isolated databases with limited interconnectivity, creating institutional barriers. Proprietary electronic health record (EHR) systems can result in vendor lock-in, posing technological challenges to data sharing and aggregation. Additionally, the lack of universal data standards hinders interoperability between different healthcare providers and systems. Data silos restrict the development of comprehensive datasets, reducing the robustness of AI models. Fragmented data also leads to incomplete patient histories, which impacts the performance of predictive models for conditions like chronic diseases. For example, within a single health network, EHR data may exist in different formats, preventing seamless data integration for AI applications.

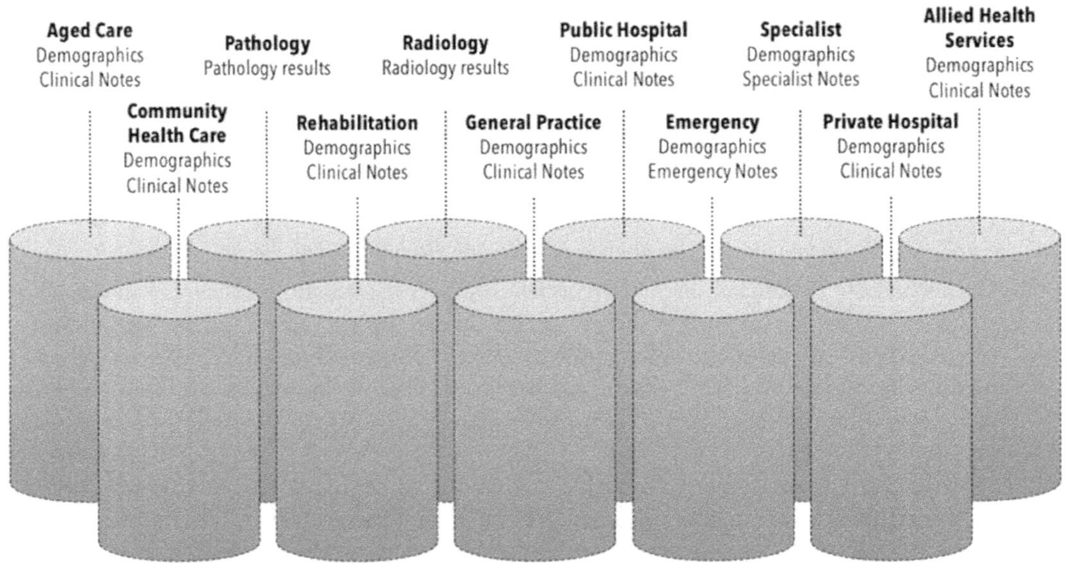

Figure 2.4 Data silos in healthcare.

- **Data Privacy and Security**: Regulatory frameworks like GDPR in Europe and HIPAA in the U.S. are essential for protecting patient privacy and ensuring data security in healthcare. However, these frameworks also present significant challenges. Stringent consent requirements can limit researchers' access to valuable patient data. Ensuring that data is de-identified while retaining its utility for AI training is a complex and delicate task. Additionally, as healthcare data becomes more digitized, it becomes increasingly vulnerable to cyberattacks, raising the risk of data breaches. These privacy concerns often restrict the pooling of data across institutions, reducing dataset diversity and impacting the performance of AI models. For example, the GDPR mandates that patients own and control their own data, requiring explicit consent for its use or sharing, which creates barriers for AI-driven healthcare innovations. Studies have noted that a lack of standardized data-sharing frameworks and strict data governance policies hinders AI implementation, delaying its potential benefits for patient care (Ahmed et al., 2023).

Additionally, distributional shifts between development and deployment settings often compromise the generalizability of AI systems. Data collected from controlled environments may not reflect the complexity or diversity of real-world clinical scenarios, leading to reduced effectiveness.

2.4.2 Integration Challenges

Integration challenges are significant obstacles to embedding AI solutions into existing healthcare workflows and IT systems. These challenges arise from technical, operational, and infrastructural issues that impede the seamless adoption of AI in healthcare environments. Addressing these barriers is essential for maximizing the potential of AI to enhance efficiency, accuracy, and patient outcomes.

- **Interoperability Issues**: AI systems often struggle to integrate with legacy electronic health records (EHRs) and other healthcare IT systems. This challenge arises from the lack of standardization across EHR platforms and data exchange formats. Many EHRs are proprietary and do not adhere to universal standards, such as FHIR (Fast Healthcare Interoperability Resources), making seamless communication between systems difficult. The fragmentation of IT systems leads to siloed data, complicating the implementation of AI models that rely on aggregated, comprehensive datasets. Without interoperability, AI tools may require extensive customization for each healthcare organization, increasing costs and reducing scalability. For example, an AI-driven clinical decision support system may fail to access patient records housed in older EHR systems, limiting its utility during patient care.
- **Scalability**: Many AI solutions are developed for specific, localized use cases and often lack the scalability required for deployment across larger healthcare networks or regions. This issue arises because models are frequently trained on datasets tailored to a single institution or demographic, limiting their generalizability to broader populations. Additionally, the infrastructure required to support scalable AI deployment—such as high-speed internet, centralized data repositories, and robust IT support—may be unavailable in many healthcare settings, particularly in low-resource areas. For example, an AI model designed to predict readmission rates in a single hospital may perform poorly when deployed across a multi-hospital network due to variations in data quality and patient demographics.
- **Workflow Alignment**: AI tools are often designed with a focus on technical capabilities rather than clinical usability, leading to misalignment with existing workflows. Instead of simplifying tasks, these tools may add complexity by requiring clinicians to input additional data or interact with unfamiliar interfaces. When AI disrupts established workflows, clinicians may perceive it as burdensome, leading to reduced adoption rates. Furthermore, the lack of clear integration points within clinical systems can result in duplicate work or inefficiencies. For example, an AI-powered diagnostic tool that requires clinicians to manually upload images from a separate system may deter adoption due to the additional time and effort required.
- **Infrastructure Gaps**: The computational infrastructure needed for AI implementation is often lacking in many hospitals and clinics, especially in rural or underfunded areas. Key infrastructure requirements, such as high-speed internet, robust servers, and secure data storage systems, may not be readily available. Furthermore, the cost of acquiring and maintaining such infrastructure can be prohibitive for smaller healthcare organizations. This digital divide exacerbates disparities in AI adoption, leaving many regions unable to benefit from AI advancements. For example, a rural clinic may lack the bandwidth or hardware to implement an AI-powered telemedicine platform, limiting access to remote consultations and advanced diagnostic tools.

Real-time decision support, which is a critical application of AI, is particularly hindered by these integration challenges, making it difficult to deliver timely and actionable insights during patient care.

2.4.3 Workforce and Cultural Resistance

Workforce and cultural resistance are key challenges to the successful adoption of AI in healthcare. These barriers stem from a combination of skepticism, knowledge gaps, fears about job displacement, and hesitance to disrupt established workflows. Building trust, addressing concerns, and empowering healthcare professionals are essential for integrating AI solutions effectively.

- **Trust Deficit**: Many clinicians view AI as a "black box" technology, where the decision-making process is opaque and lacks transparency. This skepticism is heightened when AI outputs conflict with clinical judgment or when the models fail to provide clear justifications for their recommendations. The absence of explainability can lead to mistrust, as clinicians may hesitate to rely on tools they do not fully understand.

  Additionally, automation bias—where clinicians over-rely on AI recommendations without adequate scrutiny—further complicates trust-building efforts. Past instances of AI errors or biases have exacerbated these concerns, making it harder to foster confidence in AI systems. For example, a clinician may question an AI system's diagnostic recommendation if the model cannot explain why it flagged a particular condition, or they may over-rely on a suggestion that contradicts observable clinical evidence.
- **Skill Gaps**: Healthcare professionals often lack the technical expertise required to interpret AI outputs, troubleshoot issues, or understand the underlying mechanisms of the technology. While AI tools are designed to simplify processes, their integration often requires familiarity with concepts like machine learning, data analysis, and model limitations. This skill gap can make it challenging for clinicians to confidently integrate AI into their workflows, particularly in high-stakes environments where decisions have life-or-death consequences. For example, a radiologist using an AI system for automated imaging analysis may struggle to evaluate its accuracy or identify potential errors without training in the basics of AI.
- **Job Security Concerns**: The growing use of AI in automating certain tasks has led to fears among healthcare professionals that these technologies will eventually replace their roles. This concern is particularly strong for repetitive tasks such as medical transcription, diagnostic imaging analysis, and administrative processes. While AI is intended to augment clinical decision-making and improve efficiency, the perception of job displacement can lead to resistance and a reluctance to adopt these tools. For example, medical coders may fear that AI-powered billing systems will render their expertise redundant, creating apprehension about supporting the implementation of such technologies.
- **Resistance to Change**: Healthcare workflows and clinical practices are often deeply ingrained, with established routines that have been refined over years of practice. Introducing AI tools can disrupt these routines, requiring significant adjustments that may initially seem burdensome or unnecessary to clinicians. The perceived complexity of AI tools, combined with limited time for training, can further amplify resistance to change. For example, a hospital implementing an AI-based electronic prescribing system may encounter pushback from clinicians who are comfortable with their current manual or semi-digital processes.

Real-world validation of AI tools is often lacking, further fueling skepticism among clinicians. Shadow mode testing—where AI tools operate in the background without influencing real decisions—could help build trust by demonstrating reliability in live clinical environments without direct risk.

2.4.4 Regulatory and Ethical Challenges

Regulatory and ethical challenges are critical hurdles in the deployment of AI in healthcare. These challenges arise from the rapid pace of AI advancements, which often outstrip the evolution of

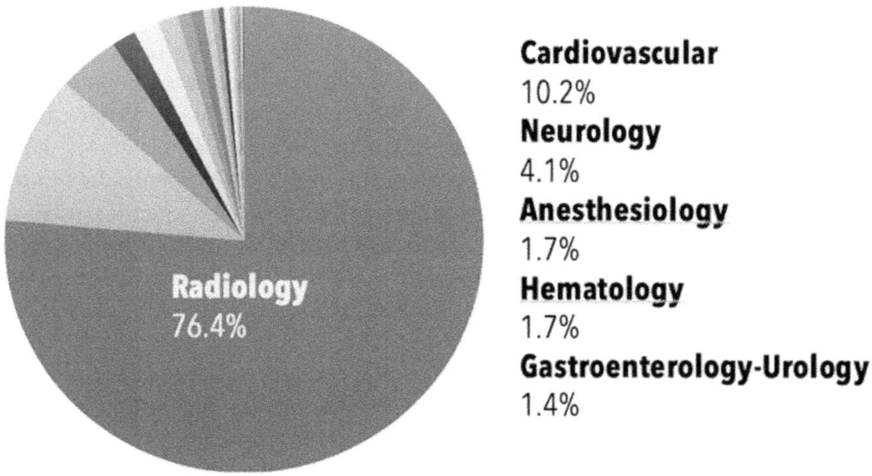

Figure 2.5 The U.S. FDA has cleared more than 1,000 AI models (current as of 12/20/2024).

regulatory frameworks, and the ethical dilemmas surrounding fairness, accountability, transparency, and patient autonomy. Addressing these issues is essential for ensuring trust, compliance, and equitable outcomes.

- **Regulatory Uncertainty**: Existing regulatory frameworks, such as those outlined by the FDA in the U.S. or the European Medicines Agency (EMA), often lag behind the rapid development of AI technologies. This regulatory lag creates ambiguity in areas such as liability, validation, and approval processes for AI systems. The dynamic nature of AI, particularly in systems that evolve through continuous learning, poses additional challenges for compliance with existing regulations. Healthcare providers and developers are often uncertain about how to navigate these frameworks, resulting in delays or barriers to deploying innovative AI solutions. For example, an AI system for detecting early-stage cancers may face prolonged approval processes due to unclear validation standards for adaptive algorithms.
- **Fairness and Accountability**: Ensuring fairness and accountability in AI systems is a complex ethical issue, as these technologies can inadvertently perpetuate or exacerbate existing healthcare disparities. Bias in training datasets, as well as design and implementation decisions, can lead to unequal outcomes for different demographic groups. Additionally, assigning accountability when AI systems make errors remains a gray area, particularly when multiple stakeholders (developers, healthcare providers, and regulatory bodies) are involved. For example, an AI algorithm used for prioritizing patient care might disproportionately deprioritize minority patients due to biases in the training data, exacerbating healthcare inequalities.
- **Transparency and Explainability**: Many AI models, especially those based on deep learning, are considered "black box" systems, where the decision-making process is difficult to interpret. This lack of explainability complicates the adoption of AI in highly regulated healthcare environments, where clinicians and regulators demand a clear understanding of how decisions are made. Transparency is essential not only for regulatory approval but also for fostering trust among healthcare providers and patients. For example, a clinician may

hesitate to rely on an AI tool for prescribing medication if the tool cannot explain why it prioritized one treatment option over another.

- **Patient Consent and Autonomy**: Balancing AI-driven recommendations with respect for patient preferences and informed consent is a delicate ethical issue. Patients must understand how AI systems influence their care decisions, but the complexity of these systems often makes it challenging to provide clear and meaningful explanations. Additionally, there is a risk of over-reliance on AI recommendations, which could undermine patient autonomy and lead to decisions being made without sufficient patient input. For example, an AI system that recommends aggressive treatment for a chronic condition might conflict with a patient's preference for conservative management, creating tension between clinical AI and patient-centered care.
- **Data Governance and Privacy**: The absence of clear data governance frameworks further complicates AI adoption. Ensuring compliance with privacy regulations like GDPR and HIPAA while safeguarding sensitive patient information is a significant challenge. Concerns about privacy violations or unauthorized use of patient data erode public trust and could stall AI progress. For example, a high-profile data breach involving an AI healthcare application could lead to widespread distrust among patients and regulators.

The successful implementation of responsible AI in healthcare requires a focus on fairness, transparency, inclusiveness, and sustainability (Siala & Wang, 2022). These principles ensure that AI technologies address ethical and societal challenges while maintaining trust and accountability. By embedding these values into AI design and deployment, healthcare organizations can align innovation with the overarching goal of improving patient care. By addressing these regulatory and ethical challenges, healthcare organizations can create frameworks that ensure AI is safe, equitable, and centered on improving patient care. Initiatives like shadow mode testing, bias auditing, and explainable AI research are critical to overcoming these barriers.

2.5 Future Opportunities

The next wave of AI in healthcare will be driven by foundation models and agentic AI, two transformative technologies with the potential to reshape patient care, optimize clinical workflows, and improve health outcomes. These advancements address longstanding challenges such as fragmented data, clinician burnout, access disparities, and inefficient care delivery.

2.5.1 Foundation Models: The Backbone of Comprehensive AI Systems

Foundation models (FMs), capable of processing multimodal data—such as imaging, genomics, and clinical notes—are poised to reshape healthcare. By integrating diverse data types into a unified framework, these models generate real-time insights that enhance care delivery. From predicting disease progression to recommending personalized treatments, they support clinical decision-making across specialties.

Unlike traditional AI, which relies on task-specific models, foundation models offer a versatile, all-in-one solution for diagnostics, preventive care, and resource optimization. By synthesizing complex datasets, they provide clinicians with actionable insights, improving accuracy, efficiency, and patient outcomes.

2.5.1.1 Examples of Foundation Model Applications

- **Predicting Disease Progression and Personalizing Treatments**: Foundation models can analyze large datasets to detect early warning signs of diseases such as cancer, cardiovascular disease, and neurodegenerative disorders—enabling earlier, more targeted interventions.
- **Enhancing Clinical Workflows**: By eliminating data silos, FM enables clinicians to quickly access and interpret patient information, reducing administrative burden and improving care coordination.
- **Accelerating Drug Discovery and Clinical Trials**: FM can process genomic and proteomic data to identify drug targets, predict treatment efficacy, and refine trial designs—reducing costs and speeding up the development of new therapies.
- **Reducing Hospital Readmissions**: A foundation model integrating imaging and lab results could predict complications in patients with chronic conditions, enabling timely interventions and improving long-term health outcomes.

2.5.2 Agentic AI

Agentic AI goes beyond recommendations, autonomously acting within predefined guidelines to assist clinicians and optimize care. Unlike traditional AI, which relies on human input to trigger actions, agentic AI actively monitors, identifies issues, and takes action—reducing clinician workload while maintaining oversight and accountability. This marks a shift from AI as a passive tool to a proactive clinical partner, capable of improving efficiency, decision-making, and patient outcomes (Zou & Topol, 2025).

2.5.2.1 Examples of Agentic AI Applications

- **Orchestrating Clinical Tools**: AI agents can integrate multiple functions, such as transcribing patient meetings, analyzing medical images, and referencing clinical guidelines, all while maintaining context from patient histories.

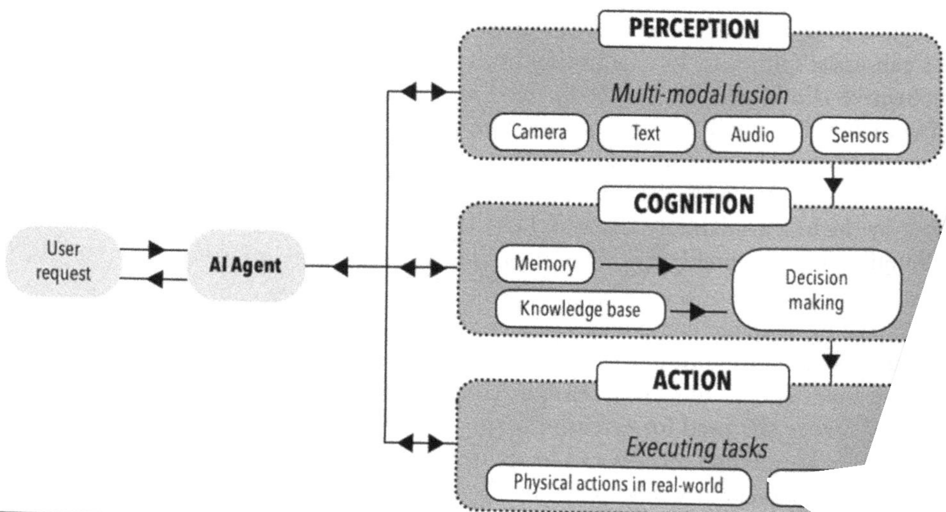

Figure 2.6 Functional architecture of an AI agent: From perception to action.

- **Automating Clinical Tasks**: AI agents can schedule follow-ups, adjust medication doses based on real-time monitoring, and triage patients during high-demand periods, reducing administrative burden.
- **Continuous Monitoring and Decision Support**: Unlike traditional AI, agentic AI maintains long-term memory and contextual awareness, tracking complex patient histories and providing timely, personalized insights.
- **Enhancing Preventive Care**: AI agents analyzing wearable data can detect early signs of conditions like atrial fibrillation, enabling timely interventions and reducing complications.

2.6 Conclusion

Foundation models and agentic AI are set to revolutionize healthcare by tackling some of its most pressing challenges—data overload, workforce shortages, and rising costs. Foundation models, with their ability to process multimodal data, enhance diagnostics, treatment personalization, and operational efficiency. Meanwhile, agentic AI goes beyond recommendations, autonomously managing tasks, optimizing workflows, and supporting clinicians in real-time.

Despite challenges around trust, regulation, and adoption, a collaborative and responsible approach can unlock AI's full potential, ensuring that these technologies drive more accurate, efficient, and accessible healthcare for all.

We envision a revolution in healthcare driven by the profound and seamless integration of advanced AI technologies to deliver precise, personalized, and equitable care. Our goal is to create scalable, robust, and adaptable AI solutions that process diverse data and provide comprehen-
sive, real-time insights, thus reshaping care delivery in transformative and sustainable ways. These
hnologies promise to revolutionize diagnostics, optimize workflows, elevate clinician decision-
ng, and personalize patient care. This will ensure AI's transformative potential translates into
e, lasting benefits for both patients and healthcare providers. With a steadfast commitment
tion, this approach will improve patient outcomes, expand access to high-quality care,
er clinicians to deliver healthcare more effectively, equitably, and efficiently.

ering healthcare providers with AI tools capable of delivering context-aware, action-
can expand access to high-quality care in underserved or remote areas. For exam-
clinicians by integrating imaging, genomics, and patient-specific data into a
cal picture, enabling them to make informed, confident decisions without
nt. This vision goes beyond simple advancements in technology; it redefines
more inclusive, adaptive, resilient, and deeply patient-centric. By embed-
lthcare providers can ensure that every diagnosis and treatment plan is
evidence and tailored to the unique needs of each patient. In doing
nce and compassion, empowering clinicians to focus on what mat-

ents and foundational technologies, healthcare systems can
I, allowing clinicians to synthesize diverse datasets in real-
rate AI development by providing pre-trained, versatile
labeled data and task-specific solutions. For instance,
uickly adapted to new applications, enabling rapid,
ealthcare systems. This evolution is not just about
g trust, ensuring transparency, and promoting inter-

Building AI literacy among healthcare professionals will be essential to instill confidence, ensure seamless integration, and maximize the benefits of these tools.

AI's transformative role extends beyond technological innovation; it is about creating a healthcare system that is both inclusive and resilient. By addressing disparities in care delivery and expanding access to advanced diagnostic capabilities, AI ensures no patient is left behind. A prime example of this is the use of these technologies in ultrasound imaging.

Traditionally, access to ultrasound imaging has been limited in underserved regions due to the high cost of equipment and a shortage of trained sonographers. Embedding advanced AI algorithms into portable devices empowers healthcare providers to perform diagnostic imaging with minimal training. This enables early detection of complications and improves outcomes for mothers and infants.

Furthermore, AI enhances human capabilities, allowing clinicians to focus on empathy and personalized care while benefiting from data-driven insights.

Responsible deployment is crucial to realizing this vision. Transparent, explainable, and accountable AI systems must align with clinical values, ensuring fairness, privacy, and inclusivity. Collaboration among technologists, clinicians, and policymakers will be key to harnessing AI as a force for equitable and sustainable healthcare.

The shift from isolated, manual processes to collaborative, data-driven workflows is central to AI's role as a transformative force in healthcare. Multimodal AI systems enable clinicians to work at the top of their expertise, focusing on delivering personalized care while supported by the unmatched analytical power of AI. This transformation will fundamentally change how care is delivered, making healthcare systems more intelligent, efficient, adaptable, and just. Whether in a rural clinic or an urban hospital, every decision will be informed by the world's most advanced insights, ensuring equity, excellence, and high-quality care for all.

AI is not just about technology—it is about empowering healthcare providers to deliver better, more accessible care for all. By embracing these technologies responsibly and collaboratively, healthcare systems can harness AI's capabilities to deliver smarter, faster, and more equitable care. As AI becomes an integral part of medicine, its success will depend on amplifying human potential while ensuring that compassion and trust remain at the heart of patient care.

Ultimately, this vision is about creating a future where AI is universally trusted, seamlessly integrated, and recognized as a foundation of modern healthcare. At the heart of this transformation are foundation models—versatile, pre-trained systems that enable rapid AI development and integration. These models provide the scalability, adaptability, and multimodal capabilities necessary to deliver on AI's promise, ensuring that the future of healthcare is fair, accessible, and deeply patient-centered.

References

Acosta, J. N., Falcone, G. J., Rajpurkar, P., & Topol, E. J. (2022). Multimodal biomedical AI. *Nature Medicine, 28*(9), 1773–1784.

Ahmed, M. I., Spooner, B., Isherwood, J., Lane, M., Orrock, E., & Dennison, A. (2023). A systematic review of the barriers to the implementation of artificial intelligence in healthcare. *Cureus, 15*(10), e46366.

Alder, S. (2025, January 20). Healthcare data breach statistics. *The HIPPA Journal*. https://www.hipaajournal.com/healthcare-data-breach-statistics/

Alnsour, Y., Johnson, M., Albizri, A., & Harfouche, A. H. (2023). Predicting patient length of stay using artificial intelligence to assist healthcare professionals in resource planning and scheduling decisions. *Journal of Global Information Management, 31*(1), 1–14.

AlSaad, R., Abd-Alrazaq, A., Boughorbel, S., Ahmed, A., Renault, M.-A., Damseh, R., & Sheikh, J. (2024). Multimodal large language models in health care: applications, challenges, and future outlook. *Journal of Medical Internet Research, 26*, e59505.

Amann, J., Blasimme, A., Vayena, E., Frey, D., Madai, V. I., & Consortium, P. (2020). Explainability for artificial intelligence in healthcare: A multidisciplinary perspective. *BMC Medical Informatics and Decision Making, 20*, 1–9.

Arora, A., Alderman, J. E., Palmer, J., Ganapathi, S., Laws, E., Mccradden, M. D., . . . others. (2023). The value of standards for health datasets in artificial intelligence-based applications. *Nature Medicine, 29*(11), 2929–2938.

Bailey, C. R., Bailey, A. M., McKenney, A. S., & Weiss, C. R. (2022). Understanding and appreciating burnout in radiologists. *Radiographics, 42*(5), E137–E139.

Beger, J. (2024). The crucial role of explainability in healthcare AI. *European Journal of Radiology, 176*(0720-048X), 111507.

Bengesi, S., El-Sayed, H., Sarker, M. K., Houkpati, Y., Irungu, J., & Oladunni, T. (2024). Advancements in generative AI: A comprehensive review of GANs, GPT, autoencoders, diffusion model, and transformers. *IEEE Access, 12:* 69812-69837. https://ieeexplore.ieee.org/abstract/document/10521640.

Bhatt, A. B., & Bae, J. (2023). Collaborative Intelligence to catalyze the digital transformation of healthcare. *NPJ Digital Medicine, 6*(1), 177.

Bommasani, R., Hudson, D. A., Adeli, E., Altman, R., Arora, S., Arx, S. v., . . . others. (2021). On the opportunities and risks of foundation models (arXiv preprint arXiv:2108.07258). https://arxiv.org/abs/2108.07258

Celi, L. A., Cellini, J., Charpignon, M.-L., Dee, E. C., Dernoncourt, F., Eber, R., . . . others. (2022). Sources of bias in artificial intelligence that perpetuate healthcare disparities—A global review. *DPLOS Digital Health, 1*(3), e0000022.

Chen, J., Hu, Y., Wang, Y., Lu, Y., Cao, X., Lin, M., . . . others. (2024). TrialBench: Multi-modal artificial intelligence-ready clinical trial datasets (arXiv preprint arXiv:2407.00631). https://arxiv.org/abs/2407.00631

Chen, R. J., Wang, J. J., Williamson, D. F., Chen, T. Y., Lipkova, J., Lu, M. Y., . . . Mahmood, F. (2023). Algorithmic fairness in artificial intelligence for medicine and healthcare. *Nature Biomedical Engineering, 7*(6), 719–742.

Chu, J., Dong, W., & Huang, Z. (2020). Endpoint prediction of heart failure using electronic health records. *Journal of Biomedical Informatics, 109*, 103518.

Dao, T., Fu, D., Ermon, S., Rudra, A., & Ré, C. (2022). Flashattention: Fast and memory-efficient exact attention with io-awareness. *Advances in Neural Information Processing Systems, 35*, 16344–16459.

Dutta, S., Lavin, B., & Wunsch-Vincent, S. (2019). *Global innovation index 2019 creating healthy lives—the future of medical innovation.* Cornell University, INSEAD, and the World Intellectual Property Organization.

Feng, D., Mo, Y., Tang, Z., Chen, Q., Zhang, H., Akerkar, R., & Song, X. (2021). Data-driven hospital personnel scheduling optimization through patients prediction. *CCF Transactions on Pervasive Computing and Interaction, 3*, 40–56.

Fredriksson, T., Mattos, D. I., Bosch, J., & Olsson, H. H. (2020). Data labeling: An empirical investigation into industrial challenges and mitigation strategies. In *International conference on product-focused software process improvement* (pp. 202–216). Springer.

GE HealthCare. (2024, December 2). GE HealthCare unveils first-of-its-kind MRI foundation model. *GE HealthCare.* https://www.gehealthcare.com/insights/article/ge-healthcare-unveils-firstofitskind-mri-foundation-model

Gokal, A., Binesmael, A., Ellis, A., Parkin, D., Levy, L., Kuylen, M., . . . Arnold, S. (2022). *Building the future getting IT Right: The case for urgent investment in safe, modern technology and data sharing in the UK's health services.* British Medical Association.

Halliday, K., Ather, S., Baldwin, D., Bramley, R., Chen, M., Chen, Y., . . . others. (2024). *AI deployment fundamentals for medical imaging.* The Royal College of Radiologists.
Han, R., Acosta, J. N., Shakeri, Z., Ioannidis, J. P., Topol, E. J., & Rajpurkar, P. (2024). Randomised controlled trials evaluating artificial intelligence in clinical practice: a scoping review. *The Lancet Digital Health, 6*(5), e367–e373.
HelloAI. (2025). *HelloAI program.* HelloAI. https://www.helloaiprofessional.com/
Hoi, S. C., Sahoo, D., Lu, J., & Zhao, P. (2021). Online learning: A comprehensive survey. *Neuralcomputing, 459,* 249–289.
Huang, K., Altosaar, J., & Ranganath, R. (2019). ClinicalBERT: Modeling clinical notes and predicting hospital readmission (arXiv preprint arXiv:1904.05342). https://arxiv.org/abs/1904.05342
Islam, T., Hafiz, M. S., Jim, J. R., Kabir, M. M., & Mridha, M. (2024). A systematic review of deep learning data augmentation in medical imaging: Recent advances and future research directions. *Healthcare Analytics, 4,* 100340.
Jebbor, S., Raddouane, C., & El Afia, A. (2022). A preliminary study for selecting the appropriate AI-based forecasting model for hospital assets demand under disasters. *Journal of Humanitarian Logistics and Supply Chain Management, 12*(1), 1–29.
Jiang, P., Xiao, C., Cross, A. R., & Sun, J. (2023). *GraphCare: Enhancing healthcare predictions with personalized knowledge graphs.* The Twelfth International Conference on Learning Representations.
Jiang, P., Xiao, C., Jiang, M., Bhatia, P., Kass-Hout, T., Sun, J., & Han, J. (2024). Reasoning-enhanced healthcare predictions with knowledge graph community retrieval (arXiv preprint arXiv:2410.04585). https://arxiv.org/abs/2410.04585
Johri, S., Jeong, J., Tran, B. A., Schlessinger, D. I., Wongvibulsin, S., Barnes, L. A., . . . others. (2025). An evaluation framework for clinical use of large language models in patient interaction tasks. *Nature Medicine, 31,* 1–10.
Joshi, H. (2025). Natural language processing of electronic health records for predicting Alzheimer's disease. In S. Ravi, N. Gayathri, A. Kumar, D. Chinnathambi, & R. Kumar (Eds.), Deep generative models for integrative analysis of Alzheimer's biomarkers. IGI Global. Hershey, PA. (pp. 141–174).
Kaye, J., Shah, N., Kogetsu, A., Coy, S., Katirai, A., Kuroda, M., . . . Yamamoto, B. A. (2024). Moving beyond technical issues to stakeholder involvement: Key areas for consideration in the development of human-centred and trusted AI in healthcare. Asian Bioethics Review, 16(1), 1–11.
Kirillov, A., Mintun, E., Ravi, N., Mao, H., Rolland, C., Gustafson, L., . . . others. (2023). *Segment anything.* Proceedings of the IEEE/CVF International Conference on Computer Vision, pp. 4015–4026.
Kumar, A., Mani, V., Jain, V., Gupta, H., & Venkatesh, V. (2023). Managing healthcare supply chain through artificial intelligence (AI): A study of critical success factors. *Computers & Industrial Engineering, 175,* 108815.
Kumar, T., Brennan, R., Mileo, A., & Bendechache, M. (2024). Image data augmentation approaches: A comprehensive survey and future directions. *IEEE Access, 12: 187536-187572*
Lawry, T. (2023, July 25). *The future of AI in medicine and what it means for physicians and practices with Tom Lawry.* AMA. https://www.ama-assn.org/practice-management/digital/future-ai-medicine-and-what-it-means-physicians-and-practices-tom-lawry
Le, M. H., Chen, J., Wang, L., Wang, Z., Liu, W., Cheng, K.-T. T., & Yang, X. (2017). Automated diagnosis of prostate cancer in multi-parametric MRI based on multimodal convolutional neural networks. *Physics in Medicine & Biology, 62*(16), 6497.
Lee, J., Yoon, W., Kim, S., Kim, D., Kim, S., So, C. H., & Kang, J. (2020). BioBERT: A pre-trained biomedical language representation model for biomedical text mining. *Bioinformatics*, 36(4):1234–1240.
Lei, C., Chen, L., Cen, J., Chen, X., Lei, Z., Heide, F., . . . Zhang, Z. (2024). SimCMF: A simple cross-modal fine-tuning strategy from vision foundation models to any imaging modality (arXiv preprint arXiv:2411.18669). https://arxiv.org/abs/2411.18669
Li, C., Gan, Z., Yang, Z., Yang, J., Li, L., Wang, L., & Gao, J. (2024). Multimodal foundation models: From specialists to general-purpose assistants. Foundations and Trends® in Computer Graphics and Vision, 16, 1–214.

Li, F., Jin, Y., Liu, W., Rawat, B. P., Cai, P., Yu, H., & others. (2019). Fine-tuning bidirectional encoder representations from transformers (BERT)--based models on large-scale electronic health record notes: An empirical study. *JMIR Medical Informatics, 7*(3), e14830.
Lin, T., Wang, Y., Liu, X., & Qiu, X. (2022). A survey of transformers. *AI Open, 3*, 111–132.
Lipková, J., Angelikopoulos, P., Wu, S., Alberts, E., Wiestler, B., Diehl, C., . . . others. (2019). Personalized radiotherapy design for glioblastoma: integrating mathematical tumor models, multimodal scans, and Bayesian inference. *IEEE Transactions on Medical Imaging, 38*(8), 1875–1884.
Lipkova, J., Chen, R. J., Chen, B., Lu, M. Y., Barbieri, M., Shao, D., . . . others. (2022). Artificial intelligence for multimodal data integration in oncology. *Cancer Cell, 40*(10), 1095–1110.
Lucini, F. R., Reis, M. A., Silveira, G. J., Fogliatto, F. S., Anzanello, M. J., Andrioli, G. G., . . . Schaan. (2020). Man vs. machine: Predicting hospital bed demand from an emergency department. *PLoS One, 15*(8), e0237937.
Lundberg, S. M., & Lee, S.-I. (2017). *A unified approach to interpreting model predictions.* Proceedings of the 31st International Conference on Neural Information Processing Systems, pp. 4768–4777.
Luo Y, Mao C, Sanchez-Pinto LN, et al. Northwestern University resource and education development initiatives to advance collaborative artificial intelligence across the learning health system. *Learn Health Sys.* 2024; e10417. DOI: 10.1002/lrh2.10417.
Mahesh, N., Devishamani, C. S., Raghu, K., Mahalingam, M., Bysani, P., Chakravarthy, A. V., & Raman, R. (2024). Advancing healthcare: the role and impact of AI and foundation models. *American Journal of Translational Research, 16*(6), 2166.
Maleki Varnosfaderani, S., & Forouzanfar, M. (2024). The role of AI in hospitals and clinics: Transforming healthcare in the 21st century. *Bioengineering, 11*(4), 337.
Mathenge, W., Whitestone, N., Nkurikiye, J., Patnaik, J. L., Piyasena, P., Uwaliraye, P., . . . others. (2022). Impact of artificial intelligence assessment of diabetic retinopathy on referral service uptake in a low-resource setting: The RAIDERS randomized trial. *Ophthalmology Science, 2*(4), 100168.
Miao, Z., Sealey, M. D., Sathyanarayanan, S., Delen, D., Zhu, L., & Shepherd, S. (2023). A data preparation framework for cleaning electronic health records and assessing cleaning outcomes for secondary analysis. *Information Systems, 111*, 102130.
Mohammadi, I., Firouzabadi, S. R., Hosseinpour, M., Akhlaghpasand, M., Hajikarimloo, B., Tavanaei, R., . . . Eghbali, F. (2024). Predictive ability of hypotension prediction index and machine learning methods in intraoperative hypotension: A systematic review and meta-analysis. *Journal of Translational Medicine, 22*(1), 725.
Montoya, L. N., Roberts, J. S., & Hidalgo, B. S. (2024). Towards fairness in AI for melanoma detection: Systemic review and recommendations (arXiv preprint arXiv:2411.12846). https://arxiv.org/abs/2411.12846
Najjar, R. (2023). Redefining radiology: A review of artificial intelligence integration in medical imaging. *Diagnostics, 13*(17): 2760. https://www.mdpi.com/2075-4418/13/17/2760.
Nerella, S., Bandyopadhyay, S., Zhang, J., Contreras, M., Siegel, S., Bumin, A., . . . others. (2024). Transformers and large language models in healthcare: A review. *Artificial Intelligence in Medicine*, 154: 102900. https://www.sciencedirect.com/science/article/pii/S0933365724001428
Nguyen, D. C., Pham, Q.-V., Pathirana, P. N., Ding, M., Seneviratne, A., Lin, Z., . . . Hwang, W.-J. (2022). Federated learning for smart healthcare: A survey. *ACM Computing Surveys, 55*(3), 1–37.
Nimri, R., Battelino, T., Laffel, L. M., Slover, R. H., Schatz, D., Weinzimer, S. A., . . . Phillip, M. (2020). Insulin dose optimization using an automated artificial intelligence-based decision support system in youths with type 1 diabetes. *Nature Medicine, 26*(9), 1380–1384.
Olatunji, I. E., Rauch, J., Katzensteiner, M., & Khosla, M. (2024). A review of anonymization for healthcare data. *Big Data, 12*(6), 538–555.
Omega Medical Imaging. (2021, February 2). Comparison of radiation profiles between AI image-guided x-ray system and non-AI guided x-ray system. *Omega Medical Imaging.* https://www.omegamedicalimaging.com/comparison-of-radiation-profiles/#:~:text=Conclusion%3A%20In%20all%20modes%20of,%25%20and%20-51%25%20radiation%20reduction
Pai, S., Bontempi, D., Prudente, V., Hadzic, I., Sokač, M., Chaunzwa, T. L., . . . others. (2023). Foundation models for quantitative biomarker discovery in cancer imaging. *medRxiv.*

PubMed. (2024, April 30). *MEDLINE PubMed production statistics*. National Library of Medicine. https://www.nlm.nih.gov/bsd/medline_pubmed_production_stats.html

Qian, X., Pei, J., Zheng, H., Xie, X., Yan, L., Zhang, H., . . . others. (2021). Prospective assessment of breast cancer risk from multimodal multiview ultrasound images via clinically applicable deep learning. *Nature Biomedical Engineering, 5*(6), 522–532.

Ravishankar, H., Patil, R., Melapudi, V., & Annangi, P. (2023). *SonoSAM-segment anything on ultrasound images*. International Workshop on Advances in Simplifying Medical Ultrasound, pp. 23–33.

Ribeiro, M. T., Singh, S., & Guestrin, C. (2016). *"Why should i trust you?" Explaining the predictions of any classifier*. Proceedings of the 22nd ACM SIGKDD International Conference on Knowledge Discovery and Data Mining, pp. 1135–1144.

Robertson, A. J., Mallett, J, r., Stark, Z., & Sullivan, C. (2024). It Is in Our DNA: Bringing Electronic Health Records and Genomic Data Together for Precision Medicine. *JMIR Bioinformatics and Biotechnology, 5*: 23-30. https://bioinform.jmir.org/2024/1/PDF

Romero-Brufau, S., Wyatt, K. D., Boyum, P., Mickelson, M., Moore, M., & Cognetta-Rieke, C. (2020). Implementation of artificial intelligence-based clinical decision support to reduce hospital readmissions at a regional hospital. *Applied Clinical Informatics, 11*(4), 570–577.

Sarvamangala, D., & Kulkarni, R. V. (2022). Convolutional neural networks in medical image understanding: A survey. *Evolutionary Intelligence, 15*, 1–22.

Sasseville, M., Ouellet, S., Rhéaume, C., Sahlia, M., Couture, V., Després, P., . . . Gagnon, M.-P. (2025). Bias mitigation in primary health care artificial intelligence models: Scoping review. *Journal of Medical Internet Research, 27*, e60269.

Schubert, T., Oosterlinck, T., Stevens, R. D., Maxwell, P. H., & van der Schaar, M. (2025). AI education for clinicians. *eClinicalMedicine, 79*, 102968.

Seoni, S., Jahmunah, V., Salvi, M., Barua, P. D., Molinari, F., & Acharya, U. R. (2023). Application of uncertainty quantification to artificial intelligence in healthcare: A review of last decade (2013–2023). *Computers in Biology and Medicine*, 165: 107441. https://www.sciencedirect.com/science/article/pii/S001048252300906X

Sharma, S., Zhang, Y., Ríos Aliaga, J. M., Bouneffouf, D., Muthusamy, V., & Varshney, K. R. (2020). *Data augmentation for discrimination prevention and bias disambiguation*. Proceedings of the AAAI/ACM Conference on AI, Ethics, and Society, pp. 358–364.

Siala, H., & Wang, Y. (2022). SHIFTing artificial intelligence to be responsible in healthcare: A systematic review. *Social Science & Medicine, 301*, 114782.

Sinsky, C., Colligan, L., Li, L., Prgomet, M., Reynolds, S., Goeders, L., . . . Blike, G. (2016, 165). Allocation of physician time in ambulatory practice: a time and motion study in 4 specialties. *Annals of Internal Medicine, 11*, 753–760.

Stempniak, M. (2020, June 29). Physician specialist shortage—including radiologists—could climb to almost 42,000 by 2033. *Radiology Business*. https://radiologybusiness.com/topics/healthcare-management/healthcare-economics/physician-specialist-shortage-radiologists-aamc

Teoh, D. (2018). Towards stroke prediction using electronic health records. *BMC Medical Informatics and Decision Making, 18*, 1–11.

Theodorou, B., Glass, L., Xiao, C., & Sun, J. (2024). FRAMM: Fair ranking with missing modalities for clinical trial site selection. *Patterns, 5*(3): 100944.

Theodorou, B. P., Xiao, C., & Sun, J. (2023). *TREEMENT: Interpretable patient-trial matching via personalized dynamic tree-based memory network*. Proceedings of the 14th ACM International Conference on Bioinformatics, Computational Biology, and Health Informatics, pp. 1-111–9. https://www.cell.com/patterns/fulltext/S2666-3899(24)00043-6

Valeriano, E. (2024, October 21). Latest advances in research: Building a multimodal X-ray foundation model. *GE HealthCare*. https://www.gehealthcare.com/insights/article/latest-advances-in-research-building-a-multimodal-xray-foundation-model

van der Wal, I., Meijer, F., Fuica, R., Silman, Z., Boon, M., Martini, C., . . . Gozal, Y. (2023). Intraoperative use of the machine learning-derived nociception level monitor results in less pain in the first 90 min after surgery. *Frontiers in Pain Research, 3*, 1086862.

Vorisek, C. N., Lehne, M., Klopfenstein, S. A., Mayer, P. J., Bartschke, A., Haese, T., & Thun, S. (2022). Fast healthcare interoperability resources (FHIR) for interoperability in health research: Systematic review. *JMIR Medical Informatics, 10*(7), e35724.

Wang, E., Zaman, N., Mcgee, S., Milanese, J.-S., Masoudi-Nejad, A., & O'Connor-McCourt, M. (2015). Predictive genomics: A cancer hallmark network framework for predicting tumor clinical phenotypes using genome sequencing data. *Seminars in Cancer Biology, 30*, 4–12. Elsevier.

Whooley, S. (2023, September 18). Gates foundation backs GE HealthCare AI-based ultrasound. *Mass Device*. https://www.massdevice.com/bill-melinda-gates-foundation-gives-ge-healthcare-44m-to-develop-ai-based-ultrasound/

Wijnberge, M., Geerts, B. F., Hol, L., Lemmers, N., Mulder, M. P., Berge, P., . . . others. (2020). Effect of a machine learning--derived early warning system for intraoperative hypotension vs standard care on depth and duration of intraoperative hypotension during elective noncardiac surgery: the HYPE randomized clinical trial. *JAMA, 323*(11), 1052–1060.

Wilson, P. F., To, M. N., Jamzad, A., Gilany, M., Harmanani, M., Elghareb, T., . . . Mousavi, P. (2024). ProstNFound: Integrating foundation models with ultrasound domain knowledge and clinical context for robust prostate cancer detection. In *International conference on medical image computing and computer-assisted intervention* (pp. 499–509). Springer Nature Switzerland.

Wojtara, M., Rana, E., Rahman, T., Khanna, P., & Singh, H. (2023). Artificial intelligence in rare disease diagnosis and treatment. *Clinical and Translational Science, 16*(11), 2106–2111.

Xiao, C., Choi, E., & Sun, J. (2018). Opportunities and challenges in developing deep learning models using electronic health records data: A systematic review. *Journal of the American Medical Informatics Association, 25*(10), 1419–1428.

Yan, A., McAuley, J., Lu, X., Du, J., Chang, E. Y., Gentili, A., & Hsu, C.-N. (2022). RadBERT: Adapting transformer-based language models to radiology. *Radiology: Artificial Intelligence, 4*(4), e210258.

Yang, J., Soltan, AS, r., Eyre, D. W., Yang, Y., & Clifton, D. A. (2023). An adversarial training framework for mitigating algorithmic biases in clinical machine learning. *NPJ Digital Medicine, 6*(1), 55.

Yang, M., Wu, Z., Zheng, H., Huang, L., Ding, W., Pan, L., & Yin, L. (2024). Cross-modality medical image segmentation via enhanced feature alignment and cross pseudo supervision learning. *Diagnostics, 14*(16), 1751.

Yang, Z., Mitra, A., Kwon, S., & Yu, H. (2024). ClinicalMamba: A generative clinical language model on longitudinal clinical notes (arXiv preprint arXiv:2403.05795). https://arxiv.org/abs/2403.05795

Yue, L., Xing, S., Chen, J., & Fu, T. (2024). *Clinicalagent: Clinical trial multi-agent system with large language model-based reasoning.* Proceedings of the 15th ACM International Conference on Bioinformatics, Computational Biology and Health Informatics, pp. 1–10.

Yue, L., Xing, S., Chen, J., & Fu, T. (2024). *Trialenroll: Predicting clinical trial enrollment success with deep \& cross network and large language models.* Proceedings of the 15th ACM International Conference on Bioinformatics, Computational Biology and Health Informatics, pp. 1–9.

Zhang, A., Xing, L., Zou, J., & Wu, J. C. (2022). Shifting machine learning for healthcare from development to deployment and from models to data. *Nature Biomedical Engineering, 6*(12), 1330–1345.

Zhou, C., Li, Q., Li, C., Yu, J., Liu, Y., Wang, G., . . . others. (2024). A comprehensive survey on pretrained foundation models: A history from BERT to ChatGPT. *International Journal of Machine Learning and Cybernetics*, 1–65. https://doi.org/10.1007/s13042-024-02443-6

Zhou, L., Guo, Z., Wang, B., Wu, Y., Li, Z., Yao, H., . . . Cui, Y. (2021). Risk prediction in patients with heart failure with preserved ejection fraction using gene expression data and machine learning. *Frontiers in Genetics, 12*, 652315.

Zou, J., & Topol, E. J. (2025). The rise of agentic AI teammates in medicine. *The Lancet, 405*(10477), 457.

Chapter 3

Unlocking the Power of AI in Transforming Patient Access and Staff Engagement

Crystal Broj, CPDHTS

3.1 Overview

AI is shaking up healthcare in a big way, and at the Medical University of South Carolina (MUSC), we've seen firsthand how it can make a difference in patient access and staff engagement. With over 250 open patient access roles across South Carolina and a growing demand for care, we needed a smarter way to work. AI wasn't just about filling gaps—it was about rethinking how we do things, making processes more efficient, and giving staff the tools to focus on what really matters: patient care.

This chapter walks through our journey at MUSC—why we turned to AI, how we rolled it out, and what we learned along the way. From automating preregistration and streamlining scheduling to reducing no-show rates and cutting administrative burden, we've seen real results: a 50% boost in pre-registration, an 11% drop in no-shows, and a 97% patient satisfaction score. But it wasn't all smooth sailing. We tackled resistance, scaled strategically, and worked closely with vendors to build the right solutions.

AI isn't a magic fix, but when done right, it can transform healthcare. This chapter breaks down what worked, what didn't, and what's next—because this is just the beginning.

3.2 Introduction

Artificial intelligence (AI) is transforming the way healthcare systems deliver care, improve access, and engage staff. In my role as Chief Digital Transformation Officer at the Medical University of South Carolina (MUSC), I've seen firsthand how AI can help tackle some of the biggest challenges we face—especially in patient access and staff engagement. This chapter walks through our

DOI: 10.4324/9781003621294-4

journey at MUSC, showing how we've leveraged AI to address these persistent issues. We'll cover everything from developing a strategy and vision to implementation best practices, early results, the challenges we faced, and where we see opportunities for the future.

So, why AI? Let's start with the basics. As of this writing, there are over 250 open positions in patient access centers across South Carolina. That's a staggering number. When you've got that many unfilled roles, the ripple effects are felt everywhere—existing staff are stretched thin, burnout becomes a serious issue, and ultimately, patient care suffers. Automating some of the administrative tasks can help lighten the load. By streamlining processes and cutting down on manual labor, we can free up our teams to focus on what really matters: delivering exceptional care. This isn't just about solving staffing shortages; it's about making the whole system more efficient and improving the patient experience at the same time.

But it's not just a staffing issue. Access to care is becoming more important than ever, and we have to find creative ways to meet that demand. The number of people seeking care from MUSC physicians and nurses is growing—and fast. According to the U.S. Census Bureau (2023), South Carolina saw a 1.7% population increase from July 2022 to July 2023, making it the fastest-growing state in the country during that period. Combine that with an aging baby boomer population, and we're staring down a tsunami of patients coming our way.

Sure, part of the access problem is the shortage of physicians and advanced practice providers, and we know that's something we can only fix through recruitment and smarter workforce deployment. But there's another side to this—we need to get the repetitive, low-value work out of the system. Not just for our doctors, but for every member of the care team. If we can automate the routine stuff, we can give our teams more time to focus on what really matters: patient care.

On top of all that, consumer expectations are changing fast. People are used to the ease and convenience of booking a flight or ordering something online in just a few clicks. And guess what? Those same people are our patients. They expect the same kind of seamless, hassle-free experience when scheduling a doctor's appointment. Quality care is still non-negotiable, but it's no longer enough on its own to attract and retain patients. If we don't make the process easy and convenient, they'll find a provider who will.

3.3 Background

Over the past 20 years, we've seen healthcare go through a massive shift. First, we moved from paper to digital, and then we hit the era of consumerization, with a big push for better patient experiences. But let's be honest—despite all that progress, most people still find the healthcare system frustrating. It's full of friction and barriers that make even simple tasks feel complicated.

And the numbers back that up. Even with the widespread adoption of electronic health records (EHRs), staffing ratios and productivity haven't really improved. Why? Because when we rolled out EHRs, all we did was digitize our old analog processes. We didn't stop to fundamentally rethink the work or figure out how to make it faster, easier, or better. Instead, we just ended up with digital versions of the same clunky workflows. It's like putting a shiny new engine in an old car but never fixing the brakes—you're not really solving the problem.

That's where AI comes in. It gives us the chance to move beyond just digitizing what we've always done and start reimagining how healthcare *could* work. It's not just about technology for technology's sake—it's about making real, meaningful improvements that benefit both our staff and our patients. And that's the journey we're on at MUSC.

3.4 Strategy and Vision for AI

AI isn't a magic wand that will instantly solve healthcare's biggest challenges. But when combined with a clear strategy, it can bring tremendous value to health systems. By taking over repetitive, time-consuming tasks, AI frees up resources so providers and staff can focus on what truly matters: delivering exceptional care and creating transformative patient experiences.

At MUSC, we've embraced automation strategically—not just to digitize processes but to drive efficiency and innovation. This shift came from a real need to meet growing healthcare demands, improve patient care, and enable our team to work at the top of their license. With manual processes eating up time and complex regulations adding layers of difficulty, we saw automation as a must-have for faster, more efficient, and patient-centered care.

Our journey started with choosing a partner who wasn't just right for the present but could grow with us. We began by automating preregistration to create a strong foundation for operational improvements. Our goal was clear: to find a software partner capable of streamlining processes like prior authorizations, referrals, and care gap outreach—freeing our staff to focus on higher-value work. We wanted a platform where we could start small but scale up seamlessly, without needing a patchwork of point solutions to get there.

From there, it was all about having a solid strategy, a clear vision, and a steady north star to guide the way.

So we've shaped our vision for AI around three core goals:

1. **Improving Patient Access**: Making it easier for our patients to connect with the care they need by cutting through administrative red tape and optimizing workflows.
2. **Enhancing Staff Engagement**: Reducing the day-to-day grind of repetitive administrative work so our staff can spend more time on meaningful, patient-centered tasks.
3. **Driving Efficiency and Innovation**: Rethinking processes to save time, cut costs, and deliver better outcomes for both patients and staff.

Our strategy is straightforward: prioritize patients. But as we implement technology, we must make sure we consider the providers or staff who will be using it. Instead of making things more difficult, technology should make them easier. Instead of replacing humans, we see AI as a tool to empower them. AI will never run on its own; there's always a "human in the loop", so it's all about integrating AI into existing systems in a way that feels natural and useful, while fostering a culture of innovation and adaptability.

To get started, we identified areas where inefficiencies were most frustrating, things like preregistration, prior authorizations, and care gap outreach. These areas offered quick wins while paving the way for bigger transformations down the line.

Let's be honest—while electronic health records (EHRs) have revolutionized how we handle patient information, they've also added a lot of extra work for providers and support staff. Burnout isn't just a provider issue; it impacts front-desk teams, patient access centers, and back-office staff as well.

Here's how we're addressing this:

1. **Patients today expect convenience**: People are used to ordering groceries, booking vacations, and managing their lives online—at any time of the day. But in healthcare, many systems still require patients to call during office hours to get what they need. By offering seamless, digital-first options, we reduce friction and let patients find the right care when and where it works for them.

2. **Providers want to focus on care, not clerical work**: Doctors didn't become doctors to spend hours entering into an electronic health record; they want to concentrate on providing care rather than administrative tasks. Similarly, patient access and back-office personnel should not be burdened with repetitive duties when they could be assisting patients with complicated referrals and appointments. AI can take the more tedious work out of the equation, allowing providers to work at "the top of their license" and do what they really love to do—take care of patients.
3. **Efficiency isn't just about automation—it's about improvement**: Before adding AI to a workflow, it's critical to take a step back and rethink the process. Is the workflow designed as efficiently as possible? Once that's done, AI can take over the repetitive tasks, saving time, cutting costs, and even boosting job satisfaction.

3.5 Implementation Best Practices

The successful implementation of AI in healthcare requires a thoughtful and methodical approach. At MUSC, we adopted the following best practices:

3.5.1 Stakeholder Engagement

From the outset, we involved stakeholders across all levels of the organization—from executive leadership to frontline staff. This ensured alignment on goals and fostered buy-in. In workshops, we reviewed current workflows and outlined how we could improve the experience for both providers and patients. We collaborated with our Patient and Family Action Council to create experiences that truly connect with our patients, avoiding heavy clinical language. We meet with leadership and teams in regular meetings and feedback sessions to share key performance indicators (KPIs) and sentiments expressed by both patients and staff to address concerns and gather insights.

3.5.2 Change Management

For true transformation to make an impact on an organization, it is essential to have a true plan for change management. This became integral to our implementation strategy. We appointed a dedicated change manager to oversee training, communication, and the rollout of new solutions. This role was critical in bridging the gap between technology and its users, ensuring smooth transitions and sustained adoption. While creating detailed plans with timelines and deliverables for each project, the change manager also educated both the project team and leaders on the importance of having a solid process for change, allowing team members to take on change tasks as projects progressed.

3.5.3 Data-Driven Decision-Making

AI thrives on data, and its implementation necessitated robust data governance practices. We needed to know what change we were trying to achieve, from increasing patient engagement to decreasing no-show rates. By capturing the existing metrics, we were able to observe the change the technology brought to the processes and make adjustments along the way to ensure we were achieving the desired outcomes. This is not a one-time process, and we continue to monitor and tweak the AI on a regular basis.

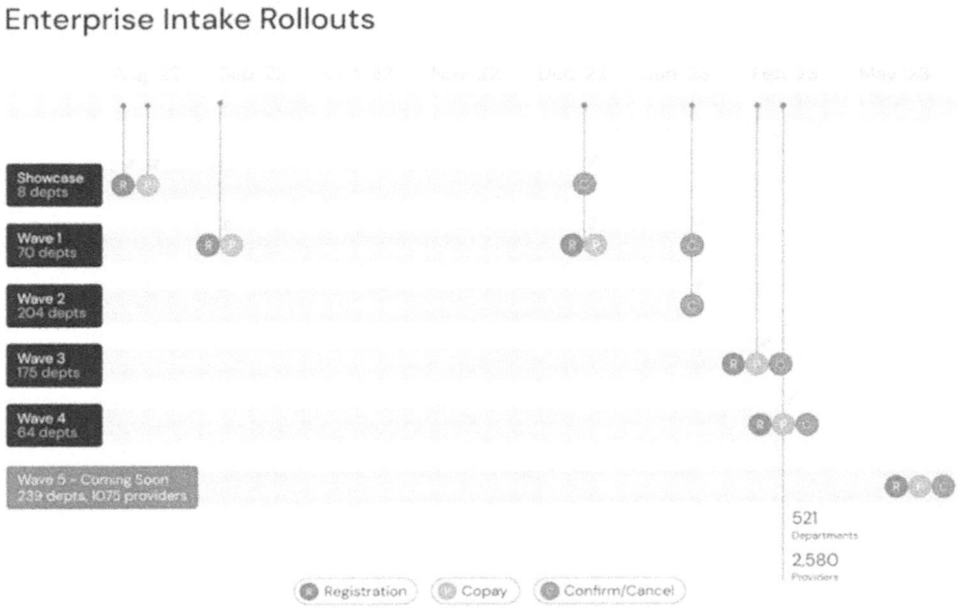

Figure 3.1 Installing preregistration in waves.

3.5.4 Iterative Development

Rather than aiming for perfection from the start, we embraced an iterative approach. Pilot projects were used to test and refine solutions before scaling them across the organization. Our first project was launched with limited capabilities in just five offices. This very controlled approach allowed us to work closely with the initial launch sites to work out processes, updates, and training before expanding. As we expanded the next wave to 70 offices, we continued to modify the approach, and we also added functionality. (*See* Figure 3.1) This allowed us to adapt to real-world challenges and incorporate user feedback. As new waves were initiated, they received all the new technology updates along with their software rollout. We also retrofitted early adopters with new features. It was essential to have good communication so teams would know where they were in the rollout and to share updates and enhancements in the system as we grew.

3.5.5 Focus on Equity

We know that not everyone can adapt to technology the same way, and as such, we worked on solutions that were very easy to use for all our patients. To bridge the digital divide, we designed solutions that prioritized accessibility. For example, once the preregistration process was stabilized, we translated it into Spanish and delivered the texts and experience in Spanish for those patients who identified that as their preferred communication language. This resulted in a great experience for those patients who commented on how happy they were to complete this on their own, in Spanish, in their own time.

But we also knew that technology was not a one-size-fits-all opportunity, and we could not digitize every workflow. There will always be patients who prefer to interact with a human instead of technology, and as such, we need to maintain the consistency of experience that is customer-focused from both the digital and physical interactions. This thought process helped us remain grounded in assisting all of our community.

3.6 Initial Results

The impact of AI implementation at MUSC has been transformative. Some of the key outcomes include:

3.6.1 Improved Preregistration Rates

Prior to implementing AI, only 24% of patients completed preregistration online or in our EHR application. We changed the process with automation, and 3 days before a patient's appointment, we send a text with a link to complete their pre-registration, from verifying demographic information like current address to uploading the driver's license and insurance card. By automating this process, we doubled the completion rate to 50%, significantly reducing the manual workload for our front desk staff because all this work was completed before the appointment, saving approximately 3–5 minutes per encounter and improving the patient experience by not handing a clipboard and making the patient fill out all information in the waiting room.

3.6.2 Decreased No-Show Rates

The preregistration process allows the patient to confirm or cancel their appointment. If the patient cancels, they are currently asked to call to reschedule (automated rescheduling will be rolled out soon). By giving the patient the option to cancel, we decreased no-show rates by 11%. However, by instituting a "fast pass" waiting list, we were also able to offer the canceled appointment to other patients on the waiting list, filling schedules and cutting down appointment wait times.

3.6.3 Enhanced Efficiency

As stated above, the amount saved between having a patient fill out a clipboard or completing the process electronically saved an average of 3–5 minutes per patient. When rolling out system-wide, we saw departments reporting saving an average of seven hours per month on administrative tasks. While this is impressive savings, it is important to note that this did not mean we reduced positions; instead, this provided the opportunity to reallocate the time to higher-value activities, such as patient care and referral processing. This shift provides both care team members and patients with a more satisfactory experience.

3.6.4 Increased Patient Engagement

Feedback from patients highlighted the user-friendly nature of our solutions. We ask our patients to rate their experience at the end of their encounter and receive a consistent 97% patient satisfaction. More importantly, we provide an open-ended comments section, which has provided amazing insights. While comments such as, "Very step-by-step and phone-friendly! Great work to the designers", underscored the positive reception of our initiatives. More importantly, there were comments expressing unhappiness about repetitive questions or even receiving multiple notifications for multiple appointments in a single week. These allowed us to iterate on the design to change the process to pull information and display it to the patient with a "validate and edit if necessary" as well as combining multiple appointments in a week into a single check-in for all appointments.

3.6.5 Confidence to Expand

Our goal was simple: execute the preregistration experience successfully and use it as a strong foundation to build on. Once that was up and running, we moved on to care gap outreach for breast cancer screenings. Using the same "AI Agents" and user interface from our registration process, we started small again, but the results were so impressive that we expanded the program across the entire region.

Building on that momentum, we took things further. We began leveraging the platform to tackle back-office tasks for our revenue cycle team, focusing on one of the most time-consuming jobs: prior authorizations. We started with radiology authorizations at a single hospital and quickly saw real results—40% of the authorizations processed through AI were handled automatically, without any human intervention. That's huge when you consider that each authorization typically takes a person up to 30 minutes to extract information from the EHR, input it into the payer portal, and update the patient record. With an AI Agent, that same process takes under a minute, allowing staff to focus on the more complex cases that require a human touch.

Both initiatives followed a phased approach. We started small with smaller groups, building confidence and ironing out any kinks before rolling them out on a larger scale. It's been a game changer for both efficiency and patient care.

3.6.6 Enhancing Preventive Care through Technology

Our AI-driven care gap outreach campaigns have made a significant impact, especially in addressing delayed preventive care following COVID-19.

One of our first initiatives focused on breast cancer screenings, enabling patients to schedule mammograms via text in their preferred language. In our initial outreach, we had 167 mammograms scheduled overnight—completely automated, without human intervention. To date, this campaign has scheduled nearly 3,000 appointments, and we continue to remind women who are overdue to schedule.

What's even more remarkable is the outcome: over 180 cases so far required further review and additional intervention, potentially preventing more serious diagnoses down the road. This demonstrates how technology can simplify healthcare access while delivering life-saving results.

Building on this success, we've expanded the program to include outreach for well-child visits and vaccination reminders, with plans to broaden its scope even further. These efforts not only support healthier lifestyles for our population but also ensure that preventive care remains a priority.

3.7 Challenges

The journey to AI adoption has not been without its challenges.

3.7.1 Addressing Resistance and Building Confidence

When we introduce new technologies, it's natural for both staff and patients to have concerns. Overcoming that resistance isn't just about flipping a switch and hoping for the best—it takes clear communication, thorough training, and ongoing support to really get everyone on board. However, we often think that we've put the product into production and we are done, but AI journeys are not "set it and forget it"; they do need updating, and those updates need to be shared with the teams.

Of course, like any tech project, we hit a few bumps along the way. During one of our pilot projects, things didn't always go as smoothly as we'd hoped, and that started to chip away at staff confidence. For instance, we had patients who received texts about our new process and came in with questions, only to be told by staff to ignore the messages and just fill out the same paperwork when they arrived. In other cases, staff missed the flag in the EHR that showed the process was already completed online, and they asked patients to redo the paperwork because, well, "that's how we've always done it". Think about walking into the doctor's office; you have already filled out all that paperwork online, and you are given the "dreaded clipboard" to fill out again. It's easy to imagine how frustrating that was for patients who had taken the time to complete everything ahead of time.

We realized quickly that communication had to be more than just troubleshooting when something went wrong. It was about making sure staff understood *why* we were doing this and how it could actually make their jobs easier—explaining the *how* and *why* behind the solution and highlighting *what's in it for them*—like freeing up more time to focus on meaningful customer service instead of shuffling papers. Giving them the right talking points and explaining the benefits in a way that mattered to them made a huge difference in getting buy-in.

But communication isn't just about what you say—it's about *how* you say it and how you interact with the team. Sending out a perfectly crafted email newsletter with all the latest updates might feel like checking the box, but let's be honest: there's a good chance it never gets read. Just like we think about how our patients prefer to be communicated with—whether that's voice, text, or email—we need to do the same for our staff. Everyone has different learning styles, time constraints, and preferences for how they like to receive information. So, we need to contact them to make the best impact. Sometimes it's a quick team huddle, other times it's a dedicated learning session, maybe a department meeting, and occasionally it's as simple as putting up a poster in the break room. What we've found is that repeating the message in different ways really helps the ideas stick. The more touchpoints we have, the more likely it is that people will absorb and adopt the information.

Another big lesson was the need for consistent, ongoing training. Staff turnover happens, and new team members often missed out on the initial rollout, which meant they didn't have the context for why the automated process was in place. Without that background, they weren't as likely to encourage patients to use it. To tackle this, we put together quick reference cards and a super simple five-minute online tutorial. It walks staff through how the system works, what the patient experience looks like, and why it matters.

These tools have been a hit. Staff feel more informed, supported, and included in the project's ongoing success. When they understand the process and see the benefits firsthand, they become ambassadors for the technology. And that shift has made a noticeable difference—not just in how the tools are being used, but in overall patient satisfaction, too.

3.7.2 Scalability

Scaling AI solutions across a large healthcare system posed both logistical and technical challenges. To navigate these complexities, we relied on iterative testing and phased rollouts. While we aimed to avoid being stuck in "pilot mode", each new phase often felt like another pilot due to the introduction of a new feature—which sometimes meant a new API or service requiring more time from our IT department. This isn't as easy as "plugging in and turning it on".

While the initial setup of connections was prioritized with our IT department, securing the necessary resources for subsequent phases proved more difficult. Unlike traditional healthcare IT projects, AI initiatives operate in agile environments where functionality is continuously developed, deployed, and refined. This agile approach can be challenging for IT departments accustomed to waterfall workflows, where upgrades or feature implementations follow a structured and regimented process.

For instance, adding new offices might require an update to a data extract or the connection of an API between the vendor and the EHR. Although these tasks are typically small—often taking less than 20 hours—they can occur sporadically over time, maybe 2 hours one week and 4 hours two weeks later. As software evolves, additional updates or changes may be necessary, and troubleshooting potential issues often defies the predictability of traditional IT staffing models.

Collaboration with our IT counterparts and the Project Management Office (PMO) was essential for balancing the resource demands of AI projects with ongoing operations and planned priorities. This partnership allowed us to align agile development cycles with the realities of IT staffing, ensuring the successful scaling of AI solutions while maintaining daily operations. It's not perfect, but this is another place where communication from both sides helps form a partnership and understanding to make it work out.

3.7.3 Partnering with Vendors

In the world of healthcare, especially when integrating AI, choosing the right vendor isn't just about picking a software provider—it's about finding a true partner. The rapid pace of technological advancements means that no single solution is static, and success often depends on building a relationship rooted in mutual growth, trust, and adaptability.

First and foremost, it's critical to select a vendor whose mission and approach align with your organization's goals. Look for partners who are committed to patient-centered care, operational efficiency, and innovation. A good vendor isn't just selling a product—they're offering a collaborative opportunity to tackle real-world healthcare challenges. By bringing them into your team, they become more than just external providers; they're stakeholders in your success.

No vendor is perfect, and that's okay. When you view a vendor as part of your team, you create space for honest dialogue. Be willing to challenge them on their solutions, push for improvements, and share critical feedback. But also be open to being challenged yourself—vendors bring expertise from other implementations and may offer insights or approaches you hadn't considered. This back-and-forth exchange leads to better outcomes and fosters a culture of continuous improvement.

In healthcare, we often assume that because everyone uses an Electronic Health Record (EHR), integrating new technology should be straightforward. But here's the reality: while many health systems use the same EHR vendors, each system configures its EHR differently. This means that connecting to one EHR doesn't guarantee a seamless connection to the next. Vendors need to be flexible and capable of navigating these unique configurations, and healthcare organizations need to be patient and understanding of the complexity involved.

AI is evolving at lightning speed, and most vendors are continuously refining what their software can do. While they may have developed something similar to what you need, it might not be an exact fit. This is where agile development comes into play. Instead of expecting a perfect solution out of the box, be prepared for a process of trial and error. Working side by side with your vendor, you'll discover new capabilities together, iterate on solutions, and adapt as both your needs and the technology evolve.

When buying something, you choose a vendor that can deliver a product. Building a vision for a software platform with AI is something entirely different—you need a partner that will walk the journey together. From the first pilot and the struggles of testing and redoing things to helping you scale the solution, to sitting with you as you expand the scope to help other areas of your organization, you need to trust a partner to be with you and support your vision the entire way. This means that you need to dedicate time to the relationship—and they do too. It's necessary to create daily stand-ups with the system project managers and the developers—especially during critical time periods. It means providing timely feedback, as much information as you can, and being as transparent as possible. It's honestly admitting mistakes and truly celebrating the successes.

My favorite parts of these relationships are when we challenge our partners to be better. Sometimes, it's to write better documentation, or help with training, and other times it is to create a new feature that didn't exist before and provide reasons why it is useful in the tool. But you have to be willing to accept challenges too, remembering that you selected this partner for their experience, and they have seen other systems and other implementations from which you can learn. When both sides are committed to a partnership, the end result is not just a product or an AI tool—it becomes a unique solution for your organization that is crafted to meet your unique needs. AI provides the option to do this and make these types of unique solutions and partnerships more than ever before.

Healthcare AI is evolving so quickly and is always changing, and it's impossible to "go it alone". By developing these partnerships with patience, openness, and a willingness to learn and grow together, healthcare organizations can unlock the full potential of AI with these partners to transform patient care and operational efficiency.

3.8 Looking Ahead: The Future of AI in Healthcare Transformation

We have already seen the potential AI has to change the processes in healthcare, offering practical solutions to reduce administrative burden and improve patient care. As we look ahead, here are some of the key areas we are planning to focus on for AI to drive further transformation:

3.8.1 AI-Driven Chart Scrubbing

Healthcare providers are stretched thin, facing burnout and the overwhelming task of keeping up with ever-growing medical knowledge. Consider this: Medical knowledge has been expanding at an unprecedented rate. In 1950, it doubled every 50 years, but by 2020, it was doubling approximately every 73 days (Densen, 2011). That's staggering!

How can we use AI to help providers in their day-to-day interactions with patients?

- **Patient Prep**: AI can analyze charts, labs, prescriptions, and other data to create concise summaries for providers before a visit. We are excited for this technology to create a visit pre-summary for a provider, saving the provider time by highlighting past action plans, flagging follow-up questions, and identifying care gaps or medication updates. This allows providers to focus on delivering informed, efficient care rather than wading through pages of records. As we move into other phases, it will also be able to review the patient data and even help with the coding of the types of things that should be billed for this visit, making the provider more efficient and helping to save coding errors.
- **Provider Co-Pilot**: By scanning libraries of data, curated specifically by providers for providers, an AI module can take the notes a provider makes during a visit (perhaps even with Ambient listening) and offer suggestions for next best steps based on standard protocols. Of course, these would be reviewed by the provider and implemented only afterwards.
- **Specialized Referrals**: Referrals often involve extensive paperwork, much of it arriving via fax. Staff spend hours sifting through these documents, scanning or typing data into charts, and identifying any pre-visit tests that need to be ordered. With Optical Character Recognition (OCR) and AI chart scrubbing, this process—which can take an hour or more—can be completed in minutes. AI empowers providers by eliminating these tedious tasks, giving them more time to focus on patient care.

3.8.2 Care Gap Outreach for Chronic Conditions

Expanding care gap outreach beyond preventive screenings to chronic condition management is a natural next step. By sending automated reminders to patients with diabetes or heart conditions, providers can encourage patients to stay engaged with their care.

AI can enable simple text interactions where patients input data such as weight, glucose readings, or blood pressure measurements. This data can be monitored in real time, and patients who require additional support can be flagged for outreach. This proactive approach helps improve outcomes and ensures patients feel supported in managing their conditions.

3.8.3 Revenue Cycle Automation

Building on our success with prior authorization automation, we're scaling up statewide and broadening the scope of automation in our revenue cycle. Our next focus areas include:

- **Underpayments**: AI can quickly identify and correct instances where payers have underpaid providers, saving significant time and ensuring proper reimbursement.
- **Denial Management**: Automating the process of reviewing denied claims, adding necessary documentation, and resubmitting can drastically reduce the administrative burden and improve cash flow.

These efforts allow staff to spend less time on manual revenue cycle processes and more time on higher-value tasks.

3.8.4 Enhanced Rescheduling Options

Improving patient access includes making appointment rescheduling simple and seamless. Instead of canceling and calling to rebook, patients should be able to reschedule with ease. However, this requires accounting for various factors, such as provider availability, linked appointments, and any orders tied to the visit. AI can streamline this process by balancing these complexities automatically, reducing patient frustration and freeing up staff resources.

3.8.5 End-to-End Referral Automation

The ultimate goal is a fully automated referral process. Imagine a system where a provider makes a referral, all necessary orders are automatically submitted, and the patient is guided through scheduling the tests and appointments in the correct sequence. Once all prerequisites are complete, the patient can schedule directly with the referred provider—without multiple staff touchpoints.

Using the automation foundations we've already built, we're working toward refining this process. By reducing manual interventions, we can create a smoother, more efficient experience for both patients and staff.

3.9 Conclusion

The future of AI in healthcare is incredibly bright, and the opportunities truly feel endless. From simplifying workflows and closing care gaps to optimizing revenue cycles and rethinking how we approach patient access, AI has the power to completely transform how we deliver care. But what makes these advancements so exciting isn't just the technology itself—it's the opportunity to build a healthcare system that empowers providers, deeply engages patients, and focuses on what really matters: delivering exceptional care.

This chapter has walked through the beginning of the journey of AI at MUSC, covering everything from the "why" behind using AI in healthcare transformation to the strategy and vision that guided us. We dove into best practices for implementation, shared the impact of initial results, and emphasized the importance of building on lessons learned with agile processes, strong change management, and stakeholder engagement. At every step, we've focused on using AI not as a replacement for people but as a tool to enable them to do what they do best.

AI's potential to revolutionize patient access and staff engagement is undeniable, but success requires thoughtful implementation and collaboration. At MUSC, we've seen firsthand how leveraging AI to automate administrative tasks, improve accessibility, and enhance care delivery can make a real difference. These efforts have set a strong foundation for a more efficient, equitable, and patient-centered healthcare system. And just as importantly, the lessons we've learned provide a blueprint for other healthcare systems to unlock the transformative power of AI in their own journeys.

It's also incredible to reflect on how far AI has come in such a short time. When MUSC first started this work, AI was just beginning to make its way into healthcare operations. Since then, the technology has evolved rapidly, and with it, our ability to dream bigger and tackle challenges that once felt out of reach. As we look ahead, we're excited to continue embracing these advancements, adapting to new technologies, and pushing ourselves to find even better ways to serve our patients.

Ultimately, the journey with AI is ongoing, and that's part of what makes it so inspiring. The opportunities are boundless, and every step forward brings us closer to creating a healthcare system that's more connected, innovative, and compassionate. It's not just about the technology—it's about the people it serves and the difference it makes. That's what keeps us motivated, and that's the future we're working toward.

References

Densen, P. (2011). Challenges and opportunities facing medical education. *ResearchGate.* https://www.researchgate.net/figure/Estimated-Doubling-Time-of-Medical-Knowledge-by-Year-Students-starting-medical-school-in_fig 2_328078870

U.S. Census Bureau. (2023, December 19). *U.S. population trends return to pre-pandemic norms.* https://www.census.gov/newsroom/press-releases/2023/population-trends.html

Chapter 4

Delivering AI Responsibly in Clinical Settings across the Health Continuum

Lisa Lucadamo Jarrett, MBA, MIS

4.1 Strategy and Vision for AI

Imagine a future where artificial intelligence supports and enhances clinical care across healthcare settings, resulting in a smoother patient experience, better-informed care, and happier patients and clinicians. That's a small example in a very big opportunity space for how artificial intelligence can improve healthcare and outcomes.

In this chapter, you will understand through practical applications what Responsible AI is, why it is important, and how to build trust with clinicians and health systems. This chapter will also cover the broad framework of responsible AI principles and how, when applied effectively, they can transform the health ecosystem for better health outcomes, lower risk, and streamlined communication. A critical part of any successful AI adoption is to thoughtfully consider the different roles that will interact with the AI feature and design to the unique perspectives across roles.

The focus of this chapter is to highlight principles and dimensions of responsible AI from practical application in care settings. The perspectives are my own, derived from experience implementing AI across multiple health segments: post-acute, acute, payer, and life sciences. The primary example is a machine learning algorithm identifying patients at risk of re-hospitalization from Skilled Nursing Facilities (SNFs) in the post-acute segment.

4.2 Strategy

The potential impacts that AI may bring to healthcare are game-changing; from automating repetitive tasks for efficiency, enabling scarce clinical resources to have more time to provide care, to helping improve health outcomes with predictive and preventative risk management, and much more. An effective strategy for AI-enabled capabilities in healthcare needs to consider not just

 DOI: 10.4324/9781003621294-5

the functionality, the data, and the context of usage, but also how to deeply engage with users to build trust, gather feedback, and adapt based on that feedback. This will help gain buy-in that AI is effectively supporting their care delivery and creating efficiencies based on their needs and use cases.

Targeting clinical workflows and tasks for effective use of AI requires thoughtful consideration, since health delivery settings and use cases vary widely, requiring higher standards for critical care and more flexibility for less critical workflows. A few dimensions to consider for variation are:

- **Information type**—Personal Health Information (PHI) requires the highest levels of security and accuracy; Personally Identifiable Information (PII) also requires a high level of security.
- **Time Sensitivity**—The time sensitivity of activities ranges from being significantly time-sensitive in critical care settings to less time-sensitive for more routine activities. A hospital Emergency Department requires rapid results for patients, while Skilled Nursing Facilities are driven more by shifts and operations that can be more flexible regarding the timing of AI algorithm results.
- **Drift**—Both machine learning (ML) and natural language processing (NLP) models can experience drift, where model performance deviates from expected behavior or gold data sets over time. Drift is broader than just accuracy, including metrics for performance (F1 scores, precision, recall) or predictions. Like accuracy, monitoring frequency and alerting levels are driven by the criticality level, particularly for clinical workflows based on acuity or impact. Appropriate alerting is required both for clinicians and operational roles that need to be aware of potential inaccuracies and for the developer to investigate and correct them. In all care settings, performance needs to be high, even for more administrative or operational use cases.

Clinicians in various care settings may have different expectations, requiring tailored model results and user experiences to drive broad AI use. The same AI model supporting nurses in Skilled Nursing Facilities may need to have a different user experience or additional data to be valuable and successfully adopted in another care setting or by a different role such as case managers. A broad strategy can identify a problem area to solve with AI, but its execution and user experience need to be researched and adapted to be successful with different roles in different clinical care settings.

In my experience, the best strategy is one that starts small and expands to broader problem areas. For example, a strategy that focuses on staff efficiency starts with a specific task or problem, like reviewing notes from other care providers in the same department. Solving one use case, earning trust, and adapting help grow adoption. Then, applying lessons learned to a broader problem area, such as taking actions based on the note type or content, expands the value delivered, which also supports adoption. In clinical settings, trust is essential for adoption, so incrementally expanding AI capabilities enables users to become comfortable with the technology and grow into more complex use cases.

An example for life sciences is use cases that find candidates for clinical trials. Instead of starting with sophisticated models searching across hundreds of parameters from cohort data to identify trial candidates, it's more effective to start from simpler problems. To identify specific patients in a health system who could be candidates, it's possible to start with annotation of clinical notes with entity recognition for rapid searching and summarization, and entity recognition in medical texts for finding applicable research, both of which are needed to enable solutions to complex problems.

For payers, the usual AI strategy is to start with repetitive administrative tasks to reduce execution time, then move on to more complex tasks. There are certain payer domains where AI has been overused, making it more challenging for authorizations to be reviewed for clinical need ahead of claim denial, as noted by (Mello & Rose, 2024). The broad outcry from this action across multiple payers is a hard lesson to ensure that use cases are thoroughly examined by all the stakeholders, not just the stakeholder using AI.

4.3 Vision

Drivers for applying AI in the workflow of clinicians are manifold, surfacing critical information in the context of care delivery for prevention and risk management, making workflows more efficient to spend more time on care and interaction, and more. There are multiple aspects to account for in the workflow for AI to be effective and support care providers in prioritizing the most meaningful actions to take to help improve care outcomes. The fundamental principles of responsible AI (RAI) for US markets come from the Assistant Secretary for Technology Policy and the Office of the National Coordinator for Health Information Technology (ASTP/ONC) (Office of National Coordinator [ONC], 2024). They are:

- Fair
- Appropriate
- Valid
- Effective
- Safe

Let's start with an understanding of what these principles are and how they are executed.

4.3.1 Fair

The model does not exhibit biased performance, prejudice, or favoritism based on a person's inherent or acquired characteristics. Practically, that means that the model has a similar impact across the same or different populations or groups. For example, an acuity rating for a patient or resident delivers similar results across a cohort that has similar demographics (e.g., age, weight, gender, co-morbidities, etc.).

4.3.2 Appropriate

The model is well matched to specific contexts and populations to which it is applied.

4.3.3 Valid

The model is proven to estimate accurate and expected values for both internal and external data.

4.3.4 Effective

The model has demonstrated benefits and significant results in real-world conditions.

4.3.5 Safe

Model use has probable benefits that outweigh any probable risks.

With the activation of the US HHS ONC HTI-1 Part 3 regulation (ONC, 2024), additional elements were added to the use of AI features in Electronic Health Records:

- Transparency of source attributes used
- Risk Management for AI features
- Customers opt in/out of the use of AI
- Accessible Customer feedback

The specific requirements of the regulation defined a starting point for healthcare users to understand at a deeper level the algorithm data source, bias, fairness, and risks. Users might directly communicate with the company creating the AI algorithm. While these capabilities are a start to building trust with clinicians, there's more required for successful adoption beyond this information, including user walkthroughs, accessible communication, education for buyer/executive roles, and proactive responsiveness to customer feedback.

Since the use of AI in healthcare depends on successful adoption by users, the rule's focus on collecting users' feedback on evidence-based interventions (DSI) is a valuable contribution to the management of health AI. The direct communication from users to product managers and model developers is an essential input to the effective management and adoption of health AI models. The rule also requires accessible feedback for organizations to download for their own assessment of models and user reactions to the model. This enables adopting organizations to understand the sentiment of their users and allows developers to analyze comments across organizations as a critical input to model monitoring and evaluation.

In responsible AI, ensuring that the model can both be easily explained and interpreted by the user is essential to helping those leveraging AI see its benefits to their daily care delivery; in doing so, it will help build trust in AI as a technology that benefits both the provider and patient/member. Explainability is how the model reached a decision, recommendation, or prediction. It's based on how the model operates and the types of training data used. Interpretability focuses on understanding the inner workings of the model. Both need to be understood by the users and buyer personas for them to develop a point of view on the validity and efficiency of the model results. Assessing the model needs to be done both by clinicians and users, as well as by IT, since both are involved in the acquisition of AI-enabled tools. There should be clear information in the sales process, during solution evaluation, and enablement of clinicians about:

- Explainability
- Interpretability
- What clinical data the model uses
- How the model should be used, within workflow and by role
- Any subpopulations where the model should not be used
- How it is updated and maintained

A best practice for organizations that are considering AI solutions is to ensure early participation of clinical users, as their standards for fairness, validity, effectiveness, and risks are unique to the clinical setting. IT roles will be assessing the security, privacy, IT risks, and lifecycle management of the model.

Beyond these practical actions, there are other considerations such as social impact and accountability. Often, the lens of analyzing the impact of any AI model is ideally measured in clinical impact, but that doesn't consider the social impact of a model. An example is a nurse utilizing mobile devices to support evaluations of skin and wound infections. There are clear time efficiencies to be gained by the nurse, as well as more detailed clinical information that is gathered from mobile images, where the AI can detect subtle changes in measurements that could be an indication of infection. There's a broader context to consider in relation to the patient's experience that isn't reflected in those efficiencies and could materially impact the interaction with the nurse. For elderly patients who don't have the same level of experience or use of mobile devices and are in a Skilled Nursing Facility or assisted living, there could be concern or fear over what else the device may record, either in image or with voice recognition from their surroundings. Patients often feel providers are not paying attention to their needs and are merely on their phones. These factors may mean the nurse needs to materially change her approach to engaging with the patient and how the technology is used. He/she may need to help the patient understand the benefits of this approach to help build the patient's trust in the technology and ensure their cooperation isn't inhibited. Generational and demographic impacts need to be examined across personas in the design of, and desired user experience of, the AI feature.

Accountability is the underlying fabric that pulls together both developer work and users of the AI feature. For the developer, accountability includes adjusting for bias in training data, ensuring appropriate use rights for model training, and engaging clinicians at the start (from data labeling through to results and assessment for quality). Ahead of release, the team needs to ensure that the model results are safe and effective for the users, and analyze and mitigate risks. After launch, the team needs to ensure continuous monitoring for drift and accuracy, including alerts to users when model performance falls below the accepted baseline in clinical workflows.

For the consumer, accountability exists at multiple levels of the organization, for buyers and users. Buyers need to consider how the model was developed, if they have sufficient transparency into the data and how the model works to trust its results. A critical practice during procurement for clinically oriented models is to engage clinicians in the buying organization to participate in model evaluation and understand whether there's sufficient model and clinical alignment to build trust among clinical users. These steps are critical to successful adoption and ongoing engagement.

Similarly, for models targeting operations and administration, buyers should still assess transparency, risk management, ongoing monitoring, and model results as they impact critical business practices such as scheduling, revenue management, etc. For meaningful adoption, it's important to appropriately engage users in the procurement and evaluation stages to ensure that users see the benefits of the model and its results.

There is a wide range of information that must be clearly understood by developers, buyers, and users to be transparent about the AI model and set expectations. The elements listed above all come into play in building more confidence in how AI is embedded into clinical workflows and in health operations. This requires time, energy, and resources, both from developers and consuming organizations, to appreciate how the technology is applied, creates efficiencies, and achieves improvements. With the high expectations for how AI can deliver better care outcomes and management, along with Return on Investment (ROI), it's important that all stakeholders in the lifecycle are proactively educated throughout the process. The execution of those principles is what makes the difference between successful adoption and potential indifference or misuse.

4.3.6 The Village for RAI

It takes a village, reaching across many functions, to design, develop, and deliver on the principles of RAI. Appropriately identifying and managing bias extends from the earliest stages all the way through to adoption and ongoing monitoring. Similarly, privacy and security must be included from design through development and deployment. Transparency also requires collaboration and clear documentation between many functions to communicate clearly on the inputs, algorithm details, and expected results. This requires commitment from a variety of functions: data scientists, product managers, corporate privacy, legal, security, engineers, and leadership. Commitment across all these functions and governance between them is required to execute properly. Beyond development and delivery, there are important roles for sales, marketing, and professional services to appropriately set expectations and convey parameters for effective use to buyers and users.

4.4 Implementation Best Practices

4.4.1 Ecosystem

When developing and implementing health AI models, there's an array of federal and state laws and regulations that need to be factored in. Much like the rapid rate of change in technology, there are constant shifts in federal and state laws and regulations applicable to health AI. For developers of health AI models or features adhering to core principles mentioned earlier in the chapter, it's imperative to provide a solid common foundation that can be extensible and adaptable to changing laws, regulations, and customer needs. Despite the changing environment, keeping ethics, effectiveness, fairness, and accuracy at the center of the AI lifecycle model will guide teams to higher-quality model results and, therefore, also help improve real-world outcomes.

The National Institute of Standards and Technology (NIST) Risk Management Framework (NIST, 2024) provides a practical approach to incorporate core principles of responsible AI into practice, incorporating them into lifecycle stages: Map, Manage, and Measure, supported by governance and risk management. Security and privacy by design need to be applied from the earliest stages through launch and ongoing management. In Map, early design and exploration in a model concept incorporate appropriate clinical and health management roles for setting objectives, evaluating training data for fairness and potential risk identification. In Manage, model development and testing with end users provide a greater opportunity to evaluate fairness and model results with subject matter experts. These learnings provide insights into potential risks from the model to inform ongoing risk management.

The final stage, Measure, relates to the ongoing monitoring, adaptation, and management of the model and its results. This stage requires corporate and product focus on responsible AI to ensure that models used in health delivery settings and management are appropriately monitored, with changes and revisions made as needed to not only maintain but also improve the model's performance. It also includes taking actions beyond measuring, including updating documentation and communicating changes in an understandable way to buyers and users.

Beyond legal, regulatory, and model delivery frameworks, industry perspectives are quickly evolving based on inputs from doctors, nurses, health systems, and industry consortiums that must be evaluated and factored into the health AI's model design, development, launch, and ongoing management. For example, the American Medical Association promotes using artificial intelligence as augmented intelligence, where it supplements and keeps physicians at the center of decision-making.

Similarly, the American Nurses Association's Center for Ethics promotes the use of artificial intelligence to support and enhance their core values of caring and compassion, ensuring that AI doesn't compromise the human interactions and relationships required for effective care delivery. As nurses play a critical role with patients and families, they must clearly understand the "what" and "how" of AI to build confidence and trust in its successful use in care settings. The Association also emphasizes the criticality of including nurses throughout the design, development, and adoption of AI features, as well as being aware of the data used in these features so they can assess its validity in practice.

For vulnerable populations such as older adults or those with severe disabilities, the health ecosystem is a broad and diverse array of health delivery settings. Home care, residential programs, skilled nursing, assisted living, acute settings, and the many transitions that occur between these facilities form a dynamic continuum for humans to receive care. Transfers between these groups can be frequent, and each setting has different roles with different needs. For effective implementation across health delivery settings, AI models need to be evaluated from the perspective and needs of the multiple roles involved—such as facility Medical Directors, Emergency Department MDs, nurses in different settings, health administration roles, and those in supportive cost containment roles among payers. Each has different goals, with a unique emphasis on different data and results, and one AI model will likely require a different focus for enablement and transparency.

4.4.2 Unique Perspectives across the Care Journey

For AI models that are designed to span health care settings, it's critical to include the array of roles throughout the lifecycle to ensure their unique needs and concerns. With the staffing challenges impacting many parts of the health delivery chain, from nursing to physicians and allied caregivers in between, AI models need to be tested to span different languages and skill levels. This is particularly true as care delivery increasingly is supported by a wide range of provider roles to ensure usability and effective results.

Product, User Experience (UX) discovery needs to be executed in partnership with data science, with consideration to the staffing and skill pressures in care settings. This requires a deeper investment of effort in the early stages of AI models. For models that are directed at fewer personas, it's more straightforward for discovery, feedback, and adaptation. A gradual adoption path leads to higher success in implementing models across different settings and personas. When segmentation by role or setting is researched, there are more opportunities for recalibration based on feedback, which may vary widely across users. The incremental approach also allows for adaptation of enablement information and documentation, which could also vary based on the role.

4.4.3 Considerations for Healthcare Settings and across the Continuum

Accuracy, safety, and performance requirements for AI models for health are always high based on the criticality of health outcomes, risk levels, and use cases. Beyond these must-have areas, the context of the healthcare use case and setting will heighten or change the needs for the model characteristics. For example, Skilled Nursing Facilities operations may not be as time-sensitive as emergency departments, where seconds matter to care delivery. For any clinical case, accuracy, safety, and fairness standards won't shift much from the high standards required by the industry.

4.4.3.1 Skilled Nursing Facilities (SNFs)

Operations at SNFs are centered more around staff shifts and the challenges of ensuring appropriate communication and information sharing between rotations of clinicians and external medical providers who together manage the care of patients. Sensitivity to the timing of events, understanding the prior shifts' observations and assessments, and carrying that knowledge into patient interactions is essential to observe and track patient progress or regression. Pertinent information spans different units of time across multiple days and shifts. The focus of clinical leadership is on days and weeks, while administrative and operations staff are likely to be focused across longer time spans for their work. Accuracy, safety, and transparency for AI are make-or-break for this segment, given the different levels of clinicians involved with care delivery, management, and how intertwined operations are with care delivery.

4.4.3.2 Assisted Living (AL)

Operations at Assisted Living occur at a different pace than SNFs, with meal schedules driving much activity, resident monitoring, reviews, and active visits from care providers, alongside programs for more independent residents. Depending on the use case for this segment, information may not be PHI or care-centric, but transparency is important so users in operational and administrative roles can "interpret" what the algorithm does to better understand how it can positively impact efficiencies and experiences of residents. For residents, if AI is used in their interactions, there should be simple, clear information on model basics: information used and results expected. Fear of AI is real and may be particularly important to reassure older residents that it is used for a beneficial purpose and its limits.

4.4.3.3 Acute

Standards are higher in acute settings for performance, transparency in clinical workflows, and in operational and administrative applications. If AI is used in patient interactions, it should also be clear to the patient what the AI's function is, and the results will be embedded into care delivery workflows and patient recommendations for closing gaps in care.

4.4.3.3 Payer and Risk-Bearing Entities

With value-based care (VBC) models advancing, payers and risk-bearing entities are also interested in shifting risk identification and mitigation to earlier in the member's care plan, for a higher probability that care intervention improves outcomes and has a direct impact on how they will be reimbursed for closing gaps in care and delivering improved results for their members. Insights that will matter to them are patterns for rising acuity, members' prescriptions and implications with multiple co-morbidities, understanding trends in member cohorts, predicting risk that could result in a costly intervention or more expensive care setting, and monitoring interventions and activities of daily care. Timeliness is important to this segment as they have a vested interest in achieving positive member outcomes.

4.5 Initial Results

This example is focused on post-acute care settings targeting older and disabled populations. In these settings, care delivery is executed in shifts, creating a critical need to have clear and up-to-date information as nurses start their shifts. The problem targeted is to support nurses in identifying and acting on risks for patients. The predictive machine learning algorithm developed needed to be trustworthy to gain adoption by nurses, with transparency on the drivers of an increase in risk.

The solution ranked patients by rehospitalization risk (identifying who needed to be seen first to prevent rehospitalization), including identifying why the risk was high with specific insights that were clear, so nurses knew what actions needed to be taken. With nursing resources scarce, a key design principle was to use data already collected in daily care to drive predictions that didn't require additional data input outside the normal course of care. The model had many features which, for usability, were organized into clinical groupings so clinical leadership could more easily interpret and use the predictions. Across the clinical groupings, similar measures to indicate trends and range were provided on hover to support quick scans during routine shift meetings.

The risk of rehospitalization is useful to different roles: bedside nurses, nurse leaders, physicians, administrative and operational staff, and care coordinators. Collaboration across the broad health ecosystem supporting care for older and disabled populations is one of the keys to materially improving health outcomes. To illustrate how rehospitalization risk supports different roles enabling collaboration, let's start by understanding how the information helps a nurse leader and acute care coordinators.

For a nurse leader, using information from the predictive model enables adjustment of care based on changes in risk in a timely way (daily) that has a higher probability of successful intervention to change the risk trend. With clear organization by patient and risk groups, nurse leaders can more effectively communicate with care team members and, as needed, physicians in a timely manner for better results from interventions.

For acute coordinators, the same information enables more proactive collaboration with skilled nursing facility partners for high readmission risk patients. By understanding timely changes in risk levels, coordinators can more efficiently and effectively prioritize care coordination activities for high-risk patients. The same information enables better collaboration across stakeholders to actively manage risks with the same goal of improving patient outcomes and minimizing transfers back to acute care. Such transfers can be both jarring and disruptive to older patients, costly to the health plan, and negatively impact the overall health journey of seniors.

As usage grows, new insights and sensitivities from users will emerge, often requiring reframing and changing either model outputs or user interfaces. This is an important evolution, and health AI developers need to be committed to ongoing monitoring and adjustment to ensure the highest quality results and outcomes from the model. In this example, an additional informational area was added as user feedback indicated that without it, they wouldn't see the results as complete. The additional information didn't change model results and wasn't helpful in improving model accuracy, but from the user's perspective, it was essential to be valid and help build trust. Listening to feedback and acting on that feedback is an ongoing phase of model management.

Launching AI models into health delivery settings requires significant collaboration, both in the health AI developer's work and in the purchasing organization, for a successful launch and growing adoption to achieve the impact targeted by the model consumer. Health AI developers need to effectively communicate, train, and deepen understanding of appropriate/inappropriate model use and expected results through their customer-facing teams, such as customer success, marketing, and sales, so customer expectations are set appropriately. Expectation mismatch is a frequent cause of unsuccessful adoption and realized results by customers. Buyers require a different array of information than users do, with overlap on information about accuracy, safety, expected use, and more.

In this example, significant effort was made to document, share, and answer questions both internally and to support sales in answering customer questions and concerns. Enablement and education on an ongoing basis also helped organizations expand adoption through their staff. An important learning in the expansion of use of the AI model was the importance of relationship building with key opinion leaders and users in organizations. In addition, periodic communication of successful adoption experiences from other consumers helped build trust. Prospects were able to see themselves in their peers' results, with the identification of risk enabling staff to effectively manage high-risk individuals requiring intervention and closer monitoring, resulting in reduced readmissions.

The model has demonstrated meaningful results, including achieving 90–120 minutes per week saved for organizations moving from manually creating "watch lists" to the AI feature. Further details on the impressive results of this model can be found in the peer-reviewed article (Kandel et al., 2025).

In the evolution of the readmission risk model, user feedback indicated that a change was needed to make the interface simpler and to mimic clinical thinking (adding clinical categories). The original design presented information in descending order of risk, which clinicians didn't find helpful, requiring the addition of categories for ease of use.

The team created different forms of information, with varying levels of detail needed for both internal roles (sales, customer success) and external roles (IT buyers, clinical leadership, floor nurses). Following up with clinical leadership in the months following implementation was essential to gain valuable insights as nurses moved beyond the initial learning stage to everyday use.

4.5.1 Best Practices

- Summarizing lessons learned from the implementation of the risk model.
- Gain hard evidence of results to gain buy-in for adoption, such as time saved.
- Simple is best. Keep user interfaces simple, conduct user research periodically as adoption expands to gather new feedback and adapt, such as adapting for data needed to support clinical thinking.
- Clinicians in the Loop is the key to success. Practical insight is needed throughout the AI product feature development, particularly early on in design through launch to maintain success.

4.6 Challenges and Future Opportunities

In my experience working across various health segments, I've observed that challenges for health AI models are both numerous and diverse. They can differ based on the specific health segment, the purchasing organization, and the targeted user persona. These obstacles emerge throughout the model's lifecycle and affect everyone involved, from the health AI developers and the organizations acquiring the technology to the clinicians, administrative staff, and patients who ultimately use it.

4.6.1 Ongoing Monitoring

In classic software development, the adage of *80% of effort to maintain and 20% to develop* has been proven over many decades. When it comes to health AI, developers frequently underestimate the effort required beyond just engineering and data science that spans organizational functions to monitor and maintain highly accurate, performant, and valid models. While proactive monitoring is required on models in production by engineering and data science, it doesn't reach the 80/20 split of maintenance to develop but it does require continuous monitoring for the safety of model results and drift, and updates when data or model features change to documentation, etc. As mentioned earlier in the chapter, the patterns of resources shift right for design, ethics, risk mitigation, and early testing to ensure effectiveness, safety, and validity. With those shifts, there's a heavier load at the beginning of a model's lifecycle, perhaps closer to 40% than 20%, but that still requires ongoing resources for maintenance and adaptation. AI Operations software can automate measurements and generate alerts; however, teams from data science, product, and engineering must collaborate both within their respective domains and across functions to act on these insights effectively.

Based on monitoring, other functions may need to engage to help with customer communications, expectation management, and explanation of changes. If a significant performance problem occurs, roles such as Customer Success and Marketing may need to be involved to assist with customer communication and explanations. While very rare, if legal or regulatory lines have been compromised, legal teams may need to engage to assess the impact.

In an environment where laws, regulations, and industry perspectives are rapidly changing and adapting, part of a healthy AI model lifecycle also involves periodic assessment by product, data science, legal, and privacy teams. This routine practice sets the organization up for success when significant changes occur such as new requirements for data rights, transparency, testing, interpretability, etc. Often, these cross-functional collaborations aren't designed and planned but occur reactively. A best practice in health AI is to align on a process-driven evaluation during strategy planning and be open to change-driven reviews. This fosters a more balanced approach to resource management and cross-functional alignment, aiming to reduce the effort required when changes occur.

4.6.2 Continuous Risk Management

AI use in health products requires continuous risk management to be integrated into the product development lifecycle and organizational processes for risk management. I've observed that risks—and their associated management strategies—generally fall into five areas: brand or marketing, regulatory/legal, product/customer, security, and IT. Most health-sector organizations already have strong risk management frameworks for marketing, regulatory/legal, security, and IT.

For product teams, AI risk management requires a different cadence of evaluation, monitoring, and mitigation. Once algorithms are deployed in production, they process ever-changing data that can lead to model drift or performance issues. While data science and engineering teams commonly handle model monitoring, product processes must also adapt. This includes increasing the frequency of monitoring reviews, incorporating user feedback into decisions about potential model revisions, and planning future model or product enhancements.

Most product lifecycle processes include less frequent reviews for mature products, but with AI models, product managers need to change from passive monitoring to active monitoring of forward-leading indicators for model adoption and user satisfaction, informed by both by model metrics and user comments. These areas of information can be incorporated into periodic product health reviews, but product managers should also set model service level indicators to stay ahead of potential problems. As mentioned earlier in the chapter, alerting is a must-have for effective risk management.

A key factor of AI-enabled products that can strain communication processes is the need to address customer-specific performance concerns. Outbound customer communications are usually a centralized push-driven process for broad messages, and while organizations may have customer success or technical account managers assigned to large customers, often the bulk of customers do not receive one-to-one attention. For risk management, it's critically important that AI in health products includes clear thresholds for acceptable and unacceptable performance and is instrumented into the software to show alerts to users so they know when results are beyond defined thresholds and can make decisions or take actions with that knowledge.

4.6.3 Skepticism in Clinical Adoption

Clinician perspectives on the use of AI in healthcare vary from enthusiastic to extreme skepticism. The clinical community has supported the notion that AI will support, not replace clinical decision-making. From the American Medical Association's position on AI as augmentation (American Medical Association, 2022) to a similar position from the American Nurses Association's from their ethics code, which states that nurses are accountable for decisions made and actions taken (American Nurses Association, 2022). The most powerful tools to increase transparency into the "black box" of AI are explainability and interpretability, so clinicians understand how the model operates and how to interpret results. However, effectively explaining a model's workings and results can be challenging—particularly for clinical audiences with varying levels of clinical and technological expertise, education, and language skills. An experienced physician will often require more detailed information for trust than a newly certified nursing assistant (CNA). In general, doctors and most nurses want answers to these questions:

- What data are the inputs?
- What is the level of data quality and validity?
- What weights do they have in the model?
- How does the model operate (for example, the steps it takes to use the data, is it generative or is it extractive)?
- What are acceptable uses for the results?
- What are acceptable values?
- What risks exist and how are they mitigated?

Investing resources in creating documentation for transparency throughout the model's lifecycle generates a significant return in building trust with clinical users. As health delivery increasingly integrates AI not only into clinical operations but also administration and operations, this information is needed both for IT, Operations, and leadership to evaluate an AI-enabled product. While levels of detail vary for different audiences, it's important to thoughtfully consider the range of roles that need this transparency and create appropriate assets to support them. Different assets are needed from evaluation and purchase, through implementation, to routine active use. Training courses, recorded demos, and explanations of models, data sheets, model cards, and other collateral will be needed for launch, adoption, and ongoing use.

4.6.4 Future Opportunities

AI in healthcare creates exciting opportunities for administrative and operational use cases that automate repetitive tasks across data entry, documentation, routine communications, process, and task automation. There are significant efficiencies, productivity gains, and cycle time reductions that can be achieved, usually with low risk. With AI agents, task-focused automation becomes more accessible for administration and operations. There is significant potential to accelerate many routine parts of healthcare processes, such as reducing lag time in communications between health ecosystem stakeholders, enabling more timely communication with clearer insights for patient transfers, execution of billing, understanding operational bottlenecks, and many more.

Given that between 15% and 30% of US healthcare spending goes to administration (Health Affairs, 2022), this represents one of the greatest opportunities for improving the amount of a dollar going to care delivery, bringing down rapidly rising healthcare spending levels. Using AI at appropriate places in administrative and operations processes, where time and repetition exist, will enable much faster execution and resource savings. That said, health systems need thoughtful attention when selecting where to use AI in their workflow. For example, significant turmoil and delayed care have resulted from the use of AI in insurer denials, revolving around opacity in decision-making from AI algorithms. A wiser choice is to focus on areas not requiring humans in the loop, as mentioned by (Mello & Rose, 2024).

Beyond the benefits of AI for health administration and operations, exciting yet challenging opportunities exist for using AI in clinical workflows. There are many opportunities to save time that clinicians can use to focus more on care, with positive benefits both for patients and clinicians. Another high-impact area is to go further with AI than predictive analytics has in the past to support and enable clinical decision-making. Each clinical decision workflow has many variables, such as specific data needed, different requirements for timeliness, single or multiple roles involved, different levels of acuity, and much more. Thoughtful consideration of the process is needed for where AI supports, informs, and surfaces potential risks for clinical decision-making in the clinicians' workflow.

With the shift to Value-Based Care, the focus on optimizing health outcomes creates new pressure on proactive risk management across providers, health systems, and payers. In this chapter, the example highlighted is a predictive machine learning algorithm that enables nurses and other roles to focus care on patients with higher or increasing risk of return to the hospital, with transparency into the drivers of risk scores, so they understand what to evaluate in patient interactions.

4.7 Summary

Implementing AI-enabled products in clinical care settings has its challenges, but the potential opportunities for improved health outcomes, more efficient administration, and communication across the health continuum are so impactful that the challenges must be overcome. Predictive analytics has long been an important tool for clinicians and operators without AI. While AI can support clinicians with many more capabilities, the principles learned from decades of technology and analytics implementation in healthcare apply to AI as well. Clear and understandable information at the right level for the user about what the model is, what data it uses, how it gets results, what's expected and what's unexpected, and risks helps build understanding, a precursor to trust. Focusing on user understanding is a good start to encouraging adoption, supported by user experience research and adaptation to customer feedback. As adoption grows, new insights, concerns, and opportunities will emerge for model improvements, corrections, and potential new use cases.

References

American Medical Association. (2022). *Augmented intelligence in health care H-480.939.* https://policysearch.ama-assn.org/policyfinder/detail/artificial%20intelligence?uri=%2FAMADoc%2FHOD.xml-H-480.939.xml

American Nurses Association Position Statement. (2022). *The ethical use of artificial intelligence in nursing practice.* https://www.nursingworld.org/globalassets/practiceandpolicy/nursing-excellence/ana-position-statements/the-ethical-use-of-artificial-intelligence-in-nursing-practice_bod-approved-12_20_22.pdf

Health Affairs. (2022). *The role of administrative waste in excess US healthcare spending.* https://www.healthaffairs.org/content/briefs/role-administrative-waste-excess-us-health-spending

Mello, M., & Rose, S. (2024). Denial- artificial intelligence tools and health insurance coverage decisions. *JAMA Health Forum,* 5(3), e240622. https://doi.org/10.1001/jamahealthforum.2024.0622

Kandel, B., et al. (2025). Development of a predictive hospitalization model for skilled nursing facility patients. *Journal of the Post-Acute and Long Term Care Medical Association, 26*(1). https://doi.org/10.1016/j.jamda.2024.105288

National Institute of Standards and Technology. (2024). *AI risk management framework (RMF).* https://www.nist.gov/itl/ai-risk-management-framework

Office of the National Coordinator in Health and Human Services Department. (2024, January). Requirements for decision support interventions and predictive models. *Algorithmic Transparency* (PowerPoint slides). https://www.healthit.gov/sites/default/files/page/2024-01/DSI_HTI1%20Final%20Rule%20Presentation_508.pdf

Chapter 5

Reimagining Primary and Specialty Care with AI

John R. Williford and David Kim, MBA

5.1 Introduction

Artificial intelligence (AI) is poised to transform the administration and delivery of healthcare from scheduling, clinical chart review, and diagnosis to care coordination and quality improvement. Traditional electronic health record (EHR) systems have established foundational building blocks but have also introduced administrative burdens while leaving vast amounts of valuable data locked in unstructured formats. Recent advances in AI, particularly in natural language processing (NLP) and large language models (LLMs), offer new and powerful tools enabling users to extract actionable insights from data, automate chart reviews, close care gaps, streamline prior authorizations, and improve decision-making. While AI holds the promise of reducing clinician burnout and improving patient outcomes, challenges remain such as ensuring data privacy, enabling interoperability with existing EHRs, and mitigating algorithmic bias. Successful implementation will require robust governance, diverse training datasets, user-friendly design, and strong provider buy-in. By leveraging thoughtful integration and stakeholder collaboration, AI can serve as a reliable co-pilot by reducing manual documentation, supplementing provider expertise, and personalizing patient engagement to elevate the overall quality of care. This chapter explores the role of AI in reshaping the healthcare industry while addressing some hurdles that must be overcome to realize its promise.

5.2 Strategy and Vision for AI

The healthcare industry is in the midst of a data revolution. Every second of every day, there is a staggering amount of information being generated by smartphones, wearables, and connected medical devices. The potential for this data to revolutionize patient care is immense, yet so much of it remains locked away as unstructured data, making it difficult to retrieve and analyze. Just two decades ago, most medical practices relied on paper charts, handwritten notes, and phone calls to

DOI: 10.4324/9781003621294-6

coordinate patient care. The introduction of electronic health records (EHRs) was seen as a major step forward, promising to streamline documentation, improve care coordination, and provide a foundation for data-driven decision-making. Today, EHRs are embedded in healthcare, yet their impact has seen mixed results (The Lancet Digital Health, 2025). While automation and electronic data storage have been established, EMRs have also introduced new administrative burdens that have contributed to clinician burnout and workflow inefficiencies (Sarkar & Bates, 2024). If this were simply due to limitations of specific EHR vendors, it would be relatively straightforward to address. Unfortunately, this is largely due to the information being documented. A vast majority of documented healthcare data, including clinical notes, medical histories, lab result interpretations, and prescriptions, is written and stored as free text in an unstructured form, meaning they do not conform to a standardized format, facilitating easy extraction of discrete data elements. This makes it extremely challenging to sort, interpret, and generate reportable/actionable outputs from this documentation. The solution has been to rely heavily on manual review of medical records, resulting in overburdened providers and reduced time with patients, which in turn can lead to critical patient information or opportunities for care intervention being missed (Payerchin, 2024).

Artificial intelligence (AI) is emerging as a powerful tool to address these challenges by reshaping the way primary and specialty care providers manage patient populations, coordinate care, and optimize practice efficiency. Although AI initially relied on straightforward symbolic, rule-based algorithms, it has now progressed into highly sophisticated solutions capable of multimodal information processing—combining structured and unstructured data to tackle complex healthcare tasks, as illustrated in Figure 5.1.

Recent advances in AI, particularly in the combination of machine learning (ML) and artificial reasoning for natural language processing (NLP), are beginning to enable providers to automate chart reviews, streamline scheduling, and proactively close care gaps. Modern generative AI models such as large language models (LLMs) promise to interpret massive quantities of unstructured data and use context-aware reasoning to synthesize summaries, valuable insights, and actionable recommendations with previously unimaginable versatility, reliability, and speed (Clusmann et al., 2023). LLMs are trained on vast datasets including medical literature and research, clinical

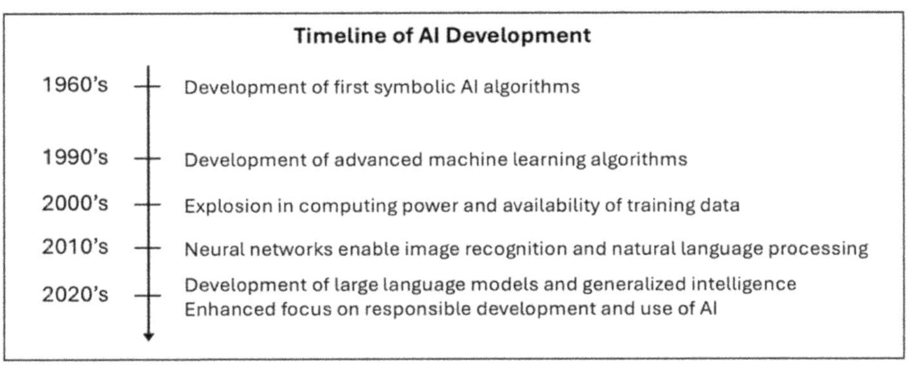

Figure 5.1 The evolution of AI—from early symbolic, rule-based systems to today's deep learning and advanced neural networks—underscores how the technology's development underpins its capacity to address these enduring data challenges (Alaita, 2024).

notes, and structured health data, allowing them to rapidly scan, interpret, and synthesize complex medical information and produce critical insights that providers and administrators need to deliver high-quality care. With LLMs, providers are beginning to summarize patient histories, extract key diagnostic details, and reconcile information across different systems. Leveraging the power of LLMs, therefore, could allow healthcare organizations to unlock insights currently buried within vast amounts of disparate text (Agatstein, 2023). AI-driven chart review systems are starting to surface clinically relevant information to ensure that providers have immediate access to critical patient insights at the point of care. The vision is for AI to examine and reconcile patient histories, diagnostic details, and notes across different systems ("AI May Help Researchers," 2024). AI-powered scheduling tools may soon be able to predict patient needs, optimize appointment timing, and reduce missed appointments by automating follow-up reminders. Beyond individual practices, AI is positioned to drive systemic improvements in population health management (PHM). By integrating AI with health information exchanges (HIEs), payers, and others across the provider continuum, there can be a more comprehensive understanding of patient populations to enhance performance on quality measures and implement targeted interventions at scale. Reflecting this expanding role, market forecasts suggest that cutting-edge AI in healthcare could grow nearly fivefold by 2030 (Pangarkar, 2025), underscoring the rapidly increasing confidence and investment in these transformative technologies, as illustrated in Figure 5.2.

AI-driven automation has the potential to help alleviate administrative burdens associated with prior authorizations, documentation, and compliance reporting, allowing providers to focus on high-value clinical tasks (Sarkar & Bates, 2024).

Despite its transformative potential, AI adoption in primary and specialty care also comes with challenges. Ensuring data privacy, mitigating biases in AI models, and integrating these technologies seamlessly into clinical and administrative workflows requires careful planning and thoughtful implementation. Provider education and engagement are essential to ensuring that AI enhances rather than disrupts the patient-provider relationship. As healthcare continues to evolve in an increasingly data-rich environment, AI offers a compelling pathway to enhance efficiency, improve patient outcomes, and redefine the future of clinical practice.

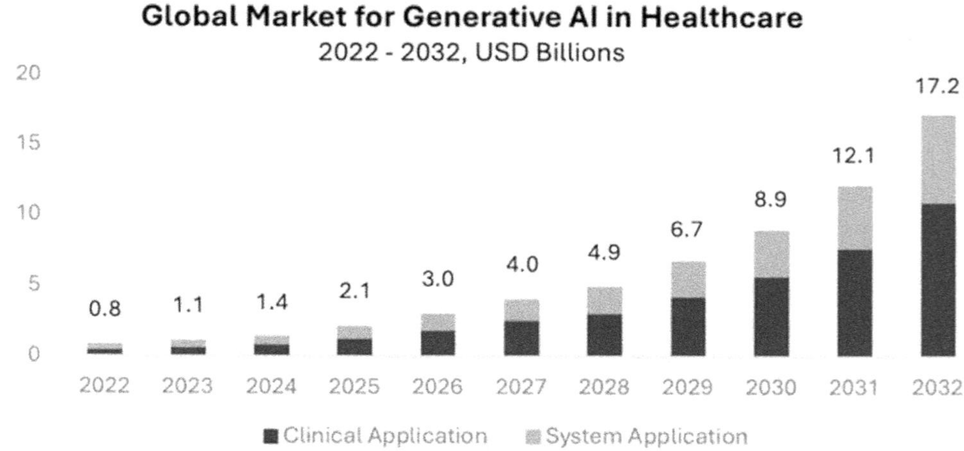

Figure 5.2 The projected year-by-year growth in the global generative AI healthcare market reinforces the dramatic increase in both clinical and system-level applications anticipated over the next decade (Pangarkar, 2025).

5.2.1 Implementation Best Practices and Initial Results: Chart Review

One of the most immediate and potentially impactful applications of AI in healthcare is the automation of time-consuming administrative tasks. Physicians and healthcare staff spend a substantial portion of their time on documentation, data entry, and compliance reporting (Overhage & McCallie, 2020). AI-powered voice recognition tools and natural language processing (NLP) algorithms are starting to enable capabilities that will listen to patient interactions, transcribe clinical notes in real time, and populate EHR fields automatically. This not only reduces the manual documentation workload but also allows providers to focus more on patient care.

One early example of this is with AI-assisted chart reviews to enable scanning of patient records and highlighting of relevant information before an appointment. Chart review is an essential but time-consuming task in both primary and specialty care settings. Providers must sift through extensive amounts of EHR data to extract relevant clinical insights, reconcile patient histories, identify care gaps, and document findings for compliance and billing. By reducing the cognitive load associated with navigating EHRs, AI has the potential to alleviate mental fatigue and increase efficiency for clinicians and staff. AI can also begin to help flag missing or outdated information, ensuring that care teams have the most accurate and up-to-date data available (Agatstein, 2023). Traditionally, this process has been a manual effort requiring hours of physician and administrative time that could otherwise be spent on direct patient care. AI is poised to revolutionize this process by transforming chart review from a burdensome administrative task into a streamlined, efficient, and highly accurate ecosystem of workflows ("AI May Help Researchers," 2024).

5.3 Chart Review—Automating Extraction and Summarization of Clinical Data

One of AI's most immediate benefits in chart review is the ability to extract and summarize large volumes of clinical data rapidly. Rather than requiring providers to manually search through pages of notes, lab results, imaging reports, and medication histories, AI-powered tools could instantly analyze a patient's record, identifying key diagnoses, relevant lab trends, and treatment plans. This would allow providers to focus on clinical decision-making rather than on the mundane task of data retrieval. For example, an AI system may highlight a patient's history of hypertension for a cardiologist, retrieve the most recent echocardiogram results, and flag any abnormal cholesterol levels, all within seconds. Similarly, in primary care, AI could also summarize a patient's chronic conditions, vaccination history, and recent lab results to ensure that nothing critical is overlooked during a visit.

Physician burnout is a growing concern in healthcare, with documentation and administrative tasks being among the leading contributors. AI-driven chart review can help to reduce this burden by automating much of the tedious data entry and reconciliation work. Rather than manually inputting patient histories or updating problem lists, providers can begin to look to AI systems to maintain accurate and up-to-date records, freeing them to focus on patient interactions. Additionally, natural language processing (NLP) technologies allow AI to interpret free-text clinical notes and integrate them into structured fields within the EHR. This means that physicians can dictate or type notes in their preferred style, and AI can automatically extract relevant details, ensuring consistency and completeness without requiring additional manual input.

Beyond improving efficiency, AI-powered chart review can play a critical role in enhancing clinical decision-making and patient safety. By continuously analyzing a patient's chart, AI may be able to identify inconsistencies, potential medication errors, and missed diagnoses (Choudhury & Asan, 2020). An AI system reviewing an oncology patient's chart may detect discrepancies between the prescribed chemotherapy regimen and the latest treatment guidelines, which can then prompt a physician to reassess the plan. AI can flag a patient who has been prescribed two contraindicated medications by different providers and help to prevent a potential adverse drug reaction. AI has the potential to also identify at-risk patients by recognizing subtle patterns in their medical history, such as a patient with increasing HbA1c levels, rising blood pressure, and a sedentary lifestyle who may be flagged as at risk for developing cardiovascular disease, prompting proactive intervention by the provider.

5.4 Chart Review—Supporting Population Health Management (PHM) and Value-Based Care

AI-driven chart review plays a crucial role in supporting population health management and value-based care initiatives. By continuously analyzing EHR data, AI has much potential in its ability to track quality measures, monitor patient populations for chronic disease management, and identify trends that inform care management. An example of this is in analyzing charts to determine the percentage of diabetic patients who have received their annual foot and eye exams. If gaps are identified, AI could support the generation of targeted outreach lists to ensure that patients receive necessary preventive care. In a specialty practice such as endocrinology, AI could also support tracking medication adherence among patients with thyroid disorders, identifying those who may need additional follow-up or education.

AI-enabled chart review also has the potential to streamline pre-visit preparation by summarizing a patient's medical history, flagging overdue screenings, and identifying outstanding care gaps. This allows providers to enter patient encounters fully informed, improving the odds of a more focused and efficient visit. As part of post-visit follow-up, AI can help prioritize post-visit actions by analyzing clinical notes and automatically generating referral requests, lab orders, and patient instructions. If a specialist recommends additional imaging or a medication adjustment, AI can help ensure that these recommendations are accurately documented and followed up on, thereby reducing the risk of missed interventions.

From a financial and administrative standpoint, accurate medical coding is essential for reimbursement and regulatory compliance. Manual chart review often results in missed billing opportunities or errors that lead to claim denials (Nguyen, 2024). AI-driven chart review enhances coding accuracy by automatically identifying billable services, ensuring proper documentation, and flagging missing or incorrect codes before claims are submitted. For an orthopedic practice, AI could review surgical notes and ensure that all relevant procedures are properly coded, thereby reducing the likelihood of reimbursement delays. In a primary care setting, AI can potentially identify preventive screenings and chronic disease management services that qualify for additional reimbursement, maximizing revenue under value-based contracts.

5.5 Challenges and Considerations for Chart Review and AI

Despite its numerous benefits, the implementation of AI-driven chart review comes with challenges. One key concern is data accuracy and reliability. AI models must be trained on high-quality, diverse datasets to ensure they accurately interpret and summarize patient records without introducing errors (Lee et al., 2024). Integration with existing EHR systems also presents a technical challenge, as many legacy platforms are not designed to support advanced AI applications. Ensuring seamless interoperability between AI tools and EHR systems is essential to maximizing effectiveness. Another critical consideration is patient data privacy and compliance with regulations such as the Health Insurance Portability and Accountability Act (HIPAA). AI systems handling sensitive patient information must have robust security measures to prevent breaches and unauthorized access.

Physician and staff buy-in is crucial for successful AI adoption. The end-users must feel confident that AI-driven chart review enhances their workflow rather than adding complexity. Robust training, user-friendly interfaces, and transparent AI decision-making processes can help build trust and encourage adoption. While AI has the potential to significantly enhance efficiency, it should be viewed as a tool to supplement and augment rather than a replacement for clinical judgment. Providers must be trained to interpret AI-generated insights critically, ensuring that human oversight remains central to patient care decisions.

As AI technology continues to advance, its role in chart review will only expand. Future developments may include real-time AI assistants that support providers during patient encounters by automatically generating visit summaries and treatment recommendations. AI-driven decision support tools may also integrate with wearable device data, providing a more comprehensive picture of a patient's health beyond traditional EHR records. AI's ability to process and interpret unstructured data such as imaging reports, pathology results, and genetic testing data will further enhance its value in specialty practices, enabling more personalized and precise care delivery. AI-driven chart review represents a major step forward in improving healthcare efficiency, reducing clinician burnout, and enhancing patient outcomes. The challenge now lies in ensuring thoughtful implementation, ongoing refinement, and continuous collaboration between technology developers and healthcare providers to unlock AI's full potential in patient care.

5.5.1 Implementation Best Practices and Initial Results: Quality and Care Gaps

Ensuring that patients receive timely, appropriate, and comprehensive care is a persistent and pervasive challenge in healthcare. Care gaps, which include missed screenings, overdue vaccinations, unmanaged chronic conditions, and unaddressed social drivers of health (SDOH), all pose significant risks to patient outcomes and can drive up healthcare costs. Addressing these gaps is critical to improving population health and achieving success in value-based care models. Historically, identifying and closing care gaps has relied on manual chart reviews, population health reports, dashboards, and provider-initiated outreach efforts. However, these methods are often labor-intensive, reactive, and prone to inefficiencies. AI is beginning to change this by enabling proactive and automated interventions that enhance patient care and drive better health outcomes (Barr, 2024).

5.6 Care Gap Automation and Identification

One of AI's most powerful applications in care gap closure is its ability to analyze vast amounts of patient data in real time to identify gaps that might otherwise go unnoticed. Traditional care gap identification often depends on static reports and periodic audits, which often become quickly outdated. AI has a goal of continuously processing EHR data, claims, lab results, and unstructured notes to pinpoint patients who have missed preventive services or require follow-up care. AI would flag patients who are overdue for colorectal cancer screening based on age, medical history, and prior test results, or may identify high-risk patients with undiagnosed atrial fibrillation based on subtle trends in past ECG readings. By providing real-time alerts, AI would seek to ensure that care gaps are identified proactively rather than retrospectively (Lee et al., 2024).

Once care gaps are identified, the challenge then becomes how to engage patients effectively. Traditional outreach such as mass emails or robocalls often results in low response rates. AI has immense potential for enhancing patient engagement by personalizing outreach based on patient preferences, behaviors, and risk profiles. AI could help determine whether a patient is more likely to respond to a text message, phone call, or patient portal notification. AI-driven chatbots can also provide automated yet interactive communication by allowing patients to schedule appointments, ask questions about recommended screenings, and receive educational materials tailored to their needs. In a specialty practice such as endocrinology, AI-driven outreach can be particularly impactful for managing chronic conditions. If an AI system detects that a diabetic patient has not had an HbA1c test in over six months, it could enable triggering a personalized reminder through the patient's preferred communication channel. If the patient does not respond, AI can support escalating outreach by generating a task for a care coordinator to follow up with a phone call.

5.7 Care Gap Closure: Helping to Enable Care Coordination Workflows and PHM

Care gaps often arise due to fragmented workflows where patients receive treatment from multiple providers who may not always have access to the same information. AI-powered interoperability helps to bridge these gaps by aggregating data across disparate systems and ensuring that all relevant providers have a comprehensive view of a patient's health history. A patient discharged from a hospital following a stroke may need follow-up care with a neurologist, cardiologist, and primary care physician. AI can assist in ensuring that all relevant providers are informed of the discharge and track whether the patient has kept up with their follow-up appointments. If any step is missed, AI can trigger reminders or escalate outreach efforts to prevent the patient from falling through the cracks. AI can also assist in managing social determinants of health, which are often overlooked in traditional care models. If an AI system detects that a patient with diabetes has frequently missed medical appointments and has a documented history of housing instability, it may be able to alert care managers to connect the patient with social services and community resources.

One of the major barriers to care gap closure is the complexity of integrating insights into clinical workflows to enable real-time decision support. AI has the potential to address this by embedding real-time alerts and decision support tools directly into the EHR user interface that providers and staff use (Agatstein, 2023). As an example, when a primary care provider sees a patient for a routine visit, an AI-powered assistant would automatically generate a list of recommended actions such as ordering a mammogram or discussing smoking cessation. The provider can then act on these recommendations within the same workflow, minimizing disruption to their routine and ensuring care gaps are closed seamlessly. Similarly, in an oncology setting, AI could create an alert for oncologists if a patient has missed a follow-up imaging study or has not yet been referred for genetic counseling despite meeting criteria for hereditary cancer risk. This real-time support ensures that critical interventions are not overlooked.

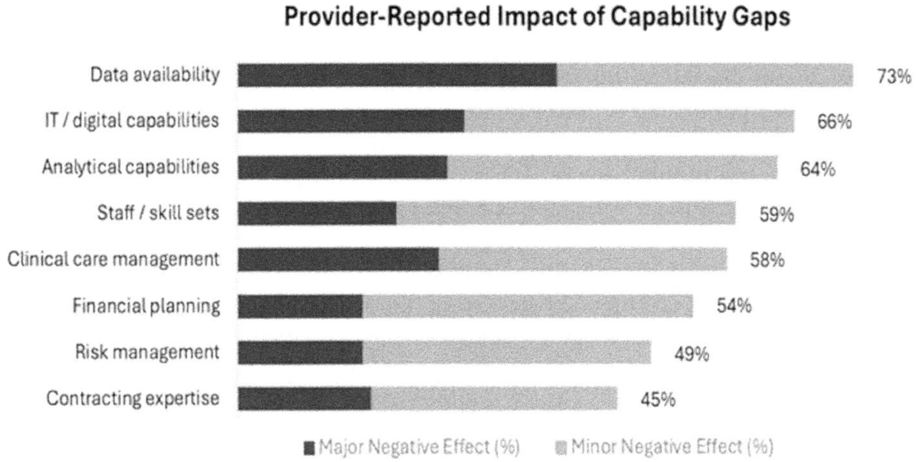

Figure 5.3 Results from a survey of providers asking about capability gaps that have negatively affected the performance of value-based care programs (Jackson, 2024).

The shift toward value-based care models places a strong emphasis on preventive care and chronic disease management. While value-based care has the potential to benefit both patient populations and providers, limited data availability and insufficient IT and analytics capabilities are proving to be hurdles. These gaps make it challenging for providers to track patients' journeys and deliver the comprehensive analysis required under two-sided risk arrangements, ultimately limiting performance and adoption (Jackson, 2024).

AI-driven care gap closure aligns perfectly with these goals by enabling healthcare organizations to track quality metrics, stratify risk, and implement targeted interventions at scale. Using AI to continuously monitor key performance indicators such as breast cancer screening rates and annual wellness visit completion can help generate actionable insights and allow providers to implement focused outreach campaigns and optimize resource allocation. AI-driven care gap closure also plays a crucial role in managing high-cost conditions such as heart failure and chronic kidney disease. By identifying patients at risk of disease progression and ensuring they receive timely interventions, AI helps reduce hospitalizations, emergency department visits, and overall healthcare costs.

5.8 Challenges and Considerations for Care Gaps and AI

AI implementation in care gap closure is also not without challenges. The accuracy and fidelity of data remain a primary concern as incomplete or inconsistent EHR records can lead to incorrect care gap identification (Khan et al., 2023). Ensuring AI systems are trained on high-quality representative datasets is essential for minimizing false positives and false negatives. Provider adoption is another critical factor as AI-driven alerts and recommendations must be seamlessly integrated into clinical and administrative workflows without contributing to alert fatigue or excessive administrative burden. If providers perceive AI recommendations as irrelevant or intrusive, they may be less likely to engage with the technology. Thoughtful and user-friendly interfaces, along with robust provider education, are key to fostering trust and maximizing the impact of AI-driven care gap closure. Patient engagement also presents a challenge, especially among populations with limited digital literacy or access to technology. AI outreach strategies must account for these barriers by adopting multiple communication modalities and leveraging community-based resources to reach underserved populations effectively. Regulatory and ethical considerations must also be addressed to ensure that AI-driven care gap closure aligns with privacy standards and avoids biases to support equitable healthcare delivery. Transparent algorithms, robust data security measures, and ongoing performance monitoring are essential for responsible AI deployment (Khan et al., 2023).

AI's role in care gap closure will likely be driven by advancements in predictive analytics, machine learning, and natural language processing. Future developments may include AI-driven virtual health assistants that proactively engage patients in self-care or advanced predictive modeling that anticipates care gaps before they even occur. AI is not just a potential enabler for transforming the way care gaps are identified; it has potential to reshape the entire care delivery model, making healthcare more proactive, personalized, and efficient. By leveraging AI to close care gaps, primary and specialty care practices can improve patient outcomes, enhance provider efficiency, and advance the broader goal of value-based, patient-centered care.

5.8.1 Implementation Best Practices and Initial Results: Appointment and Follow-Up Scheduling

Ensuring that patients receive timely follow-up care is critical to maintaining continuity of treatment, improving outcomes, and preventing unnecessary hospitalizations (Kripalani et al., 2019). However, coordinating follow-up appointments, particularly for patients seeing multiple providers, remains a significant challenge. Traditional scheduling processes often rely on manual efforts from administrative staff, leaving room for inefficiencies and scheduling conflicts that result in missed appointments. AI is also able to facilitate major improvements in follow-up scheduling by automating workflows, analyzing patient data to predict future appointment needs, and then proactively engaging patients to ensure compliance. One of the most significant advantages AI brings to appointment follow-up scheduling is automation. Historically, scheduling a follow-up visit required front-desk staff to manually coordinate dates, check provider availability, and then reach out to patients via phone or email. This process can be time-consuming and prone to human error, leading to scheduling bottlenecks or missed appointments. AI-driven scheduling tools can streamline this process by automatically analyzing patient history, provider recommendations, and availability to suggest optimal follow-up dates (Toker et al., 2024). One example may be after a routine check-up; AI-driven scheduling can instantly book a patient's next visit based on clinical guidelines and provider availability, or AI could track complex treatment schedules and ensure patients receive follow-ups for tests, imaging, and medication adjustments without delay from a specialty perspective. AI might also be able to help with predicting scheduling needs based on historical patterns. If a diabetic patient typically requires an endocrinology visit every three months, AI can proactively schedule the next visit before the patient leaves their current appointment. Again, this would help to eliminate gaps in care and ensure better adherence to treatment plans.

Missed follow-up appointments are also a pervasive issue in healthcare (Triemstra & Lowery, 2018) and can often lead to worsened outcomes or lost revenue. AI can potentially help reduce no-shows by sending personalized, automated reminders via text, email, or voice call based on a patient's preferred communication method. Unlike traditional, more generic reminder systems, AI-driven tools use behavioral data to optimize engagement. For example, if a patient is more likely to confirm appointments via SMS rather than email, AI can help prioritize text reminders.

In addition, AI could also analyze historical patterns to identify patients at risk of missing appointments, such as those with a previous no-show history, and then implement additional interventions, such as offering transportation assistance or same-day scheduling flexibility. In specialty areas where delays in follow-up can impact disease progression, AI may even be able to go a step further by alerting care coordinators when a high-risk patient misses a critical appointment. This allows for immediate outreach and rescheduling, thereby reducing the likelihood of gaps in treatment.

5.9 Patient-Centered Scheduling and Care Coordination

AI not only makes follow-up scheduling more efficient for providers but also enhances the patient's experience by offering greater flexibility and convenience. Traditionally, scheduling an appointment often requires multiple phone calls and long hold times. AI-powered self-scheduling platforms can potentially mitigate this frustration by allowing patients to book or reschedule visits through an intuitive online portal or mobile app. Advanced AI chatbots can further enhance patient convenience by answering scheduling-related questions, suggesting optimal appointment times, and even possibly integrating with personal calendars. A patient undergoing physical therapy after surgery may receive automated messages suggesting follow-up sessions based on their progress, with the ability to confirm or modify appointments in real time. AI-powered scheduling systems are seeking to incorporate external factors such as travel time, prior authorization requirements, and provider availability across multiple locations. This is particularly beneficial in multispecialty practices where patients often need to coordinate visits with multiple providers. AI can ensure that follow-up appointments are scheduled efficiently in order to reduce unnecessary delays and improve care coordination.

Enabling AI-driven follow-up scheduling requires integration directly with electronic health records (EHRs) to ensure that appointment recommendations are based on real-time data. This integration allows providers to receive automated scheduling prompts within their workflow and eliminates the need to toggle between multiple systems. For instance, when a primary care physician orders a follow-up cholesterol test for a patient with hyperlipidemia, AI can likely support scheduling automation for the lab appointment and a follow-up visit to review results.

For patients receiving care from multiple providers, follow-up scheduling becomes even more complex. AI can help to streamline coordination by synchronizing appointments across different specialties to ensure patients receive comprehensive and timely care. A patient recovering from a heart attack may need follow-ups with a cardiologist, Primary Care Physician (PCP), and a physical therapist, so AI can analyze provider availability and schedule these visits in a way that minimizes travel time. AI can also flag any conflicts in follow-up recommendations and suggest alternative dates to avoid overloading the patient with multiple appointments on the same day.

AI's role in follow-up scheduling extends beyond just convenience, as it can also help address barriers to care by identifying social drivers of health (SDOH), which may impact a patient's ability to attend appointments. If AI detects that a patient frequently misses appointments due to a lack of transportation, it can seek to integrate with ride-sharing services or community support programs to help. AI can also potentially flag financial barriers that may prevent patients from scheduling necessary follow-ups. If a patient with chronic kidney disease is at risk of missing a nephrology appointment due to high out-of-pocket costs, AI might also enable the notification of care coordinators to explore financial assistance options or adjust scheduling based on insurance coverage changes.

5.10 Challenges and Considerations in AI-Driven Scheduling

Despite its many advantages, data quality remains a key concern regarding AI-driven scheduling, which relies on accurate, up-to-date patient information. Discrepancies in EHR data can lead to inappropriate scheduling recommendations, while ensuring interoperability between different healthcare systems is crucial to maximizing AI's effectiveness. While AI may automate many aspects of scheduling, clinicians and administrative staff must be trained to use AI-generated recommendations effectively. Resistance to change or concerns about over-reliance on automation can slow adoption, necessitating clear education on AI's role as a complement to human decision-making and not a replacement. Privacy and security concerns also need to be addressed, particularly in AI-driven patient outreach (Khan et al., 2023). Ensuring compliance with HIPAA regulations and protecting patient data from breaches is essential for maintaining trust in AI scheduling solutions.

As AI continues to evolve, scheduling will likely become even more sophisticated, incorporating predictive modeling, voice-assisted scheduling, and real-time patient feedback. Future AI systems may use biometric data from wearables to determine optimal follow-up times based on a patient's health status. Additionally, AI-driven scheduling could become more integrated with telehealth by automatically transitioning in-person follow-ups to virtual visits when appropriate. For example, a post-operative check-in that does not require a physical exam could be converted to a telehealth visit based on AI recommendations, improving patient convenience and reducing unnecessary clinic visits. AI's role in follow-up scheduling is not just about efficiency but also about ensuring patients receive the care they need and when they need it. By reducing the administrative burden, enhancing patient engagement, and improving care coordination, AI is looking to transform follow-up scheduling from a logistical challenge into a seamless, patient-centered experience.

5.10.1 Implementation Best Practices and Initial Results: Prior Authorization Workflows for Primary and Specialty Practices

Prior authorization (PA) remains one of the most cumbersome and time-consuming administrative burdens in healthcare, often leading to treatment delays, increased provider frustration, and worsened patient outcomes. The traditional PA process requires providers to submit extensive documentation to insurance payers that justifies the medical necessity of treatments, medications, or procedures. These requests often involve a back-and-forth exchange of medical records, payer-specific forms, and clinical justification, leading to inefficiencies that drain time and resources from both providers and staff ("AI and Health Insurance," n.d.). AI helps streamline and optimize the PA workflow by automating documentation processes, extracting relevant clinical information from EHRs, and facilitating real-time decision-making. By leveraging AI-powered tools, healthcare providers can enable the submission of prior authorizations more quickly and accurately to reduce administrative burden while ensuring that patients receive timely access to necessary treatments (McKinsey & Company, 2022).

5.11 Prior Authorization Submission

Historically, PA submissions require significant manual effort from healthcare providers and administrative teams. Staff members needed to gather patient medical records, confirm payer requirements, fill out forms, and submit documentation via fax, phone, or online portals. This inefficient process often resulted in delays, with prior authorization approvals taking days or even weeks before patients could receive their treatment. AI can automate the PA submission process by extracting relevant clinical data directly from EHRs and mapping it to payer-specific requirements. AI-driven platforms would be able to compile a complete and accurate prior authorization request much more quickly by analyzing a patient's medical history, diagnostic codes, and clinical notes. Instead of manually searching for justification documents, providers can rely on AI algorithms to retrieve and format necessary information automatically. In primary care, providers frequently request authorizations for imaging studies, specialty referrals, and various medications. AI could then significantly reduce the time required to complete and submit these requests. In specialty practices, where PAs are required for high-cost treatments, AI can help ensure that all necessary documentation is submitted in a standardized format, thus reducing the likelihood of denials or follow-up requests from payers.

5.12 Reducing Denials and Appeals

Another major frustration of the traditional PA process is the high rate of denials due to incomplete or incorrect submissions. Payers often reject requests due to missing documentation, incorrect coding, or failure to meet specific criteria (Nguyen, 2024). These denials force providers to spend additional time on appeals, resulting in further delays with patient care. AI-powered PA solutions can potentially improve approval rates by ensuring that all required documentation is included in the initial submission. Machine learning algorithms would be able to analyze previous PA requests and payer policies to predict whether a submission will be approved or denied before it is sent. If AI identifies missing information or potential red flags, it can then alert providers, allowing them to correct errors before submission. AI systems may also be able to track payer-specific trends and recognize patterns in approval and denial rates. For example, if a payer frequently denies PA requests for a certain medication unless a step therapy requirement is met, then AI could automatically flag this requirement and ensure that alternative treatments are documented before submission. This proactive approach would minimize the number of appeals and help providers navigate payer policies more effectively.

5.13 Real-Time Prior Authorization

A promising advancement in AI-driven PA workflows is the potential for real-time decision-making. Traditional PA often involves multiple days of waiting for payers to manually review documentation submitted. AI-driven solutions, along with payer-integrated automation, can facilitate immediate approvals for certain treatments by cross-referencing medical necessity criteria against payer guidelines. For example, AI systems integrated with payer decision-support tools can automatically approve routine procedures or medications that meet predefined criteria. A patient with type 2 diabetes who requires a refill of an already approved medication should not have to wait for a manual PA review each time a prescription is renewed. AI would be able to analyze the patient's history and confirm that the medication meets payer guidelines to instantly approve a request and therefore eliminate unnecessary delays. This type of real-time automation is particularly beneficial in specialty practices, where delays in treatment authorization can have severe consequences. For example, Oncology patients requiring chemotherapy may face extended waiting periods due to PA requirements. AI-driven real-time approvals ensure that cancer patients receive life-saving treatments without unnecessary bureaucratic hurdles.

5.14 Enhancing Operational and Administrative Efficiency

AI-driven prior authorization tools free up considerable time for providers and administrative staff by allowing them to focus on patient care instead of paperwork. Physicians and staff spend a lot of their time on prior authorizations, with many practices requiring dedicated staff members to manage these requests. By automating much of the PA process, AI can potentially reduce the manual workload associated with gathering documentation, completing forms, and following up with payers (Granston, 2024). In many cases, AI-powered PA tools can be embedded directly within EHR workflows, allowing providers to initiate and track authorizations without leaving the patient record. AI-driven chatbots and virtual assistants may be able to handle provider-payer communications to reduce the need for time-consuming phone calls to insurance companies. These AI tools can answer provider inquiries, check authorization statuses, and even escalate urgent requests to further streamline the PA process.

5.15 Challenges and Considerations in AI-Driven Prior Authorization

While AI holds immense promise in transforming PA workflows, challenges remain. One key issue is the variability in payer policies and requirements. Insurance companies often have different criteria for approving the same treatment, requiring AI systems to continuously update their algorithms to reflect changing policies. Sufficient interoperability represents another major challenge since AI-driven PA solutions must integrate seamlessly with multiple EHR systems and payer IT platforms, which require collaboration between technology vendors and payers/providers (McKinsey & Company, 2022). Standardization of prior authorization data exchange, such as the adoption of Fast Healthcare Interoperability Resources (FHIR) standards, can and will likely help mitigate these issues. Another consideration is the trust of providers in AI-driven decision-making. While automation can improve efficiency, healthcare professionals must retain control over clinical decisions, so AI should function as an assistive tool that can provide recommendations and help streamline workflows without overriding provider judgment.

In addition to these technical and organizational hurdles, ethical considerations are paramount. AI-driven authorization systems must be designed and implemented in a manner that ensures fairness and transparency, so automated decisions do not inadvertently reinforce biases or cause harm through excessive denial. A majority of physicians recently surveyed by the American Medical Association believe AI is increasing or will increase denial rates, reflecting concerns over abuse of the technology and insufficient human supervision (American Medical Association, 2025). Many of these physicians worry that automated systems, if left unchecked, place unnecessary barriers between patients and needed care. Establishing clear oversight mechanisms and maintaining human-in-the-loop review are essential steps to safeguard patient rights and uphold ethical standards in claims approval and denial processes.

Provided that these concerns are addressed and adequate oversight mechanisms are put in place, integration of AI technology into prior authorization workflows could hold the potential to reduce barriers to care. Future advancements may include AI-powered predictive analytics that anticipate when a patient will need PA approval for a treatment before the provider even submits a request. Increased collaboration and trust between AI vendors and payers could lead to fully automated, payer-integrated solutions that allow for real-time approvals across a broader range of services. AI could also expand into voice-assisted PA workflows, enabling providers to initiate authorizations through voice commands within EHR systems. With careful design and ongoing human review, AI-driven automation is well-positioned to transform the prior authorization process from a bureaucratic bottleneck into a more efficient system of workflows. By reducing administrative burden, minimizing delays, and improving access to necessary treatments, AI will shape the future of prior authorization for both primary and specialty practices.

5.15.1 Overall Challenges and Future Opportunities: Where Are We and Where Do We Go from Here?

As we stand on the precipice of a new era in healthcare, the integration of artificial intelligence (AI) into primary and specialty care offers a beacon of hope for a more efficient, patient-centered, and equitable healthcare system. The transformative potential of AI is not merely a distant dream but a tangible reality that is already reshaping the way healthcare providers deliver care, manage administrative burdens, and engage with patients. While challenges remain, the opportunities presented by AI are vast, and the benefits—ranging from reduced clinician burnout to improved patient outcomes—are too significant to ignore. As we look to the future, AI will play an increasingly leading role in healthcare, acting as a powerful co-pilot for providers and a catalyst for systemic change.

For primary and specialty care providers, the promise of digital transformation remains largely unfulfilled. Although healthcare is now one of the most data-rich industries in the world, clinicians often struggle to harness this wealth of information effectively. EHRs, initially designed as repositories for storing patient records, were not built to facilitate real-time decision-making, automate administrative processes, or proactively identify patients in need of intervention. The result is a system where providers spend more time navigating complex interfaces than engaging with patients (Overhage & McCallie, 2020), and care teams must sift through extensive datasets to identify care gaps, manage follow-ups, and coordinate across multiple specialties.

5.16 The Promise of Artificial Intelligence

The potential benefits of AI in primary and specialty care are vast, being able to touch nearly every aspect of clinical practice, from administrative efficiency to patient engagement and care coordination. By automating time-consuming tasks such as documentation, chart review, and prior authorization, AI alleviates an administrative burden that has long plagued healthcare providers. This reduction in mental stress allows clinicians to focus more on what truly matters—their patients. The result may not only improve job satisfaction for providers but also create more meaningful patient-provider interactions that foster a healthcare environment prioritizing human connection over paperwork.

As we look to the future, the opportunities for AI in healthcare are many. The rapid advancements in natural language processing (NLP), machine learning (ML), and generative AI models such as large language models (LLMs) are opening new doors for innovation. These technologies are not only seeking to improve the accuracy and efficiency of existing applications but also enabling entirely new use cases that were once considered more science fiction. AI's role in supporting value-based care initiatives should not be overstated. By automating care gap closure, improving coding accuracy, and streamlining prior authorization processes, AI can enhance financial sustainability for healthcare practices. In an era where value-based reimbursement models are becoming the norm, AI's potential to improve quality measures and reduce costs could be a significant enabler for both providers and patients (Wachter & Brynjolfsson, 2024).

AI's ability to enhance patient engagement could be equally transformative. Through personalized outreach, virtual health assistants, and remote monitoring tools, AI will be able to empower patients to take an active role in their own care. For individuals managing chronic conditions, AI-driven reminders and tailored recommendations could make the difference between adherence and neglect, leading to better or worse health outcomes. Other examples include the development of real-time AI assistants that support providers during patient encounters, where AI-powered tools could automatically generate visit summaries, suggest evidence-based treatment recommendations, or even predict potential complications based on real-time data from wearable devices. These AI assistants could act as intelligent co-pilots, augmenting human expertise and ensuring that providers have all the information they need to make informed decisions at the point of care.

The integration of AI with telehealth and remote monitoring technologies is another area of potential focus. AI can play a crucial role in optimizing virtual care delivery by using AI-driven tools to analyze data from wearable devices, flag anomalies, and then provide real-time feedback to both patients and providers. Continuous monitoring not only could enhance patient engagement but also can enable early detection of health issues, reducing the need for in-person visits and improving access to care for underserved populations (Marzban et al., 2022). AI in healthcare is not limited to clinical applications, as there continue to be AI-driven innovations in drug discovery, medical imaging, and genomics that are poised to revolutionize the way we diagnose and treat diseases. By analyzing vast datasets and identifying patterns that would be impossible for humans to detect, AI can accelerate the development of new therapies and improve diagnostic accuracy.

5.17 Navigating the Path Forward Carefully

While the opportunities presented by AI are immense, it is also important to constantly remind ourselves of the challenges that lie ahead. The successful integration of AI into healthcare requires careful planning, thoughtful implementation, and ongoing collaboration among key stakeholders. One of the most pressing challenges is ensuring data privacy and security as AI systems handle sensitive patient information. Compliance with regulations such as the Health Insurance Portability and Accountability Act (HIPAA) is essential, but it is merely a first step. Healthcare organizations should also invest in advanced cybersecurity measures and ensure that AI systems are designed with privacy in mind. Another area to be watchful of is the potential for bias in AI algorithms. AI models are only as good as the data they are trained on, and if that data is biased or incomplete, resulting algorithms may perpetuate or even exacerbate existing inequities in healthcare (Wubineh et al., 2024). To mitigate this risk, it is essential to train AI models on diverse and representative datasets and to continuously monitor their performance for signs of bias. Interoperability is another significant challenge. Many healthcare organizations still rely on legacy EHR systems that were not designed to support advanced AI applications. Ensuring seamless integration between AI tools and existing systems is essential for maximizing their effectiveness. This requires collaboration between technology vendors, healthcare providers, and policymakers to develop standardized data exchange protocols and promote interoperability across the healthcare ecosystem. Provider

Table 5.1 Key Opportunities and Challenges for AI applications in Healthcare

Key Opportunities	*Key Challenges*
• Automation of administrative tasks • Enhanced clinical decision-making • Proactive care gap detection • Optimized scheduling • Increased patient engagement • Streamlined utilization management • Integration of data from disparate sources	• Ensuring high-quality data from legacy systems • Protecting the privacy and security of sensitive data • Mitigating bias in AI algorithms • Thoughtfully integrating into provider workflows • Navigating regulatory and standardization hurdles • Addressing legal liability and accountability • Educating on limitations and setting expectations for human supervision

adoption is another critical element that will determine the success of AI in healthcare. While AI has the potential to enhance clinical workflows, providers must feel confident that these tools are reliable and aligned with their needs.

5.18 A Bright and Hopeful Future

Despite there being a number of areas to carefully monitor and address, the future of AI in healthcare is bright. The potential for AI to enhance efficiency, improve patient outcomes, and reduce costs is too great to ignore. Looking ahead, we should expect to see AI become an integral part of everyday clinical practice. AI-driven tools will enable more personalized and precise care by helping providers tailor treatment to individual patient needs and preferences. At the same time, AI will empower patients to take a more active role in their own care by fostering a sense of ownership and accountability that is essential for long-term health. As AI continues to evolve, it will also play a crucial role in addressing some of the most pressing challenges facing healthcare today, from the rising burden of chronic diseases to the growing demand for mental health services. By enabling early interventions and optimizing resource allocation, AI has the potential to transform healthcare from a reactive system focused on treating illness to a proactive system focused on promoting wellness. In the future, providers will have more time to spend with their patients, free from the burdens of administrative tasks, and healthcare organizations will be better equipped to manage the complexities of modern medicine by delivering high-quality care that is both cost-effective and outcomes-driven.

The success of AI in healthcare will depend on our ability to navigate the challenges and seize upon opportunities that lie ahead. This will require collaboration among technology designers, payers, providers, policymakers, and patients to ensure that AI is implemented in a way that is ethical, equitable, and aligned with the needs of all stakeholders. It will also require a commitment to ongoing innovation as we continue to explore new applications for AI and refine existing ones. Together, these critical stakeholders can build a healthcare system that is not only smarter but also more compassionate, more equitable, and more focused on the well-being of every individual. The future of healthcare is bright, and AI is leading the way. By embracing the potential of AI and working together to overcome the challenges, we can unlock a future where healthcare is not only more effective but also more human-centered.

References

Agatstein, K. (2023). Chart review is dead; long live chart review: How artificial intelligence will make human review of medical records obsolete, one day. Population Health Management, 26(6), 438–440. https://doi.org/10.1089/pop.2023.0227

AI and health insurance prior authorization: Regulators need step-up oversight. (n.d.). Health Affairs Forefront. https://www.healthaffairs.org/content/forefront/ai-and-health-insurance-prior-authorization-regulators-need-step-up-oversight

AI may help researchers with medical chart review, Stanford Medicine study finds. (2024). Mednews. https://med.stanford.edu/news/all-news/2024/12/ai-pediatric-adhd.html

Alaita, F. (2024, May 1). Demystifying AI: Exploring the origins, evolution, and impact of artificial intelligence [LinkedIn post]. LinkedIn. https://www.linkedin.com/pulse/demystifying-ai-exploring-origins-evolution-impact-francisca-alaita-bdlqf/

American Medical Association. (2025, February 24). Physicians concerned AI increases prior authorization denials. https://www.ama-assn.org/press-center/press-releases/physicians-concerned-ai-increases-prior-authorization-denials/

Barr, M. (2024, November 27). Industry voices—reaching for the (Medicare) stars: Leveraging AI for better quality outcomes. Fierce Healthcare. https://www.fiercehealthcare.com/payers/industry-voices-reaching-medicare-stars-leveraging-ai-better-quality-outcomes

Choudhury, A., & Asan, O. (2020). Role of artificial intelligence in patient safety outcomes: Systematic literature review. *JMIR Medical Informatics, 8*(7), e18599. https://doi.org/10.2196/18599

Clusmann, J., Kolbinger, F. R., Muti, H. S., et al. (2023). The future landscape of large language models in medicine. *Communications Medicine, 3*, Article 141. https://doi.org/10.1038/s43856-023-00370-1

Granston, T. (2024, September 18). Closing the AI gap: How intelligent prior authorization is transforming health care. BenefitsPro. https://www.benefitspro.com/2024/09/18/closing-the-ai-gap-how-intelligent-prior-authorization-is-transforming-health-care/?slreturn=20250213141839

Jackson, R., & Dotson, K. (2024, June 5). The key role of downside risk in the success of value-based care. *HFMA*. https://www.hfma.org/payment-reimbursement-and-managed-care/value-based-payment/the-key-role-of-downside-risk-in-vbcs-success/

Lancet Digital Health. (2025). Exploring electronic health records to study rare diseases. *The Lancet Digital Health, 7*(2), Article e008. https://doi.org/10.1016/j.landig.2025.01.008

Khan, B., et al. (2023). Drawbacks of artificial intelligence and their potential solutions in the healthcare sector. *Biomedical Materials & Devices, 1*(2), 731–738. https://doi.org/10.1007/s44174-023-00063-2

Kripalani, S., et al. (2019). A transition care coordinator model reduces hospital readmissions and costs. *Contemporary Clinical Trials, 81*, 55–61. https://doi.org/10.1016/j.cct.2019.04.014

Lee, C., et al. (2024). Prospects for AI clinical summarization to reduce the burden of patient chart review. *Frontiers in Digital Health, 6*, Article 1475092. https://doi.org/10.3389/fdgth.2024.1475092

Marzban, S., et al. (2022). Impact of patient engagement on healthcare quality: A scoping review. *Journal of Patient Experience, 9*, Article 23743735221125439. https://doi.org/10.1177/23743735221125439

McKinsey & Company. (2022, April 19). AI ushers in next-gen prior authorization in healthcare. McKinsey & Company. https://www.mckinsey.com/industries/healthcare/our-insights/ai-ushers-in-next-gen-prior-authorization-in-healthcare

Nguyen, K. (2024, July 10). How to prevent healthcare claim denials. *Experian Healthcare Blog*. https://www.experian.com/blogs/healthcare/how-to-prevent-healthcare-claim-denials/

Overhage, J. M., & McCallie, D. (2020). Physician time spent using the electronic health record during outpatient encounters. *Annals of Internal Medicine, 172*(3), 169–174. https://doi.org/10.7326/M18-3684

Pangarkar, T. (2025, January 14). AI in healthcare statistics and facts (2025). *Market.Us Scoop*. https://scoop.market.us/ai-in-healthcare-statistics/

Payerchin, R. (2024, June 10). Physicians say documentation burdens are impeding patient care. *Medical Economics*. https://www.medicaleconomics.com/view/physicians-say-documentation-burdens-are-impeding-patient-care

Sarkar, U., & Bates, D. W. (2024). Using artificial intelligence to improve primary care for patients and clinicians. *JAMA Internal Medicine, 184*(4), 343. https://doi.org/10.1001/jamainternmed.2023.7965

Toker, K., et al. (2024). A solution to reduce the impact of patients' no-show behavior on hospital operating costs: Artificial intelligence-based appointment system. *Healthcare, 12*(21), Article 2161. https://doi.org/10.3390/healthcare12212161

Triemstra, J. D., & Lowery, L. (2018). Prevalence, predictors, and the financial impact of missed appointments in an academic adolescent clinic. *Cureus, 10*(11), e3613. https://doi.org/10.7759/cureus.3613

Wachter, R. M., & Brynjolfsson, E. (2024). Will generative artificial intelligence deliver on its promise in health care? *JAMA, 331*(1), 65. https://doi.org/10.1001/jama.2023.25054

Wubineh, B. Z., et al. (2024). Exploring the opportunities and challenges of implementing artificial intelligence in healthcare: A systematic literature review. *Urologic Oncology: Seminars and Original Investigations, 42*(3), 48–56. https://doi.org/10.1016/j.urolonc.2023.11.019

2

AI ACROSS THE HEALTHCARE ECOSYSTEM

The day healthcare can fully embrace AI is the day we have a revolution in terms of cutting costs and improving care.

Fei-Fei Li, Professor of Computer Science at Stanford University

DOI: 10.4324/9781003621294-7

Chapter 6

The Impact of Artificial Intelligence on Dentistry

Zahid Lalani, DDS, MBA, PhD and Archita Jain, BSc, DDS

6.1 Overview

Use of artificial intelligence in dentistry and the oral health sciences has been increasing over the last decade, mainly in the areas of diagnostics, predictive analytics, treatment planning, as well as practice management. This chapter explores the different types of AI models, improvements and advances in these models and how their combinations can provide dentists and oral health professionals with the tools to diagnose oral health diseases with better precision and to design more efficient and effective treatments. Judicious use and applications of AI will improve oral healthcare and allow oral health clinicians to provide more efficient and effective care for their patients.

6.2 Introduction

Artificial intelligence (AI) is a broad term for a type of technology that enables machines to perform tasks that are usually performed by and requiring human intelligence. AI is a broad field of computational science that utilizes a variety of techniques to examine and solve a spectrum of tasks. The use of AI in dentistry has grown over the past decade in the areas of diagnostics, predictive analytics, treatment planning, practice management and most recently in the use of robotics for treatment. The focus of AI utilization has been in treatment planning, the use of robotics to achieve planned treatment outcomes and practice management, as these are areas where commercial applications of the burgeoning technology have the most impact.

AI-based methods can be classified into four broad groups: statistical learning, artificial neural network-based learning, genetic algorithm-based learning and hybrid AI methods (Ghaffari et al., 2024; Nguyen et al., 2023).

Principles and concepts of statistics are utilized by the statistical learning model to make predictions and decisions based on the provided data. Examples of statistical learning methods include logistic regression, linear regression, decision trees, support vector machines and random

DOI: 10.4324/9781003621294-8

forests. These models can assist in understanding risk factors affecting systemic diseases and oral health, predicting the risk of different diseases that can afflict oral tissues and analyzing different treatment options for different diseases affecting oral health and their effectiveness (Ghaffari et al., 2024; Nguyen et al., 2023).

Artificial neural networks are types of algorithms that use interconnected layers of artificial nodes to process and transmit information. These neural networks analyze data and learn from complex patterns and relationships by adjusting the weights of different connections. An example of a neural network-based methodology includes convolutional neural networks. These types of algorithms have been utilized for image recognition and analysis and natural language processing (Ghaffari et al., 2024; Nguyen et al., 2023).

Genetic algorithms are based on human genetics and natural selection. They are used to find optimal solutions for complex problems by using selection, crossover and mutation processes in their algorithms (Ghaffari et al., 2024; Nguyen et al., 2023).

Hybrid AI methods utilize a combination of various techniques to address complex problems by using the strengths of different methods described above (Ghaffari et al., 2024; Nguyen et al., 2023).

6.3 Background of AI in Oral Health

Let us consider the various aspects of oral health/dentistry, the impact of AI on them and the possibilities for the future.

6.3.1 General Dentistry

General dentistry, in some sense, is an amalgamation of all parts of specialized dentistry in the 21st century. The rapid technological advances in diagnostic and treatment planning modalities, partly driven by AI and a change in the structure of dental practices where a significant proportion of practices are multi-specialty groups under a single roof, have transformed the treatment that can be offered to patients in a single practice or dental office. The use of this practice model has been a product of an increasing proportion of the aging population with higher disposable income who are seeking dental treatment, economic advantages of treating patients in one office as compared to referring to specialists and the increased penetration of dental service organizations (DSO) in the US. This has led to a general dental practice today seeing a variety of patients with complex health issues and varied treatment needs under one roof. This has led to the need for advanced technology for diagnosis, treatment planning and rendering treatment with expectations for accurate and optimal outcomes by general dentists. The use of AI-enabled detection of caries based on imaging and the types of restorations best suited for patients based on imaging have been utilized for improving outcomes with more conservative treatment and minimizing the removal of healthy tooth structures (Abduo et al., 2014; Alferez et al., 2022; Butcher et al., 2022; Chen et al., 2022; Duong et al., 2021; Estai et al., 2022; Kühnisch et al., 2022; Lee et al., 2021; Mohammad-Rahimi, 2022; Reyes et al., 2022; Zheng et al., 2021). There is at present no technology that can distinguish between active and arrested caries. The use of AI-based imaging could potentially deliver a solution to this diagnostic problem by quantifying the percentage of demineralization in a carious lesion to give an indication if the area represents an active versus an arrested lesion (Abduo et al., 2014; Alferez et al., 2022; Butcher et al., 2022; Chen et al., 2022; Duong et al., 2021; Estai et al., 2022; Kühnisch et al., 2022; Lee et al., 2021; Mohammad-Rahimi 2022; Reyes et al., 2022; Zheng et al., 2021). The use of apex locators and AI-generated tools along with cone beam imaging technology has made the successful delivery of endodontic treatment predictable and routine by general dentists. The use of intraoral scanners and cone beam technology merged together to give a composite picture of teeth, oral soft tissues, jaw bones, maxillary sinus, nasal cavities and nerves has revolutionized treatment planning for the rehabilitation of patients with complex prosthetic needs. The use of this technology has now been combined with robotics to take the complex treatment plans that are developed to completion with no changes that a human hand and brain could achieve on their own with the use of robotics. 3D printing technology has allowed a reduction in treatment time and a more accurate fit of crowns and bridges on teeth and dental implants using Computer-Assisted Diagnosis - Computer-Assisted Management (CAD-CAM) technology.

6.3.2 *Endodontics*

Detecting apical diseases in relation to a tooth or teeth, accurately measuring the working length of a root canal and assessing and navigating the anatomy of the canal(s) are factors that are critical to successful endodontic treatment (Xu et al., 2022). The use of cone beam imaging technology and electronic apex locators has reduced these challenges to a significant extent. However, the availability of cone beam imaging is not ubiquitous, and the use of AI in examining a periapical image and providing guidance for measuring the working length of the canal based on knowledge gleaned from large data sets is helpful. In situations where cutting-edge technology and tools are not available, the use of AI with 2D imaging is beneficial, but the clinical experience and expertise of the dentist or endodontist is critical in making the assessment and carrying out treatment for a successful outcome (Chauhan et al., 2022; De-Deus et al., 2022; Herbst et al., 2023; Jeon et al., 2021; Qiao et al., 2020; Qu et al., 2022). Utilizing AI in detecting root fractures and assessing the quality of an existing root canal-treated tooth that has a persistent apical lesion would increase the effectiveness of diagnosis and, with it, effective communication with the patient regarding the potential prognosis of the tooth and ideal treatment (ADA, 2022). This would remove the dependence on intra-operative findings of a fracture or inadequate prior root canal therapy to then determine an appropriate plan. This would have tremendous benefits for patients regarding the potential for undergoing an unnecessary procedure and the cost of care associated with it.

6.3.3 *Orthodontics*

The specialty of orthodontics and dentofacial orthopedics involves the evaluation of individuals to examine their facial skeleton and the way their teeth come together, and to recommend treatment if indicated. Evaluating children and young adults for growth patterns of the facial skeleton at a young age is important to determine if there are interventions needed to guide growth and prevent the development of facial skeletal discrepancies that would require surgical correction and orthodontic treatment as they grow older. This is called preventative orthodontics. Individuals who present with a skeletal facial discrepancy, dental malocclusion or both and have completed their growth phase are evaluated and treated with orthodontic treatment alone or a combination of orthodontic treatment and surgery. AI can be of great value in evaluating individuals as they come in at a young age and are still growing to determine if their skeletal growth pattern is such that preventative or interceptive orthodontic treatment will help in correcting facial growth and obviate the need for surgical correction or if the pattern is such that interceptive measures will help modify the growth pattern but surgical correction will likely be needed. This requires that AI has had exposure to large data sets of cephalometric radiographic imaging and clinical pictures for different races and ethnic groups to be precise in the diagnosis, predictive analysis of growth and treatment planning for individuals (Akdeniz et al., 2022; Faber et al., 2019; Li et al., 2022; Monill-González et al., 2021). The use of AI in tracing lateral cephalometric images has been shown to be much more accurate than human tracing, making the diagnosis of growth discrepancies much more accurate (ADA, 2022). AI in concert with digital dental models and imaging from intraoral scanners and cone beam imaging data could also help with planning treatment for patients with malocclusion alone or in combination with skeletal facial abnormalities to ensure that the position of teeth in the mouth and the roots in the jawbone, occlusion/bite, airway space and nasal spaces are all optimized for individuals requiring treatment (Akdeniz et al., 2022; Faber et al., 2019; Li et al., 2022; Monill-González et al., 2021). Utilization of AI to evaluate the airway space in patients with obstructive sleep apnea and the improvement or lack thereof with jaw surgery could prove to be a powerful tool in determining the value of surgery for a patient.

6.3.4 Oral Medicine

Oral medicine is a specialty of dentistry that deals with the medical management of diseases of the tissues of the oral cavity, oro-facial pain, and disorders of the temporomandibular joint (ADA 2022). The use of AI in diagnosis, treatment planning and medical management of the wide spectrum of disorders that can manifest in the jaw, mouth, face and temporomandibular joints can be tremendously useful for providers (ADA, 2022). Diseases of oral tissues as a manifestation of systemic disorders are very common, but the presentation can be varied and having the advantage of AI in scouring through a large database of published articles to help with the diagnosis or determine what treatment plan would be ideal for a particular patient can be of tremendous value. The use of AI to assist in a diagnosis regarding temporomandibular disorders based on large data sets of CT (computerized tomography) and MRI (magnetic resonance imaging) imaging would also be of tremendous value in recommending appropriate surgical versus non-surgical treatment and discussing outcomes based on evidence.

6.3.5 Oral and Maxillofacial Pathology and Radiology

The use of AI in early diagnosis of oral cancer can be of tremendous value to patients (Adeoye et al., 2022; Alhazmi et al., 2021; Ashizawa et al., 2017; Banavar et al., 2022; Banerjee et al., 2015; Baniulyte & Ali 2022; Bhandari et al., 2020; Bourdillon et al., 2023; García-Pola et al., 2021; Hung et al., 2020; Idrees et al., 2021; Ilhan et al., 2020; James et al., 2021; Kar et al., 2020; Nayak et al., 2006; Scrobot˘a et al., 2017; Tobias et al., 2022). Oral cancers diagnosed and treated at an early stage have a remarkably different prognosis and survival compared to a late-stage diagnosis (García-Pola et al., 2021; Hung et al., 2020; Kar et al., 2020; Scrobot˘a et al., 2017). There is ample evidence that oral cancer, which for the most part presents as a non-healing ulcer in the mouth, can be diagnosed effectively in early stages using AI. The diagnosis of precancerous lesions or carcinoma in situ using AI has not been validated, as the clinical presentations can be similar, the etiology can be varied and the risk of these lesions progressing to overt oral cancer is not similar (Banerjee et al., 2015; Idrees et al., 2021; James et al., 2021; Kar et al., 2020; Nayak et al., 2006; Scrobot˘a et al., 2017). The differential diagnosis of lesions in the jaw seen on radiographic exams can also be narrowed based on adequate imaging data sets from different races, genders and ethnicities by AI (Setzer et al., 2020; Kirnbauer et al., 2022).

6.3.6 Oral and Maxillofacial Surgery

The specialty of Oral and Maxillofacial Surgery deals with the treatment of developmental and acquired jaw deformities; traumatic injuries to the facial skeleton and soft tissues; management of benign and malignant lesions involving the jaws and soft tissues of the mouth; reconstruction of jaw bones for defects due to trauma or surgical treatment of pathology; and extraction of teeth and placement of dental implants to restore missing teeth. AI can be used for accurate diagnosis and appropriate treatment planning with Orthodontist or Prosthodontists for patients with deformities to achieve ideal soft tissue, bony skeletal and occlusal outcomes using data from cone beam CT, intraoral scanners for soft and dental tissue, photography and soft tissue data from the CT scans (Shujaat et al., 2022; Tanikawa & Yamashiro 2021; Tobias et al., 2022; Wang et al., 2017). Fabricating cutting guides for accurate translation of pre-operative treatment planning to surgery, custom-designed plates for fixation of bony segments and CAD-CAM generated splints have made corrective and reconstructive jaw surgery more accurate, predictable and efficient in terms of time under anesthesia (Shujaat et al., 2022). The planning of patients who need implant-supported restorations to replace missing teeth has been transformative with the use of cone beam CT, intraoral scanners and AI assisted segmentation and planning, use of custom prefabricated surgical guides, and robot-assisted surgery (Bodhe et al., 2022; Liu et al., 2021; Lahoud et al., 2021).

6.3.7 Pediatric Dentistry

Diagnostic imaging of carious lesions in children has become more accurate with the use of AI using learning based on large digital imaging data sets (Pang et al., 2021; Park et al., 2021; Ramos-Gomez et al., 2021). Early identification of incipient carious lesions leads to less invasive procedures for children. Predictive analytics using population data for similar demographics, coupled with information on oral hygiene habits and diet, will give the pediatric dentist an idea of what to expect in the patient, and the education and counseling for the patient and parents can then be tailored individually to minimize caries.

6.3.8 Periodontics

The diagnosis and management of chronic inflammatory conditions involving the teeth and their surrounding and supporting hard and soft tissues forms the core of periodontology. The microbiology of the oral cavity and the periodontium has emerged as an area of key interest as treatment strategies have morphed to target the specific microbiome responsible for inflammation and pathology. The role of systemic disease in altering the microbiome and the effect of a changing oral microbiome on the general health of an individual are the focus of research in this specialty of dentistry.

Early detection of infection and inflammatory changes of the periodontium, and the impact of underlying systemic diseases on both these factors can make a significant difference in treatment outcomes for patients. Detection and diagnosis involve clinical examination, radiographic evaluation and collection of tissue and fluids for microbiological testing. These are complex processes that require advanced skills and technology. Clinical evaluation is based on the skills of the dentist and dental hygienist and is consequently subjective and can vary. Radiographic evaluation is more accurate with advanced imaging like cone beam technology but may not be universally available, and interpretation of two-dimensional radiography is subjective and therefore variable between clinicians. The use of AI in the evaluation of clinical imaging, descriptive terminology and probing depths based on clinical examination and radiographic features may lead to improved diagnosis and recommendations for appropriate treatment based on evidence-based parameters, leading to improved outcomes (Chang et al., 2020; Kim et al., 2019; Krois et al., 2019; Lee et al., 2018; Lin et al., 2015; Moriyama et al., 2019; Mudrov, 2022; Revilla-León et al., 2022).

6.3.9 Preventive and Community Health in Dentistry

The focus of this specialty is on preventative care, which primarily involves the prevention of dental caries, periodontal disease and early detection of oral cancer. The second focus of this specialty is the education of the population regarding health practices that decrease the incidence of dental caries, reduce periodontal disease and loss of teeth and avoid habits that predispose individuals to the development of oral cancer. We have discussed the detection of dental caries and periodontal disease in the sections above. The use of AI in designing methods that are effective in educating the population to improve health practices and minimize habits that can predispose individuals to the development of caries, periodontal disease and oral cancer can go a long way in reducing the burden of disease (Schwendicke et al., 2023; Schwendicke et al., 2020).

6.3.10 Prosthodontics and Maxillofacial Prosthetics

Prosthodontics is a specialty of dentistry that deals with the repair and replacement of missing teeth, bone and facial structures using prosthetic materials for the restoration of form and function. Patients seen by Prosthodontists have complex problems that are beyond the realm of treatment by dentists. Complex problems require accurate assessment of the dentition and hard and soft tissue to arrive at a diagnosis and devise a comprehensive treatment plan that will restore form and function while maintaining occlusal balance and harmony between teeth, bones, muscles, skin, underlying soft tissues and temporomandibular joints. The classic and traditional way Prosthodontists used to achieve these solutions was through the use of facial pictures, measurements, making impressions of teeth and facial structures using moulage and then pouring models and devising treatment based upon all of these inputs. With the advent of technological advances in soft and hard tissue scanning, material science and CAD-CAM fabrication of prostheses, the processes for what Prosthodontists can do have morphed from hand- and time-intensive techniques to digitally formatted, efficient ones. The value of AI in Prosthodontics and Maxillofacial Prosthetics would be to remove subjective bias from the planning and use digital facial morphometrics and data that are now routinely captured to design and plan prostheses that will mimic more accurately the facial form and function of an individual (Abduo et al., 2014; Memon et al., 2021; Mine et al., 2020).

6.3.11 Practice Management in Dentistry

The way in which a dental practice operates today in most parts of the world involves human contact at every step of the way, starting from a phone call by a patient to make the appointment to see the dentist; gathering personal and health information about the patient and their insurance plans; being seen and assessed for diagnosis and treatment by a dentist; taking impressions for restorative treatment or orthodontics if indicated; manual measurement and documentation of oral findings including periodontal charting, comparing these with prior exams; evaluation of radiographs and comparing them with prior imaging; follow-up appointment scheduling;

submitting claims for treatment rendered to the patient's insurance carrier; obtaining appropriate payment amounts from the patient for services rendered; reconciliation of these amounts and refund issuance, if necessary; reconciliation of practice finances based on these transactions; recall phone calls to patients; inventory ordering and management of supplies; and the list can go on as one delves into the further details. Many of these functions are mundane and can be done more efficiently and effectively by AI once the infrastructure and processes are in place, making the practice more efficient and allowing practitioners to focus on delivering care.

6.4 Education for Dental Students and Graduate Students in Dental Specialty Training Programs

AI-generated clinical and radiographic imaging can be used to train dental students and residents in the comprehensive diagnosis of a variety of ailments that affect oral tissues. They can then be educated in the various options to treat different oral health conditions, given the underlying medical issues that the patient may have. These problem-based learning scenarios would equip dental and graduate students with the knowledge to diagnose and manage a variety of problems that patients present with in a comprehensive manner. It would also allow them to understand the benefits of collaborating with their colleagues in different dental specialties and their patients' physicians to optimize outcomes for their patients.

6.5 Education of Patients in Oral Health

AI-generated patient education modules for oral cancer prevention and screening, the prevention and management of periodontal disease and dental caries in children and adults, oral manifestations of systemic disease and the systemic effects of oral health are areas where patient education can lead to significant benefits with regard to early detection of problems, more conservative treatment needed for early disease and improved outcomes with reduced costs.

6.6 Strategy and Vision for AI in Dentistry

The use of AI, regardless of the underlying model(s), generally requires the acquisition of a large amount of data for the algorithm to process in order to identify and evaluate trends related to diseases and factors that cause or contribute to the disease, similarities in disease patterns and their relationship to outcomes, comparisons of different treatment modalities and reported outcomes based on publications across languages from different parts of the world and comparisons of images of radiographs, clinical pictures and pathology slides to develop a way to diagnose diseases and recommend optimal treatment for a disease or condition with the highest rates of success that are evidence-based. Machine learning and artificial neural networks can then use the outcomes from these initial decisions to learn and improve or change recommendations, leading to best practices for a disease process with optimized outcomes (Ghaffari et al., 2024; Nguyen et al., 2023).

Disease does not occur in most individuals as an isolated problem. Every human has a similar anatomy and common basic physiology, but there are subtle differences in the protoplasm, genomes, the effect of environmental factors, cultural and dietary aspects of living and stressors of life that have a significant impact on the development of a disease process and how their body responds to it and to a type of treatment.

Consequently, the data that needs to be gathered to account for these many differences is large, and the computing power to process and continually update the effects of AI-generated recommendations is significant. The upfront cost and time to design, gather and look at the results of the data being processed by AI is likely to be very significant, and the cost of ongoing data collection and processing is not likely to be insignificant either.

Given the fact that healthcare is expensive in general, one begins to wonder if the use of AI technology in every aspect of healthcare is worth the expense. Basic aspects of clinical dentistry like caries detection and treatment, diagnosis and management of periodontal disease, and management of damaged or missing teeth with different types of prostheses can and should be managed by dentists in any part of the world. Rather than using AI to diagnose carious lesions early or give tailored recommendations for the management of periodontal disease based not just on clinical and radiographic findings, but on the microbiome of an individual, it may be prudent and more cost-effective to use the recommendations generated by AI to educate dentists across the world to view the diagnosis and treatment of oral health problems as a part of the patient's general health and help them design treatment based on a better and broader understanding of the disease process compared to abrogating the thought process of making clinical decisions to recommendations made based on data sets. The use of technology to improve diagnosis and treatment procedures involving restorative and endodontic interventions, making them more effective and efficient, is critical to improving care for patients and, over time, reducing the cost of care. A reduction in the cost of care over time improves population health, quality of life, and decreases the burden of disease in communities and nations. This has the potential for more resources to be available to individuals, communities, and governments to use the saved resources to improve the lives of their citizens in other ways.

AI-generated diagnosis and treatment recommendations have value in the treatment of precancerous lesions, cancer and benign pathology afflicting the head and neck, including the mouth, as our knowledge at this point in time, while evaluating and designing treatment, is fragmented. As the understanding of diseases at molecular, genetic and epigenetic levels improves, the value of AI in putting it all together and looking for commonalities and trends to guide treatment for optimal long-term outcomes may prove to be a game changer for patients.

Use of AI in diagnosis of potential facial skeletal abnormalities in a growing child, interventions to correct the growth pattern and the correction of malocclusion using orthodontic treatment, while ensuring the teeth, bone, soft tissues surrounding the teeth, facial muscles and the temporomandibular joint are all in harmony, may be very valuable for patients. Utilizing data on surgical management of skeletal facial deformities to achieve ideal outcomes in occlusion and facial aesthetics with stable long-term results would be another valuable application of AI.

Areas where AI can make a significant impact in dentistry involve integrating electronic dental records (EDR) with electronic medical records (EMR) and practice management. There is currently only one system that has dental modules built into electronic medical records that are primarily used by large hospital systems. Electronic dental records commonly utilized by general dentists and dental specialists do not have an interface with the electronic medical records that are used by most physicians. This leads to a significant communication gap between the patients' physicians and their dentists with regard to care. Dentistry and medicine have traditionally been separated, but in an era where people are living longer and chronic diseases are becoming more prevalent at younger ages, collaboration and communication between physicians and dentists hold the potential for a significant value-added proposition to improve care and outcomes for patients.

Using AI in EMR and EDR modules to send a note to the specialist dentist or from the specialist dentist to the general dentist to inform them of the treatment needed or rendered to the patient makes for a closed communication loop and ensures that important information about patient care is shared. Pathology and imaging reports or communications between dentists and physicians can also be shared using an integrated EMR and EDR by all treating providers so that all members of the team taking care of the patient are up to date on their healthcare.

Use of AI models for practice management holds great promise for both patients and dentists. The ability to have a system whereby patients can schedule their appointments online at their convenience, with an algorithm that looks at their dental records and questions them on what their complaint is, and allocates a time that is likely needed for the dentist to see them, is just one example of a process that can optimize the practice and delivery of care on a daily basis. The AI-generated algorithm can take a cancellation of an appointment made after the office has closed, look at the practice management software database, and send a message to multiple patients who are waiting for appointments, offering them an earlier one. This kind of optimization improves efficiency for the dental practice while allowing flexibility for patients based on changing life situations. AI-based algorithms can also be used for interoperability with insurance carriers to check patients' insurance status, claims and available benefits before the patients visit the dental office for an appointment. This information can then be shared with the patient and the dentist's office such that there is complete transparency and knowledge of the financial obligations of the patient before they come for an appointment.

Machine learning can be utilized to read notes of dentists in the EDR and generate insurance claims and submit them electronically. The algorithm can be taught based on claims-based data regarding the requirements for submission of clean claims to facilitate efficiency. AI-based technology can also be embedded into the practice management system to keep track of claim submission and receipt of reimbursement funds to allow for improved revenue cycle management. AI algorithms can show if there are issues with coding and billing for services provided, the reasons for delays in submitting claims, if any, the ratio of clean claims to those returned due to errors, types of claim errors and the time lapses from submission of clean claims to receipt of reimbursement from insurance carriers. The data obtained can identify areas where problems are occurring in the workflow and processes. AI can subsequently be utilized to change or design processes to remove the barriers to effective and efficient submission of clean claims and shorten the time for reimbursement.

Inventory management is another aspect of a dental practice that is a significant line item for expenses. AI-based technology can be used for inventory management. A number of vendors of dental supplies, dental implants and devices now provide software programs that contain details of the stock supplied, reference numbers and lot of these supplies, as well as embedded technology to bill the vendor when supplies are used by the practice and a mechanism to inform the vendor to restock the supplies when the stock reaches a certain level. An AI-generated system can merge these functions such that ordering from vendors, assessing the cost after comparing similar quality supplies, making recommendations for cost per unit, assessing expiration dates of existing supplies, utilizing supplies to ensure that no product has to be discarded due to expiration, assessing the utilization of supplies every 30 days, issuing instructions for payment to vendors and ordering restocking of inventory based on seasonal trends and practice busyness can be performed without human intervention. AI systems can also be designed to check the work described above and ensure that there are no errors, waste or fraud in inventory management and billing.

6.6.1 Implementation of Best Practices

One can build on the FDA's principles for good "AI/Machine Learning Practices" to develop best practices for the use of AI in dentistry (ADA, 2022; Ducret & Mörch, 2023; Khandare et al., 2019; Ossowska et al., 2022; Wang et al., 2022; Yang et al., 2021). These best practices can include the following.

1. Development of test data sets for various aspects of use in dentistry as enumerated above, using a diverse population group to prevent the introduction of bias.
2. Model the data sets to answer specific questions that can be used to train AI algorithms to answer questions, provide a range of solutions, and carry out specific tasks for different stakeholders in dentistry.
3. Perform testing to evaluate algorithms and utilize the results to make modifications as deemed necessary to accurately answer the questions on validation data sets.
4. Once the test sets have been perfected, develop participant data sets for the various purposes for which AI-based technologies and algorithms are to be utilized.
5. AI models should be designed to answer specific questions or carry out specific tasks utilizing the highest levels of patient data safety and security.
6. All stakeholders should have input into the development of the AI models such that there is a partnership between humans and AI to improve processes and increase efficiencies.
7. A system should be in place to update the data sets and regulatory guidelines in a dynamic fashion to allow the AI models to evolve and improve performance without errors or bias.
8. The system should have ethical guidelines in place to look for biases and processes to test quality control and performance on a routine basis.
9. Prioritize patient data, privacy, safety and security.

6.6.2 Challenges and Future Opportunities for Utilization of AI in Dentistry

There has been confusion in the dental literature between AI and emerging and developing technology that is revolutionizing dentistry and all its specialties (Ossowska et al., 2022). The advent of digital scanners for soft tissues, cone beam CT imaging for dental and bony structures, and the merging of these two technologies for CAD-CAM options for more effective and efficient restorative, orthodontic, implant dentistry and oral surgical treatment have been mistaken for advances attributed to AI.

Improving technology can give us the tools to carry out diagnoses with better precision and design treatments that are more accurate and can be delivered more efficiently. AI can help in improving technological advances and biological knowledge, and the data derived from using that knowledge and technology can help spawn data that can then be examined to improve diagnostics, treatment planning and treatment outcomes for various disease processes for our patients. These are the opportunities of the future, and they come at a cost, so judicious use and application of AI to improve oral health care, rather than supplant the use of human thought, clinical experience, and acumen, would be prudent. The greatest immediate use of AI in dentistry lies in the realm of practice management and the integration of electronic dental records (EDR) and electronic medical records (EMR). Interoperability of EDR and EMR would make a significant change in the delivery of care and utilization of AI in practice management would result in significant improvements in efficiency, cost savings and transparency with regard to patients' insurance benefits.

References

Abduo, J., Lyons, K., & Bennamoun, M. (2014). Trends in computer-aided manufacturing in prosthodontics: A review of the available streams. *International Journal of Dentistry, 2014*, 1–15. https://doi.org/10.1155/2014/783948

Adeoye, J., Wan, C. C. J., Zheng, L. W., Thomson, P., Choi, S. W., & Su, Y. X. (2022). Machine learning-based genome-wide salivary DNA methylation analysis for identification of noninvasive biomarkers in oral cancer diagnosis. *Cancers, 14*(14), 4935. https://doi.org/10.3390/cancers14194935

Akdeniz, B. S., Aykaç, V., Turgut, M., & Çetin, S. (2022). Digital dental models in orthodontics: A review. *Journal of Experimental and Clinical Medicine, 39*(1), 250–255. https://doi.org/10.52142/omujecm.39.1.48

Alferez, G., Jiménez, J., Hernández, H., González, M., Domínguez, R., & Briones, A. (2022). Application of data science to discover the relationship between dental caries and diabetes in dental records. *TechRxiv*. https://doi.org/10.36227/techrxiv.20311734.v1

Alhazmi, A., Alhazmi, Y., Makrami, A., Masmali, A., Salawi, N., Masmali, K., & Patil, S. (2021). Application of artificial intelligence and machine learning for prediction of oral cancer risk. *Journal of Oral Pathology & Medicine, 50*(5), 444–450. https://doi.org/10.1111/jop.13157

American Dental Association. (2022). Dentistry – Overview of artificial and augmented intelligence uses in dentistry (SCDI White Paper No. 1106).

Ashizawa, K., Yoshimura, K., Johno, H., Inoue, T., Katoh, R., Funayama, S., Sakamoto, K., Takeda, S., Masuyama, K., Matsuoka, T., & Ishii, H. (2017). Construction of mass spectra database and diagnosis algorithm for head and neck squamous cell carcinoma. *Oral Oncology, 75*, 111–119. https://doi.org/10.1016/j.oraloncology.2017.11.008

Banavar, G., Ogundijo, O., Julian, C., Toma, R., Camacho, F., Torres, P. J., Hu, L., Kenny, L., Vasani, S., & Batstone, M. (2022). Detecting salivary host-microbiome RNA signature for aiding diagnosis of oral and throat cancer. *MedRxiv*, 2007–2022. https://doi.org/10.1101/2022.07.22.22277771

Banerjee, S., Pal, M., Chakrabarty, J., Petibois, C., Paul, R. R., Giri, A., & Chatterjee, J. (2015). Fourier-transform-infrared-spectroscopy based spectral-biomarker selection towards optimum diagnostic differentiation of oral leukoplakia and cancer. *Analytical and Bioanalytical Chemistry, 407*(24), 7935–7943. https://doi.org/10.1007/s00216-015-8960-3

Baniulyte, G., & Ali, K. (2022). Artificial intelligence – Can it be used to outsmart oral cancer? *Evidence-Based Dentistry, 23*(1), 12–13. https://doi.org/10.1038/s41432-022-0238-y

Bhandari, B., Alsadoon, A., Prasad, P. W. C., Abdullah, S., & Haddad, S. (2020). Deep learning neural network for texture feature extraction in oral cancer: Enhanced loss function. *Multimedia Tools and Applications, 79*(39), 27867–2790. https://doi.org/10.1007/s11042-020-09384-6

Bodhe, R., Sivakumar, S., & Raghuwanshi, A. (2022). Design and development of deep learning approach for dental implant planning. In *2022 International conference on green energy, computing and sustainable technology (GECOST)* (pp. 269–274). IEEE.

Bourdillon, A. T., Shah, H. P., Cohen, O., Hajek, M. A., & Mehra, S. (2023). Novel machine learning model to predict interval of oral cancer recurrence for surveillance stratification. *Laryngoscope, 133*(7), 1652–1659. https://doi.org/10.1002/lary.30351

Butcher, M. C., Short, B., Veena, C. L. R., Bradshaw, D., Pratten, J. R., McLean, W., Shaban, S. M. A., Ramage, G., & Delaney, C. (2022). Meta-analysis of caries microbiome studies can improve upon disease prediction outcomes. *APMIS, 130*(12), 763–777. https://doi.org/10.1111/apm.13272

Chang, H. J., Lee, S. J., Yong, T. H., Shin, N. Y., Jang, B. G., Kim, J. E., Huh, K. H., Lee, S. S., Heo, M. S., Choi, S. C., Kim, T. I., & Yi, W. J. (2020). Deep learning hybrid method to automatically diagnose periodontal bone loss and stage periodontitis. *Scientific Reports, 10*, 7531. https://doi.org/10.1038/s41598-020-64509-z

Chauhan, R., Shah, T., Shah, D., & Gohil, T. (2022). A novel convolutional neural network–Fuzzy-based diagnosis in the classification of dental pulpitis. *Advances in Human Biology, 13*(1), 79. https://doi.org/10.4103/aihb.aihb_50_22

Chen, X., Guo, J., Ye, J., Zhang, M., & Liang, Y. (2022). Detection of proximal caries lesions on bitewing radiographs using deep learning method. *Caries Research, 56*(5), 455–463. https://doi.org/10.1159/000527418

De-Deus, G., Souza, E. M., Silva, E. J. N. L., Belladonna, F. G., Simões-Carvalho, M., Cavalcante, D. M., & Versiani, M. A. (2022). A critical analysis of research methods and experimental models to study root canal fillings. *International Endodontic Journal, 55*(3), 384–445. https://doi.org/10.1111/iej.13713

Ducret, M., & Mörch, C. M. (2023). Focus on artificial intelligence ethics in dentistry. *Journal of Dental Sciences, 18*(5), 1409–1410. https://doi.org/10.1016/j.jds.2022.12.003

Duong, D. L., Kabir, M. H., & Kuo, R. F. (2021). Automated caries detection with smartphone color photography using machine learning. *Health Informatics Journal, 27*, 146045822110075. https://doi.org/10.1177/14604582211007530

Estai, M., Tennant, M., Gebauer, D., Brostek, A., Vignarajan, J., Mehdizadeh, M., & Saha, S. (2022). Evaluation of a deep learning system for automatic detection of proximal surface dental caries on bitewing radiographs. *Oral Surgery, Oral Medicine, Oral Pathology and Oral Radiology, 134*(3), 262–270. https://doi.org/10.1016/j.oooo.2022.03.008

Faber, J., Faber, C., & Faber, P. (2019). Artificial intelligence in orthodontics. *APOS Trends in Orthodontics, 9*(4), 201. https://doi.org/10.25259/APOS_123_2019

García-Pola, M., Pons-Fuster, E., Suárez-Fernández, C., Seoane-Romero, J., Romero-Méndez, A., & López-Jornet, P. (2021). Role of artificial intelligence in the early diagnosis of oral cancer: A scoping review. *Cancers, 13*(18), 4600. https://doi.org/10.3390/cancers13184600

Ghaffari, M., Zhu, Y., & Shrestha, A. (2024). A review of advancements of artificial intelligence in dentistry. Dentistry Review, 4. https://doi.org/10.1016/j.dentre.2024.100081

Herbst, S. R., Herbst, C. S., & Schwendicke, F. (2023). Preoperative risk assessment does not allow to predict root filling length using machine learning: A longitudinal study. *Journal of Dentistry, 128*, 104378. https://doi.org/10.1016/j.jdent.2022.104378

Hung, M., Park, J., Hon, E. S., Bounsanga, J., Moazzami, S., Ruiz-Negrón, B., & Wang, D. (2020). Artificial intelligence in dentistry: Harnessing big data to predict oral cancer survival. *World Journal of Clinical Oncology, 11*(11), 918–934. https://doi.org/10.5306/wjco.v11.i11.918

Idrees, M., Farah, C. S., Shearston, K., & Kujan, O. (2021). A machine-learning algorithm for the reliable identification of oral lichen planus. *Journal of Oral Pathology & Medicine, 50*(10), 946–953. https://doi.org/10.1111/jop.13226

Ilhan, B., Lin, K., Guneri, P., & Wilder-Smith, P. (2020). Improving oral cancer outcomes with imaging and artificial intelligence. *Journal of Dental Research, 99*(3), 241–248. https://doi.org/10.1177/0022034520902128

James, B. L., Sunny, S. P., Heidari, A. E., Ramanjinappa, R. D., Lam, T., Tran, A. V., Kankanala, S., Sil, S., Tiwari, V., Patrick, S., Pillai, V., Shetty, V., Hedne, N., Shah, D., Shah, N., Chen, Z., Kandasarma, U., Raghavan, S. A., Gurudath, S., Kuriakose, M. A. (2021). Validation of a point-of-care optical coherence tomography device with machine learning algorithm for detection of oral potentially malignant and malignant lesions. *Cancers, 13*(14), 3583. https://doi.org/10.3390/cancers13143583

Jeon, S. J., Yun, J. P., Yeom, H. G., Shin, W. S., Lee, J. H., Jeong, S. H., & Seo, M. S. (2021). Deep-learning for predicting C-shaped canals in mandibular second molars on panoramic radiographs. *Dentomaxillofacial Radiology, 50*(6), 20200513. https://doi.org/10.1259/dmfr.20200513

Kar, A., Wreesmann, V. B., Shwetha, V., Thakur, S., Rao, V. U. S., Arakeri, G., & Brennan, P. A. (2020). Improvement of oral cancer screening quality and reach: The promise of artificial intelligence. *Journal of Oral Pathology & Medicine, 49*(8), 727–730. https://doi.org/10.1111/jop.13013

Khandare, L., Sreekantha, D. K., & Sairam, K. (2019). A study on encryption techniques to protect patient privacy in healthcare systems. In *Proceedings of the 2019 international conference on innovation in power and advanced computing technologies (i-PACT)* (pp. 1–5). IEEE.

Kim, J., Lee, H. S., Song, I. S., & Jung, K. H. (2019). DeNTNet: Deep neural transfer network for the detection of periodontal bone loss using panoramic dental radiographs. *Scientific Reports, 9*, 17615. https://doi.org/10.1038/s41598-019-53758-2

Kirnbauer, B., Hadzic, A., Jakse, N., Bischof, H., & Stern, D. (2022). Automatic detection of periapical osteolytic lesions on cone-beam computed tomography using deep convolutional neuronal networks. *Journal of Endodontics, 48*(10), 1434–1440. https://doi.org/10.1016/j.joen.2022.07.013

Krois, J., Ekert, T., Meinhold, L., Golla, T., Kharbot, B., Wittemeier, A., Dörfer, C., & Schwendicke, F. (2019). Deep learning for the radiographic detection of periodontal bone loss. *Scientific Reports, 9,* 8495. https://doi.org/10.1038/s41598-019-44839-3

Kühnisch, J., Meyer, O., Hesenius, M., Hickel, R., & Gruhn, V. (2022). Caries detection on intraoral images using artificial intelligence. *Journal of Dental Research, 101*(2), 158–165. https://doi.org/10.1177/00220345211032524

Lahoud, P., EzEldeen, M., Beznik, T., Willems, H., Leite, A., Van Gerven, A., & Jacobs, R. (2021). Artificial intelligence for fast and accurate 3-dimensional tooth segmentation on cone-beam computed tomography. *Journal of Endodontics, 47*(6), 827–835.

Lee, J. H., Kim, D., Jeong, S. N., & Choi, S. H. (2018). Diagnosis and prediction of periodontally compromised teeth using a deep learning-based convolutional neural network algorithm. *Journal of Periodontal & Implant Science, 48*(2), 114. https://doi.org/10.5051/jpis.2018.48.2.114

Lee, S., Oh, S., Jo, J., Kang, S., Shin, Y., & Park, J. (2021). Deep learning for early dental caries detection in bitewing radiographs. *Scientific Reports, 11,* 16807. https://doi.org/10.1038/s41598-021-96368-7

Li, S., Guo, Z., Lin, J., & Ying, S. (2022). Artificial intelligence for classifying and archiving orthodontic images. *BioMed Research International, 2022,* 1473977. https://doi.org/10.1155/2022/1473977

Li, S., Liu, J., Zhou, Z., Zhou, Z., Wu, X., Li, Y., Wang, S., Liao, W., Ying, S., & Zhao, Z. (2022). Artificial intelligence for caries and periapical periodontitis detection. *Journal of Dentistry, 122,* 104107. https://doi.org/10.1016/j.jdent.2022.104107

Lin, P. L., Huang, P. W., Huang, P. Y., & Hsu, H. C. (2015). Alveolar bone-loss area localization in periodontitis radiographs based on threshold segmentation with a hybrid feature fused of intensity and the H-value of fractional Brownian motion model. *Computer Methods and Programs in Biomedicine, 121*(2), 117–126. https://doi.org/10.1016/j.cmpb.2015.05.004

Liu, Y., Chen, Z., Chu, C., & Deng, F. L. (2021). *Transfer learning via artificial intelligence for guiding implant placement in the posterior mandible: An in vitro study.* Research Square. https://doi.org/10.21203/rs.3.rs-986672/v1

Memon, A. R., Li, J., Egger, J., & Chen, X. (2021). A review on patient-specific facial and cranial implant design using artificial intelligence (AI) techniques. *Expert Review of Medical Devices, 18*(10), 985–994.

Mine, Y., Suzuki, S., Eguchi, T., & Murayama, T. (2020). Applying deep artificial neural network approach to maxillofacial prostheses coloration. *Journal of Prosthodontic Research, 64*(3), 296–300.

Mohammad-Rahimi, H., Motamedian, S. R., Rohban, M. H., Krois, J., Uribe, S. E., Mahmoudinia, E., Rokhshad, R., Nadimi, M., & Schwendicke, F. (2022). Deep learning for caries detection: A systematic review. *Journal of Dentistry, 122,* 104115. https://doi.org/10.1016/j.jdent.2022.104115

Monill-González, A., Rovira-Calatayud, L., D'Oliveira, N. G., & Ustrell-Torrent, J. M. (2021). Artificial intelligence in orthodontics: Where are we now? A scoping review. *Orthodontics & Craniofacial Research, 24*(S1), 6–15. https://doi.org/10.1111/ocr.12517

Moriyama, Y., Lee, C., Date, S., Kashiwagi, Y., Narukawa, Y., Nozaki, K., & Murakami, S. (2019). A MapReduce-like deep learning model for the depth estimation of periodontal pockets. In *Proceedings of the 12th international joint conference on biomedical engineering systems and technologies* (pp. 388–395). SCITEPRESS – Science and Technology Publications. https://doi.org/10.5220/0007405703880395

Mudrov, V. P. (2022). Artificial intelligence in the immunodiagnostics of chronic periodontitis. *Russian Journal of Infection and Immunity, 12*(6), 1186–1190. https://doi.org/10.15789/2220-7619-AII-1999

Nayak, G. S., Kamath, S., Pai, K. M., Sarkar, A., Ray, S., Kurien, J., D'Almeida, L., Krishnanand, B. R., Santhosh, C., Kartha, V. B., & Mahato, K. K. (2006). Principal component analysis and artificial neural network analysis of oral tissue fluorescence spectra: Classification of normal premalignant and malignant pathological conditions. *Biopolymers, 82*(2), 152–166. https://doi.org/10.1002/bip.20473

Nguyen KTP, Medjaher K, Tran DT (2023). A review of artificial intelligence methods for engineering prognostics and health management with implementation guidelines. Artif. Intell. Rev, 56, 3659-709.

Ossowska, A., Kusiak, A., & Świetlik, D. (2022). Artificial intelligence in dentistry—Narrative review. *International Journal of Environmental Research and Public Health, 19*(6), 3449. https://doi.org/10.3390/ijerph19063449

Pang, L., Wang, K., Tao, Y., Zhi, Q., Zhang, J., & Lin, H. (2021). A new model for caries risk prediction in teenagers using a machine learning algorithm based on environmental and genetic factors. *Frontiers in Genetics, 12,* 636867. https://doi.org/10.3389/fgene.2021.636867

Park, Y. H., Kim, S. H., & Choi, Y. Y. (2021). Prediction models of early childhood caries based on machine learning algorithms. *International Journal of Environmental Research and Public Health, 18*(16), 8613. https://doi.org/10.3390/ijerph18168613

Qiao, X., Zhang, Z., & Chen, X. (2020). Multifrequency impedance method based on neural network for root canal length measurement. *Applied Sciences, 10*(21), 7430. https://doi.org/10.3390/app10217430

Qu, Y., Lin, Z., Yang, Z., Lin, H., Huang, X., & Gu, L. (2022). Machine learning models for prognosis prediction in endodontic microsurgery. *Journal of Dentistry, 118*, 103947. https://doi.org/10.1016/j.jdent.2022.103947

Ramos-Gomez, F., Marcus, M., Maida, C. A., Wang, Y., Kinsler, J. J., Xiong, D., Lee, S. Y., Hays, R. D., Shen, J., Crall, J. J., & Liu, H. (2021). Using a machine learning algorithm to predict the likelihood of presence of dental caries among children aged 2 to 7. *Dentistry Journal, 9*(12), 141. https://doi.org/10.3390/dj9120141

Revilla-León, M., Gómez-Polo, M., Barmak, A. B., Inam, W., Kan, J. Y. K., Kois, J. C., & Akal, O. (2022). Artificial intelligence models for diagnosing gingivitis and periodontal disease: A systematic review. *The Journal of Prosthetic Dentistry*, 1–9. https://doi.org/10.1016/j.prosdent.2022.01.026

Reyes, L. T., Knorst, J. K., Ortiz, F. R., & Ardenghi, T. M. (2022). Machine learning in the diagnosis and prognostic prediction of dental caries: A systematic review. *Caries Research, 56*(2), 161–170. https://doi.org/10.1159/000524167

Schwendicke, F., Chaurasia, A., Wiegand, T., Uribe, S. E., Fontana, M., Akota, I., Tryfonos, O., & Krois, J. (2023). Artificial intelligence for oral and dental healthcare: Core education curriculum. *Journal of Dentistry, 128*, 104363. https://doi.org/10.1016/j.jdent.2022.104363

Schwendicke, F., Samek, W., & Krois, J. (2020). Artificial intelligence in dentistry: Chances and challenges. *Journal of Dental Research, 99*(7), 769–774. https://doi.org/10.1177/0022034520915714

Scrobot˘a, I., B˘ aciuţ, G., Filip, A. G., Todor, B., Blaga, F., & B˘ aciuţ, M. F. (2017). Application of fuzzy logic in oral cancer risk assessment. *Iranian Journal of Public Health, 46*(5), 612–616.

Setzer, F. C., Shi, K. J., Zhang, Z., Yan, H., Yoon, H., Mupparapu, M., & Li, J. (2020). Artificial intelligence for the computer-aided detection of periapical lesions in cone-beam computed tomographic images. *Journal of Endodontics, 46*(7), 987–993. https://doi.org/10.1016/j.joen.2020.03.025

Shujaat, S., Riaz, M., & Jacobs, R. (2022). Synergy between artificial intelligence and precision medicine for computer-assisted oral and maxillofacial surgical planning. *Clinical Oral Investigations*, 1–10.

Tanikawa, C., & Yamashiro, T. (2021). Development of novel artificial intelligence systems to predict facial morphology after orthognathic surgery and orthodontic treatment in Japanese patients. *Scientific Reports, 11*, 15853. https://doi.org/10.1038/s41598-021-95002-w

Tobias, M. A. S., Nogueira, B. P., Santana, M. C. S., Pires, R. G., Papa, J. P., & Santos, P. S. S. (2022). Artificial intelligence for oral cancer diagnosis: What are the possibilities? *Oral Oncology, 134*, 106117. https://doi.org/10.1016/j.oraloncology.2022.106117

Wang, J., Suenaga, H., Yang, L., Kobayashi, E., & Sakuma, I. (2017). Video see-through augmented reality for oral and maxillofacial surgery. *International Journal of Medical Robotics and Computer Assisted Surgery, 13*(3), e1754.

Wang, S., Liu, Y., & Dong, X. (2022). Data imbalance problem in intelligent fault diagnosis: Advances and prospects. *IEEE Transactions on Industrial Informatics, 18*(7), 4723–4735. https://doi.org/10.1109/TII.2021.3095314

Xu, T., Zhu, Y., Peng, L., Cao, Y., Zhao, X., Meng, F., Ding, J., & Liang, S. (2022). Artificial intelligence assisted identification of therapy history from periapical films for dental root canal. *Displays, 71*, 102119. https://doi.org/10.1016/j.displa.2021.102119

Yang, X., Guan, R., & Gong, D. (2021). Solving data imbalance problem in fault diagnosis using generative adversarial networks. *Applied Soft Computing, 113*, 107899. https://doi.org/10.1016/j.asoc.2021.107899

Zheng, L., Wang, H., Mei, L., Chen, Q., Zhang, Y., & Zhang, H. (2021). Artificial intelligence in digital cariology: A new tool for the diagnosis of deep caries and pulpitis using convolutional neural networks. *Annals of Translational Medicine, 9*(9), 763. https://doi.org/10.21037/atm-21-119

Chapter 7

Leveraging AI in Substance Use Outreach and Treatment

Tiffany Champagne-Langabeer, PhD, RDN, FHIMSS

7.1 Introduction

AI can also play a pivotal role in substance use engagement, outreach, and treatment. In this chapter, we will discuss one innovative program: the Houston Emergency Opioid Engagement System (HEROES). HEROES was established as a coordinated intervention program designed to address opioid use disorder (OUD) by integrating emergency medical services, peer recovery coaching, medication-assisted treatment, and community outreach. Given the complexity of opioid addiction and the multifaceted approach required for effective intervention, HEROES has increasingly leveraged artificial intelligence (AI) to optimize its operations. AI enhances the system's predictive capabilities, improves patient engagement, streamlines resource allocation, and facilitates data-driven decision-making.

This chapter explores how HEROES integrates AI to improve patient retention, predict risk factors, and enhance the efficiency of emergency response and recovery efforts.

7.2 AI-Driven Predictive Analytics for Patient Retention

One of the most pressing challenges in opioid use disorder (OUD) treatment programs is ensuring that patients remain engaged in care for a sufficient duration to achieve long-term recovery. Research indicates that sustained participation in medication-assisted treatment (MAT) and behavioral therapy significantly improves outcomes, reducing relapse rates and lowering the risk of overdose-related fatalities (Langabeer et al., 2022). However, many patients disengage from treatment prematurely due to a variety of personal, social, and systemic factors. These may include transportation barriers, stigma surrounding addiction, mental health comorbidities, financial constraints, and a lack of perceived need for continued treatment after initial symptom relief. Identifying individuals at risk of treatment dropout is crucial for preventing relapses and improving retention rates (Bakos-Block et al., 2022).

DOI: 10.4324/9781003621294-9

To address this issue, HEROES employs machine learning models that leverage vast amounts of patient data to predict the likelihood of early dropout. These models analyze a combination of demographic information, clinical histories, behavioral patterns, and psychosocial variables to detect early warning signs of disengagement. Factors such as the frequency of missed appointments, self-reported stress levels, social support systems, and prior relapse history contribute to predictive modeling efforts. By integrating these variables, AI can assess an individual's risk profile with high accuracy and enable targeted interventions before disengagement occurs.

The predictive modeling process involves training AI algorithms on historical data from over 700 program participants, identifying key trends associated with patient attrition. Once a patient is flagged as high-risk, case managers and healthcare providers can implement additional measures to sustain engagement. These may include increased follow-up contacts, personalized counseling sessions, digital engagement through mobile applications, or adjustments in treatment plans to better align with the patient's needs. Additionally, AI-driven alerts can notify care teams when a patient exhibits behaviors indicative of potential dropout, allowing for real-time intervention strategies.

By utilizing AI in this capacity, HEROES enhances its ability to provide proactive and individualized support, mitigating the risk of treatment discontinuation and reinforcing the long-term stability of recovery programs. This technology-driven approach allows healthcare providers to move beyond reactive strategies and adopt a predictive, patient-centered model that fosters greater adherence to treatment and ultimately improves recovery outcomes.

7.3 Machine Learning Model Performance

The predictive models developed by HEROES rely on advanced machine learning algorithms, such as random forest classifiers, which have demonstrated high sensitivity (0.81–0.86) and specificity (0.65–0.66) in identifying patients at risk of disengagement. These models process vast amounts of data, integrating patient demographics, clinical histories, behavioral patterns, and psychosocial variables to determine the likelihood of treatment dropout. By continuously refining its predictive capabilities, HEROES enhances its ability to proactively address patient needs before disengagement occurs (Gottlieb et al., 2022).

One of the key aspects analyzed by these machine learning models is the patient's history of previous overdoses. Repeated overdose events serve as a critical indicator of treatment instability and are often linked to an increased likelihood of dropping out of care. By identifying individuals who have experienced multiple overdoses, HEROES can prioritize outreach and intervention efforts, ensuring that high-risk patients receive targeted support. This proactive approach enables healthcare providers to offer additional counseling, adjust medication regimens, and implement crisis intervention strategies to prevent future relapses.

Beyond overdose history, HEROES also evaluates quality-of-life improvements as a factor influencing patient retention. While enhanced well-being is generally considered a positive outcome, an interesting paradox emerges in some cases where patients who report improved quality of life are more likely to disengage from treatment (Gottlieb et al., 2022). This trend suggests that some individuals may perceive early treatment success as an indication that they no longer require ongoing support, leading them to prematurely exit the program. Such findings underscore the importance of sustained patient education and engagement, reinforcing the necessity of long-term treatment adherence even when initial progress is evident.

Additionally, the machine learning models assess the frequency and severity of recent relapse events. Patients who have relapsed within a short period of time may experience increased distress, feelings of failure, or a loss of confidence in their ability to recover—factors that contribute to treatment dropout. By recognizing these patterns early, HEROES can implement real-time interventions, such as increased therapy sessions, peer recovery coaching, or medication adjustments, to help patients navigate challenges and regain stability in their treatment journey.

Furthermore, the integration of predictive analytics into HEROES' treatment framework enables a continuous learning process. As more patient data is collected over time, AI models refine their predictions, improving accuracy and allowing for more precise, personalized interventions. In the near future, these advancements will facilitate the development of risk stratification tools, enabling clinicians to categorize patients based on their likelihood of dropout and tailor treatment plans accordingly. For example, patients identified as high risk may be assigned to more intensive case management programs, while those with moderate risk may benefit from additional digital engagement tools, such as AI-powered chatbots or mobile health applications.

By leveraging AI-driven predictive modeling, HEROES transitions from a reactive to a proactive care approach, significantly improving patient retention rates. This model not only enhances treatment outcomes but also optimizes resource allocation, ensuring that interventions are directed toward those who need them the most. As predictive analytics continues to evolve, its application in substance use disorder treatment has the potential to transform the way care is delivered, making it more personalized, data-driven, and responsive to the unique needs of each patient.

7.4 Enhancing Patient Engagement through AI

Looking ahead, the integration of artificial intelligence into patient engagement strategies has the potential to revolutionize how individuals interact with their treatment plans and healthcare providers. AI-driven virtual health assistants and chatbots could serve as 24/7 support systems, providing patients with real-time guidance, answering treatment-related questions, and offering motivational support to encourage adherence to prescribed regimens. These AI assistants could be programmed to recognize emotional cues in written or spoken language, allowing them to respond with empathy and personalized encouragement when patients express distress or hesitation about their treatment.

Furthermore, AI could refine patient engagement by facilitating predictive and context-aware interventions. For instance, AI models could analyze behavioral data in combination with environmental factors, such as social stressors or economic hardships, to anticipate periods of heightened relapse risk. By integrating information from electronic health records, social determinants of health, and wearable device data, AI could proactively recommend tailored interventions, such as scheduling additional counseling sessions, sending targeted educational materials, or connecting patients with peer support groups at critical moments. These hyper-personalized interventions would enhance the therapeutic alliance between patients and their care teams, fostering a greater sense of accountability and support.

However, despite its many benefits, AI-driven patient engagement also raises important ethical and practical concerns. Many patients with substance use disorder (SUD) may be reluctant to have their behaviors tracked continuously, fearing a loss of privacy or potential stigma associated with data collection. AI-powered monitoring tools rely on data from wearable health devices and smartphone applications, but not all patients are comfortable with or willing to use such technology, particularly if they feel that constant surveillance is intrusive or could be misinterpreted by healthcare providers or third parties. The sensitive nature of addiction treatment means that any AI-driven system must prioritize patient consent, autonomy, and data security, ensuring that individuals feel empowered rather than surveilled.

Additionally, financial barriers must be considered when designing AI-enhanced engagement strategies. Many patients in recovery face economic instability, which may prevent them from purchasing or maintaining wearable devices, smartphones, or internet access necessary for AI-based interventions. If digital tools become a standard part of engagement strategies, there is a risk of exacerbating existing disparities by leaving out individuals who lack access to these resources. Future AI-driven solutions should incorporate alternative, low-tech engagement strategies, such as phone-based check-ins, in-person peer support, and community outreach programs, ensuring that digital inequities do not prevent at-risk populations from receiving adequate care.

In addition to enhancing real-time engagement, AI could also play a role in optimizing long-term recovery strategies. Through deep learning and advanced analytics, AI systems could identify the most effective engagement techniques for different patient subgroups, ensuring that interventions align with individual preferences and needs. Some patients may respond better to frequent, brief digital check-ins, while others may benefit from structured, clinician-led outreach. AI-powered segmentation could allow treatment programs to refine engagement models continuously, ensuring that outreach efforts are as effective and non-intrusive as possible.

As AI technology continues to evolve, its role in patient engagement will likely extend beyond direct communication and monitoring. Future applications may include AI-powered gamification strategies to incentivize adherence to treatment plans, augmented reality (AR) therapy sessions for behavioral modification, and AI-curated wellness programs tailored to individual recovery journeys. However, as these innovations develop, ethical considerations regarding digital equity, consent, and patient autonomy must remain central to their implementation. By making engagement more interactive, responsive, and patient-centered while addressing privacy and access concerns, AI has the potential to transform substance use disorder treatment into a more adaptive and empowering experience, ultimately leading to improved retention rates and better long-term outcomes.

7.5 Evaluating Outreach Efforts Using AI Data

To ensure that outreach efforts align with community needs, HEROES integrates AI-driven insights with geographical and social vulnerability data. By analyzing emergency medical services (EMS) overdose reports and mapping them against program recruitment patterns, HEROES can assess the effectiveness of its outreach initiatives.

7.6 AI-Powered Geospatial Analysis

AI-powered geospatial analysis tools play a crucial role in the HEROES initiative by providing a comprehensive view of the geographic distribution of opioid overdose incidents and treatment program enrollments (Champagne-Langabeer et al., 2021). These tools allow researchers and healthcare providers to visualize spatial disparities in access to care and pinpoint regions that are disproportionately affected by opioid use disorder (OUD) but lack sufficient treatment resources. By integrating machine learning algorithms with geographic information systems (GIS), HEROES can generate highly detailed heat maps that highlight overdose hotspots and areas where treatment engagement is lacking (Bauer et al., 2021). These data-driven visualizations inform decision-making by identifying underserved regions, ensuring that outreach efforts are directed toward communities with the greatest need.

One of the key components of HEROES' geospatial strategy is the use of predictive modeling to assess future trends in opioid-related emergencies. AI algorithms analyze historical overdose data alongside socioeconomic and demographic indicators to forecast regions that may experience an increase in opioid-related incidents (Langabeer et al., 2024). This predictive approach enables proactive deployment of harm reduction resources, such as naloxone distribution sites, mobile treatment units, and peer recovery teams, to areas that are expected to see a surge in opioid use. By using machine learning to anticipate emerging crises, HEROES shifts from a reactive to a proactive model of intervention, reducing overdose fatalities and improving access to life-saving treatments.

To further refine outreach efforts, HEROES incorporates Social Vulnerability Index (SVI) data, which accounts for factors such as poverty rates, housing instability, and access to healthcare. By overlaying SVI data with recruitment and enrollment figures, AI systems assess whether outreach initiatives are successfully engaging individuals in high-risk communities (Lalani et al., 2022). If discrepancies emerge—such as low enrollment rates in areas with high social vulnerability—HEROES can adjust its engagement strategies to better connect with these populations. This may involve tailoring messaging campaigns, increasing community-based education efforts, or deploying culturally competent peer recovery specialists who can better relate to the needs of specific demographic groups.

In addition to assessing geographic disparities, HEROES employs a statistical measure known as the Enrollment Proportion Overdose Proportion Ratio (EPOPR) to evaluate the effectiveness of its outreach initiatives. The EPOPR compares the proportion of treatment enrollments within a given zip code to the proportion of overdose incidents occurring in the same area. A low EPOPR signals that a particular region has high overdose rates but low treatment engagement, indicating the need for increased outreach and resource allocation. Conversely, a high EPOPR suggests that outreach efforts are successfully enrolling individuals into treatment, allowing HEROES to replicate effective strategies in other areas. By continuously monitoring EPOPR values, HEROES ensures that interventions remain responsive to shifting overdose patterns and treatment access disparities.

AI-driven demographic analysis further enhances HEROES' outreach strategy by identifying population subgroups that may require tailored intervention approaches. Machine learning models analyze factors such as age, gender, race, income levels, and housing stability to determine which demographic groups are most at risk of opioid use disorder but least likely to engage in treatment. For instance, AI may reveal that young adults in a particular region are experiencing high overdose rates but have low enrollment in treatment programs, prompting HEROES to develop youth-focused outreach initiatives. Similarly, demographic insights can inform the development of gender-specific or culturally sensitive interventions that address unique barriers to care.

By integrating AI-powered geospatial analytics, predictive modeling, and demographic assessments, HEROES optimizes its approach to combating the opioid epidemic. These advanced analytical techniques enable real-time adjustments to outreach strategies, ensuring that treatment resources are allocated efficiently and equitably. As AI continues to evolve, its applications in geospatial analysis will become even more sophisticated, further enhancing the ability of healthcare providers to respond dynamically to the ongoing opioid crisis.

The following are two specific use cases where HEROES has leveraged advanced technology for unique purposes: qualitative thematic analysis and expediting complex statistical analyses.

7.7 AI-Driven Thematic Analysis in Qualitative Research

In addition to quantitative analytics, AI-driven qualitative research methodologies provide valuable insights into patient experiences, barriers to care, and program effectiveness. The research team has leveraged AI-assisted tools to analyze transcribed interviews and focus group discussions to extract themes and patterns in patient narratives.

In 2024, HEROES began testing large language models (LLMs) such as Claude Sonnet 3.5 and Chat GPT-4 to assist in thematic coding of qualitative data. These models were compared with manual thematic analysis to ensure consistency and reliability in identifying key themes. Through NLP-driven sentiment analysis, AI highlighted common concerns expressed by patients, including stigma, provider discrimination, and accessibility barriers. These insights informed modifications to program policies and ensured that outreach efforts remained responsive to patient needs. Furthermore, AI analyzed patterns in communication, enabling HEROES to refine its messaging and tailor its intervention strategies to different patient populations.

7.8 Expediting Complex Statistical Analyses with AI

In 2020, HEROES researchers conducted a rigorous statistical analysis to estimate national buprenorphine treatment access. This comprehensive study required months of extensive data collection, geocoding, and spatial modeling to assess treatment availability across the United States. Researchers meticulously gathered data from various sources, cleaned and standardized the information, and used geographic information systems (GIS) to model treatment access across different regions. The process involved overlaying provider locations with population density data, calculating travel distances, and identifying disparities in treatment availability. However, this traditional approach demanded a high level of expertise in statistical modeling, GIS, and data engineering, making it both time-intensive and resource-intensive (Langabeer et al., 2020).

With advancements in artificial intelligence, this process has been revolutionized, significantly reducing the time, effort, and expertise required to conduct complex geospatial analyses. AI-driven automation can now handle many of the most time-consuming aspects of geographic data processing, enabling rapid, high-precision evaluations of treatment access. This transformation allows policymakers, healthcare providers, and public health officials to make data-informed decisions in real-time, ensuring that treatment resources are optimally distributed to areas with the greatest need.

7.9 AI-Powered Steps for Geospatial Analysis

In order to effectively implement this technology, there needs to be a roadmap for success. AI streamlines geospatial analyses by automating key processes such as data aggregation, location mapping, and predictive modeling. If used appropriately, these enhancements can improve the accuracy, efficiency, and accessibility of treatment access studies.

Here are several examples:

1. **Data Aggregation**: AI scrapes, integrates, and processes datasets from multiple sources, including the Substance Abuse and Mental Health Services Administration (SAMHSA), the U.S. Census Bureau, state health departments, electronic health records, and emergency

medical services data. Machine learning algorithms quickly standardize and clean the data, resolving inconsistencies and ensuring that disparate datasets can be analyzed cohesively. This automation eliminates the need for labor-intensive manual data preparation, reducing errors and increasing the reliability of analysis.

2. **Automated Geocoding**: AI-powered geospatial tools instantly process provider addresses and apply precise latitude and longitude coordinates, eliminating the need for manual geocoding efforts. These systems use natural language processing (NLP) to correct formatting inconsistencies and improve address accuracy. By leveraging AI to handle location mapping, researchers can more effectively identify provider distribution patterns and assess how treatment availability aligns with population needs.
3. **Dynamic Distance Buffers**: Traditional geospatial analyses required extensive manual configuration of geographic boundaries to assess travel distances. AI simplifies this process by dynamically calculating driving distances and travel times based on real-world traffic patterns, road networks, and geographic barriers. These real-time assessments help identify underserved areas where treatment access is limited, allowing public health officials to deploy targeted interventions, such as mobile treatment units or telehealth services.
4. **Predictive Modeling for Treatment Gaps**: Machine learning algorithms analyze geographic disparities in provider distribution and assess which regions face the greatest barriers to accessing buprenorphine treatment. AI models incorporate socioeconomic indicators, opioid overdose trends, and patient mobility patterns to predict high-risk areas where additional intervention resources should be focused. Unlike traditional static analyses, AI-driven predictive modeling continuously adapts as new data becomes available, ensuring that treatment accessibility assessments remain current and responsive to shifting public health needs.
5. **Real-Time Dashboards**: AI-driven visualization tools generate interactive maps and real-time dashboards, allowing policymakers and healthcare providers to explore treatment access data in a user-friendly format. These dashboards provide decision-makers with the ability to filter data by demographic characteristics, geographic boundaries, or treatment provider type, making it easier to identify patterns and disparities. By integrating AI-powered visualization with GIS mapping, stakeholders can dynamically adjust resource allocation strategies, optimizing efforts to close treatment gaps in real-time.

Previously, conducting such an analysis required months of manual effort, specialized training in GIS, and deep expertise in spatial statistics. AI now democratizes access to these capabilities, allowing researchers, policymakers, and even local community organizations to conduct complex treatment access assessments without extensive technical training. This shift has the potential to enable rapid, data-driven decision-making in public health planning.

As AI continues to evolve, future iterations of geospatial analyses will incorporate even more advanced machine learning techniques, such as deep learning for image recognition in satellite mapping, AI-powered network optimization for transportation modeling, and automated anomaly detection to identify emerging access gaps. These advancements will further refine treatment access assessments, making healthcare resource allocation more precise, efficient, and equitable.

By harnessing AI-driven geospatial analysis, HEROES and similar initiatives can ensure that opioid treatment resources are allocated where they are most needed, closing service gaps and improving health outcomes for individuals with opioid use disorder. The continued integration of AI in public health strategy marks a paradigm shift toward a more proactive, responsive, and data-driven approach to addressing the opioid epidemic.

7.10 The Importance of Verifying Sources and the Limitations of Artificial Intelligence in Data Analysis and Decision-Making

Measure twice, cut once. Just as this proverb advises caution and verification in carpentry, it also applies to using AI-generated information. Ensuring the accuracy and reliability of insights provided by AI requires careful validation and cross-checking, essential steps in maintaining credibility and effectiveness in any health initiative.

Artificial intelligence (AI) has revolutionized numerous fields, from healthcare and finance to public policy and education. Its ability to process vast amounts of data, identify patterns, and generate predictive models makes it an invaluable tool for decision-making. However, despite its potential, *AI is not infallible*. One of the most significant challenges in leveraging AI for decision-making, particularly in sensitive areas like healthcare and public health, is ensuring the accuracy and reliability of the data it processes. AI systems are only as good as the data they are trained on, and the results they produce depend on the quality, relevance, and credibility of the input data.

Verifying sources is critical in preventing misinformation, ensuring ethical AI applications, and maintaining trust in AI-driven decision-making. In this discussion, we explore the importance of source verification, the limitations of AI, and a comparison of open-source and licensed AI options, along with their respective pros and cons.

7.11 The Importance of Verifying Sources in AI Applications

AI is powerful, but it lacks independent reasoning and critical thinking. It cannot inherently differentiate between reliable and unreliable sources unless it has been trained to do so. As a result, verifying the credibility of input data is paramount to ensuring the accuracy of AI-generated outputs.

Here are the essential keys to note:

7.11.1 Ensuring Data Accuracy and Reliability

- AI relies on structured and unstructured data for training and inference. If incorrect or misleading data is used, the AI model may generate biased, misleading, or outright false conclusions.
- AI-driven research and analytics must be built upon verified, peer-reviewed, and authoritative sources such as academic journals, government databases, and reputable institutions.

7.11.2 Preventing Bias in AI Algorithms

- Many AI systems inherit biases from their training data. If the input data is biased due to unverified or skewed sources, AI outputs will reflect and amplify these biases.
- Example: If a predictive model for substance use disorder interventions is trained on data that underrepresents certain demographics, it may fail to recommend effective interventions for those groups.

7.11.3 Mitigating the Risk of AI Hallucinations

- AI, particularly generative models, can "hallucinate" or fabricate information that sounds plausible but is factually incorrect.

- Example: A natural language processing (NLP) model tasked with summarizing medical literature may generate citations or facts that do not exist unless it is specifically programmed to verify sources.

7.11.4 Upholding Ethical and Legal Standards

- Using AI-generated insights without verifying sources can lead to ethical and legal consequences, especially in regulated fields such as medicine, finance, and law.
- Healthcare decisions influenced by AI-based diagnostics or treatment recommendations must be cross-verified with established clinical guidelines and medical literature.

7.12 The Limitations of Artificial Intelligence

While AI enhances efficiency and decision-making, it is not a substitute for human expertise. Understanding AI's limitations is crucial in ensuring its responsible and effective use.

Here are essential techniques to master:

7.12.1 Know Which Data to Input

- AI models are trained on specific datasets, and their accuracy depends on the relevance of the input data.
- Example: If an AI model predicting opioid overdose risks is trained primarily on data from urban populations, its predictions may not be applicable to rural populations.

7.12.2 Understand and Craft Effective Prompts

- Generative AI models, such as OpenAI's GPT and Google's Bard, are prompt-dependent. The quality of their output varies significantly based on how questions or prompts are framed.
- Example: Asking "What are the treatment options for opioid use disorder?" may yield generic responses, while a more precise prompt like "What are the most effective evidence-based treatments for opioid use disorder among pregnant women?" produces more targeted and useful information.

7.12.3 Recall AI Cannot Independently Verify Facts

- AI does not inherently fact-check; it generates responses based on statistical patterns in its training data.
- AI models trained on internet-scraped data may unknowingly pull from unreliable or biased sources, reinforcing misinformation if verification mechanisms are not in place.

7.12.4 Ethical Considerations in AI Decision-Making

- AI lacks ethical reasoning and moral judgment. It can only make decisions based on programmed logic and learned patterns.
- Example: An AI system allocating healthcare resources might prioritize efficiency over patient equity unless explicitly programmed with ethical frameworks.

7.12.5 Interpret and Explain

- Many AI models function as "black boxes," meaning their decision-making processes are opaque and difficult to interpret.
- This limitation is particularly concerning in high-stakes applications like medical diagnostics or legal decisions, where understanding how an AI system arrived at a conclusion is essential.

7.13 Open-Source vs. Licensed AI Options: Pros and Cons

Considering this rapidly evolving landscape, one pivotal decision confronts researchers, developers, and business leaders alike: should this technology remain open-source, or should it be safeguarded behind proprietary licenses? Open-source AI, celebrated for its transparency, collaborative spirit, and democratization of innovation, stands in stark contrast to licensed AI, valued for its controlled deployment, reliability, security, and profitability. In healthcare, the choice may seem like an easy one due to privacy and security. However, the implications of this choice extend far beyond HIPAA, PHI, financial, and mere technical considerations.

This next portion briefly explores the complexities inherent in open-source versus licensed AI technologies. Each healthcare entity is different, and use cases must be explored within local organizations for the best fit.

To start, there are two primary types of AI platforms: open-source and licensed (proprietary). Each has its advantages and disadvantages depending on the use case, budget, and expertise available.

7.13.1 Open-Source AI Options

Open-source AI platforms allow users to access, modify, and distribute the source code. Examples include:

- TensorFlow (Google)
- PyTorch (Meta)
- Hugging Face Transformers
- Apache OpenNLP
- OpenAI's GPT models (limited access for developers)

7.13.1.1 Pros of Open-Source AI

✓ **Transparency**: Users can inspect and modify the code, making it easier to identify and correct biases or inaccuracies.

✓ **Customization**: Open-source AI allows for deep customization to fit specific needs, such as training models with proprietary datasets.

✓ **Community Support**: Large developer communities provide extensive documentation, forums, and third-party tools to improve AI performance.

✓ **Cost-Effective**: Most open-source AI tools are free to use, making them accessible to organizations with limited budgets.

7.13.1.2 Cons of Open-Source AI

- ✘ **Requires Technical Expertise**: Setting up, training, and maintaining open-source AI requires advanced programming and data science knowledge.
- ✘ **Limited User Support**: Unlike licensed AI, open-source tools do not offer dedicated customer support, relying instead on community-driven assistance.
- ✘ **Security Concerns**: Without robust cybersecurity protocols, open-source AI implementations may be more vulnerable to hacking or data breaches.

7.13.2 Licensed (Proprietary) AI Options

Licensed AI platforms are proprietary, meaning they are owned and maintained by companies that charge users for access. Examples include:

- IBM Watson
- Google Cloud AI
- Microsoft Azure AI
- Amazon SageMaker
- OpenAI's GPT-4 API (fully licensed version)

7.13.2.1 Pros of Licensed AI

- ✓ **User-Friendly**: Proprietary AI tools often come with user-friendly interfaces and pre-built features, reducing the need for deep technical knowledge.
- ✓ **Customer Support**: Paid AI services typically include dedicated technical support, making it easier for organizations to troubleshoot issues.
- ✓ **Security and Compliance**: Licensed AI providers invest heavily in security features, ensuring compliance with data privacy regulations like HIPAA, GDPR, and CCPA.
- ✓ **Scalability and Reliability**: Proprietary AI solutions offer robust cloud infrastructure, allowing for seamless scalability and reliable performance for enterprise applications.

7.13.2.2 Cons of Licensed AI

- ✘ **High Cost**: Licensed AI tools can be expensive, making them inaccessible for small organizations or researchers with limited budgets.
- ✘ **Limited Customization**: Unlike open-source AI, proprietary platforms may restrict users from modifying algorithms or training models with proprietary datasets.
- ✘ **Potential Data Lock-In**: Users relying on proprietary AI tools may face challenges migrating to other platforms, especially if data formats are incompatible or services are discontinued.

7.14 Conclusion: Striking a Balance between AI Potential and Limitations

AI has transformed data analysis, predictive modeling, and decision-making across industries, but it is not a standalone solution. The reliability of AI-driven insights hinges on the verification of data sources, the expertise of users in crafting effective prompts, and the thoughtful selection between open-source and licensed AI tools.

Understanding AI's limitations is crucial in preventing misuse, mitigating biases, and ensuring ethical applications. Whether using open-source platforms for greater customization or opting for proprietary AI for enhanced security and support, organizations must assess their specific needs, resources, and technical expertise before implementing AI solutions.

As AI continues to evolve, it is essential to complement its capabilities with human oversight, rigorous validation processes, and ethical considerations. By doing so, we can maximize AI's benefits while minimizing risks, ultimately fostering responsible and effective AI-driven decision-making in healthcare, research, and beyond.

7.15 Conclusion

The integration of AI in the Houston Emergency Opioid Engagement System represents a transformative advancement in public health interventions. By harnessing AI for predictive analytics, geospatial assessments, and qualitative research, HEROES enhances its ability to engage patients, refine outreach efforts, and optimize resource allocation. AI-driven methodologies now enable analyses that once required months of expertise to be completed in a fraction of the time, fostering a more agile and responsive approach to addressing the opioid crisis. As AI technologies continue to evolve, they will play an increasingly pivotal role in shaping effective and data-driven public health strategies.

References

Bakos-Block, C., Nash, A. J., Cohen, A. S., & Champagne-Langabeer, T. (2022). Experiences of parents with opioid use disorder during their attempts to seek treatment: A qualitative analysis. International Journal of Environmental Research and Public Health, 19(24), 16660. https://doi.org/10.3390/ijerph192416660.

Bauer, C., Champagne-Langabeer, T., Bakos-Block, C., Zhang, K., Persse, D., & Langabeer, J. R. (2021). Patterns and risk factors of opioid-suspected EMS overdose in Houston metropolitan area, 2015–2019: A Bayesian spatiotemporal analysis. *PLoS One, 16*(3), Article e0247050. https://doi.org/10.1371/journal.pone.0247050

Champagne-Langabeer, T., Madu, R., Giri, S., Stotts, A. L., & Langabeer, J. R. (2021). Opioid prescribing patterns and overdose deaths in Texas. *Substance Abuse, 42*(2), 161–167. https://doi.org/10.1080/08897077.2019.1675114

Gottlieb, A., Bakos-Block, C., Langabeer, J. R., & Champagne-Langabeer, T. (2022). Sociodemographic and clinical characteristics associated with improvements in quality of life for participants with opioid use disorder. *Healthcare, 10*(1), Article 167. https://doi.org/10.3390/healthcare10010167

Gottlieb, A., Yatsco, A., Bakos-Block, C., Langabeer, J. R., & Champagne-Langabeer, T. (2022). Machine learning for predicting risk of early dropout in a recovery program for opioid use disorder. *Healthcare, 10*(2), Article 223. https://doi.org/10.3390/healthcare10020223

Lalani, K., Bakos-Block, C., Cardenas-Turanzas, M., Cohen, S., Gopal, B., & Champagne-Langabeer, T. (2022). The Impact of COVID-19 on Opioid-Related Overdose Deaths in Texas. *International Journal of Environmental Research and Public Health, 19*(21), 13796. https://doi.org/10.3390/ijerph192113796

Langabeer, J. R., Bakos-Block, C., Cohen, A. S., Alam, I., Gopal, B., Cardenas-Turanzas, M., Weltge, A. F., Persse, D., & Champagne-Langabeer, T. (2024, July 11). Disposition outcomes following prehospital use of naloxone in a large metropolitan city in the United States. Prehospital Emergency Care, 1–6. https://doi.org/10.1080/10903127.2024.2369774

Langabeer, J. R., Chambers, K. A., Cardenas-Turanzas, M., & Champagne-Langabeer, T. (2022). County-level factors underlying opioid mortality in the United States. Substance Abuse, 43(1), 76–82. https://doi.org/10.1080/08897077.2020.1740379

Langabeer, J. R., Stotts, A. L., Cortez, A., Tortolero, G., & Champagne-Langabeer, T. (2020). Geographic proximity to buprenorphine treatment providers in the U.S. *Drug and Alcohol Dependence, 213*, Article 108131. https://doi.org/10.1016/j.drugalcdep.2020.108131

Chapter 8

AI in Radiology: Shaping the Present, Defining the Future

Elisabeth R. Garwood, MD, Eric Alper, MD, and
Max P. Rosen, MD, MPH

8.1 Strategy and Vision for AI

8.1.1 Background

Between 2020 and 2023, the global market size of AI in healthcare grew from 6.7 to 20.65 billion dollars, driven by rising investment from both private and government sectors, with key market players including Amazon, Microsoft, Nvidia, and Alphabet (*AI Statistics 2024 · AIPRM*, n.d.). The US alone is forecast to generate 102.2 billion dollars in revenue by 2030 through AI implementation specifically in healthcare (*AI Statistics 2024 AIPRM*, n.d.).

Radiology has emerged as one of the most promising fields for AI integration due to its heavy reliance on imaging, pattern recognition, and data-driven insights. In 2015, deep learning techniques applied to the ImageNet large-scale visual recognition challenge, a database of over 14 million human-annotated nonmedical images, surpassed human performance for the first time (Russakovsky et al., 2015). This generated immediate and significant interest in applying AI in the analysis of clinical images and other medical data (Langlotz et al., 2019; Russakovsky et al., 2015).

Today, ten years following this seminal event, the translation of AI development into impactful AI, widely deployed in clinical environments for routine use, is occurring at a much slower pace than initially predicted (Mongan et al., 2022). However, slowly, this translational goal is being achieved, and the work of radiologists (the synthesis of substantial visual and clinical data into concise textual summaries) is being recognized as an understated challenge.

As AI continues to evolve and touch every aspect of health care delivery, continued collaboration will be essential to ensure that these technologies enhance—not replace—human expertise. Integrating AI into radiology is difficult and necessitates a well-defined strategy aligned with institutional goals, a clear vision for future workflows, and meticulous planning across various domains within health care. In addition, as many departments outside of radiology rely on and

 DOI: 10.4324/9781003621294-10

utilize imaging, coordination of any imaging-related AI implementations initiated by departments outside of radiology is essential.

8.1.2 Defining the Strategic Role of AI in Radiology

AI applications in radiology now span a broad spectrum, from automated detection of abnormalities in medical images to real-time triaging of critical cases. Beyond diagnostics, AI is transforming operational aspects of radiology, including intelligent workflow and resource allocation, quality control, and automation of the revenue cycle. This is not just a future state—our healthcare system, like many others, is experiencing this transformation in real-time. In a single patient care episode, AI health tools influence the care of our patients at multiple touchpoints, from emergency department triage and ambient listening/documentation to background tasks like MRI acceleration and prioritization of urgent medical imaging findings.

It is critical that the integration of AI into radiology is aligned with the overarching objectives of the healthcare institution. At our institution, AI initiatives in radiology align with the strategic directive to "leverage our AI and data mining capabilities to execute on our digital health, virtual medicine, and remote patient monitoring strategies to further improve business and operational efficiencies, reduce administrative burden for clinicians, and improve patient care", ensuring that AI initiatives in radiology not only address challenges faced within the department but also contribute to organizational performance and long-term goals of the institution.

Envisioning the future of radiology with AI involves conceptualizing workflows where AI augments all aspects of imaging and diagnostics, from image acquisition to communication, follow-up, and billing.

8.1.3 Key Components of a Strategic Plan

8.1.3.1 Leadership and Change Management

The integration of AI requires a systematic assessment of the existing organizational capabilities necessary for the deployment, management, and optimization of AI systems as well as thoughtful engagement of key stakeholders (see Figure 8.1).

Clinical leaders and radiologists play a pivotal role in championing AI initiatives, guiding their teams through the transition, and fostering a culture that embraces technological advancements. The role of chief health AI officer has recently emerged within some health systems to provide specialized leadership and change management for AI (Beecy et al., 2024).

Given the variability of radiology departments, conducting a thorough evaluation of the department's current infrastructure and workflows is essential to determine where AI can offer tangible improvements before pursuing the development or procurement of AI solutions. To assess the best AI tools for your ecosystem and guide integration—a multidisciplinary team is crucial. In addition to a strong implementation team, outreach to engage staff through clear communication about AI initiatives, circulating AI guidelines and references, and promoting ongoing AI education has helped us and others mitigate potential resistance and facilitate the acceptance of AI in clinical settings (Togher et al., 2025). Our institution, like others, has developed a specialized pathway for the intake, evaluation, approval, and ultimately deployment and monitoring of health AI tools (see Figure 8.2).

Stakeholder domain/expertise	Contributions	Role
Clinical (physicians, nurses, technologists)	- Provide clinical care - Use AI tools for diagnosis, treatment planning, and workflow optimization	Radiologist using a prioritization algorithm
Technical (non-IT)	Pre-imaging activities	Scheduling
IT and data management teams	Maintain data infrastructure; ensure secure and compliant data handling and integration of AI tools	IT specialists managing health IT and AI platform integration
Patients and patient advocacy groups	Care recipient Offer perspectives on patient needs and concerns Address concerns regarding AI in care delivery	Patients, organizations representing patient interests
Compliance and legal	Ensure AI systems meet regulatory standards and protect patient privacy	General counsel, compliance officers
Strategic alignment	Align with system strategy and goals	System leadership, healthcare administrators
Revenue cycle	Assess financial implications, cost-effectiveness, return on investment	Financial analyst/officer
Quality and safety	Ensure adherence to quality standards and patient safety	Quality and safety officers
Clinical informatics specialists	Translate clinical needs into technical requirements; facilitate EHR and AI interoperability	Informatics officers

Figure 8.1 Key stakeholders in a healthcare system involved in evaluating and implementing AI tools in radiology.

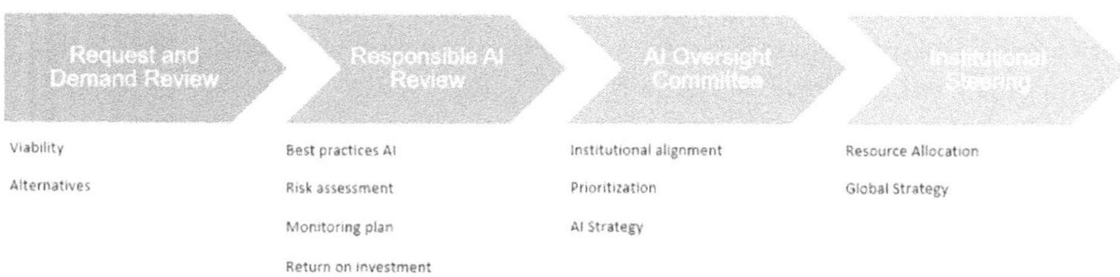

Figure 8.2 Example intake, responsible AI, and governance pathway for health AI tools (UMass Memorial Health).

8.1.3.2 Partnerships and Collaborations

In this rapidly changing landscape, it is critical for healthcare institutions and radiology departments to communicate and collaborate. Establishing collaborations with other academic institutions, technology companies, and regulatory bodies, as well as national consensus groups such as the Coalition for Health AI (CHAI) and the FUTURE-AI Consortium, groups dedicated to the operationalization of trustworthy AI in healthcare, is wise for any institution implementing AI (Lekadir et al., 2023). At a minimum, institutions should be familiar with AI best practices that encompass ethical and quality principles.

8.1.3.3 Investment and Funding Strategies

Securing funding for AI initiatives involves identifying potential sources such as grants, private investments, or institutional budgets. Conducting cost-benefit analyses and projecting returns that assess hard (financial) as well as soft returns (physician wellness, diminished malpractice liability, and trainee education (medical students, residents, and fellows)) is essential to justify expenditures and demonstrate the value of AI integration. Investments should be strategically planned as well as intermittently reassessed following deployment to ensure sustainable development and implementation of AI technologies in radiology.

8.1.3.4 Data Infrastructure

Institutional approaches to acquiring radiology AI tools vary, whether you are internally developing algorithms, purchasing vendor-developed solutions, or implementing a hybrid program; maintaining scalable and secure data pipelines is the foundation for successful AI implementation. Most current state radiology IT infrastructure operates on a less sophisticated level where imaging data resides in the picture archiving and communication (PACS) system, separate from the patient-specific information housed in the electronic medical record (EMR).

Unified healthcare data platforms are emerging as a solution to the integration of traditionally siloed data sources throughout a healthcare system, including medical imaging and reporting into a single repository. This approach allows easier leveraging of data for AI and analytics. Adherence to data governance protocols is essential to maintain patient privacy and comply with regulatory standards.

Strategically integrating AI into radiology requires a comprehensive approach that aligns with institutional goals, envisions future workflows, and meticulously plans across data management, partnerships, and investment strategies. Leadership and effective change management are crucial to foster acceptance and optimize the benefits of AI. Collaborations where institutions can learn from successful implementations in similar healthcare systems can be hugely beneficial.

8.2 AI Implementation Best Practices in Radiology

Integrating radiology AI tools requires a structured approach to avoid common pitfalls. This involves organizational readiness, having the correct technology infrastructure and support in place, workflow integration, and ongoing evaluation (Beecy et al., 2024). Best practices for implementing radiology AI align with responsible AI guidelines, which are now widely published. These guidelines emphasize core principles for integrating AI into clinical practice, prioritizing ethical considerations while enhancing healthcare outcomes (Kotter et al., 2025; Brady et al., 2024; *CHAI Responsible AI Guide*, 2025; Economou-Zavlanos et al., 2024).

8.2.1 Usefulness, Usability, and Efficacy

AI solutions must be both useful and usable within the healthcare setting, providing real value to clinicians and patients. Usefulness refers to the tool's capacity to deliver meaningful improvements in diagnosis, decision-making, or operational efficiency. Usability involves designing AI systems that are intuitive and integrated seamlessly into existing clinical workflows, ensuring that healthcare providers can interact with the technology effectively and with minimal disruption or additional training. Efficacy focuses on the AI's ability to achieve consistent, accurate, and reliable outcomes. The system should demonstrate clear performance metrics and undergo rigorous validation prior to implementation. AI tools should be designed to enhance clinician capabilities, not replace them, supporting improved patient care through augmentation rather than automation alone.

8.2.2 Fairness

AI models must be designed to operate in a manner that is equitable and just, minimizing bias and ensuring that healthcare delivery is fair across diverse populations. The Coalition for Health AI stresses that fairness must be embedded at every stage of the AI lifecycle, from data collection and model training to full-scale deployment. Data used to train AI models should be representative of diverse patient demographics, including various age groups, ethnicities, and socioeconomic backgrounds, to avoid reinforcing health disparities. Additionally, fairness involves creating systems that promote equal access to AI-driven innovations, particularly in underserved areas, without exacerbating existing inequalities in healthcare delivery.

8.2.3 Safety and Reliability

AI systems in healthcare must adhere to high standards of safety and reliability, as errors can directly impact patient outcomes. This involves testing and continuous monitoring to ensure that AI solutions perform accurately and consistently under a range of clinical scenarios. Safety considerations include mitigating risks of incorrect diagnoses, delays, or system failures that could harm patients. Existing hospital safety protocols and infrastructure may be leveraged to regulate and monitor health AI tools, incorporating established regulatory frameworks to ensure compliance (Fleisher & Economou-Zavlanos, 2024). Establishing robust safeguards in AI systems, including fail-safes and manual overrides, as well as regular performance audits and adaptation of the models to new clinical data, can improve the safety of AI tools.

8.2.4 Transparency, Intelligibility, and Accountability

Transparency and intelligibility are critical to the responsible implementation of AI in healthcare. AI solutions should provide clear, understandable insights into their decision-making processes, enhancing the radiologist's ability to interpret and act upon AI recommendations with confidence. For critical diagnosis and triage tools, this can be in the form of an AI explainability or attention map that highlights the area within the medical image that triggered the AI alert.

To address challenges surrounding the transparency of AI model development, a federated health AI registry that includes details on how models are trained and tested has been proposed—to ensure that each adopter of health AI has all the information necessary for responsible management of these solutions in clinical care (Pencina et al., 2024). Additionally, accountability is a vital principle in responsible AI use; healthcare organizations must establish clear lines of responsibility for both the deployment and outcomes of AI systems, which includes defining accountability for errors or adverse events that may arise from AI-driven decisions.

8.2.5 Technology Infrastructure and Data Management

The successful integration of AI in radiology demands a robust and scalable technology infrastructure capable of supporting high-complexity algorithms and large-scale imaging datasets.

This infrastructure must facilitate seamless interoperability with systems such as picture archiving and communication systems (PACS), radiology information systems (RIS), and electronic health records (EHRs) to enable efficient data access and processing. High-performance computing environments, including cloud and edge computing solutions, are essential to handle the computational load of AI models, particularly in resource-constrained settings. Additionally, ensuring compliance with data privacy regulations is critical for safeguarding patient information during system integration and data exchange across platforms. Implementing data management protocols—encryption, traceability, and anonymization—ensures compliance with regulatory requirements and data integrity.

By implementing a comprehensive approach based on the core principles of responsible health AI, radiology departments can maintain safety, accuracy, and human oversight while leveraging the new capabilities of AI technology.

8.3 Initial Results

8.3.1 Overview of AI Tools Currently Deployed in Radiology

Broadly, AI applications in radiology can be categorized into interpretive and non-interpretive uses (Richardson et al., 2021). Interpretive AI primarily focuses on tasks directly related to image analysis, diagnosis, classification, or prioritization (Table 8.1).

In contrast, non-interpretive AI in radiology aids radiologists, technologists, and administrative staff by automating various aspects of radiology workflows (Table 8.2).

This section provides an overview of specific AI use cases within each category as they pertain to current practices in radiology.

8.3.2 Interpretive AI

Disease detection and prioritization: The first radiology AI tool implemented at our institution in 2019 was a detection and prioritization algorithm for acute intracranial hemorrhage. Since that time, the use of AI for disease detection and prioritization has expanded significantly, particularly for those with potentially critical findings. These conditions demand urgent attention, yet they can sometimes be missed or delayed amid the high volume of routine cases. To address this challenge, AI systems leverage deep learning algorithms to analyze CT scans and flag potentially critical findings for radiologists, thereby facilitating the prioritization of cases that require immediate review.

Currently, machine learning techniques are being employed to detect a wide range of pathologies on both X-ray and CT imaging. A non-exhaustive list includes intracranial hemorrhage, ischemic stroke, pulmonary embolism, pneumothorax, intra-abdominal free air, malpositioned lines and tubes, fractures, and aneurysms. In addition to detecting acute and potentially life-threatening conditions, emerging algorithms are being developed to identify noncritical findings that may warrant follow-up, such as pulmonary nodules. By automatically evaluating medical imaging and categorizing cases according to urgency, these AI systems help streamline the radiology workflow and reduce the risk of delayed diagnoses.

The ability to accurately detect and prioritize critical findings has the potential to improve patient outcomes by expediting the review of high-risk cases. However, this approach requires continuous monitoring to ensure accuracy and reliability. While AI tools can aid in triage and prioritization, radiologists remain essential for confirming diagnoses and integrating imaging findings with the broader clinical context (Chekmeyan et al., 2023).

Table 8.1 Interpretive AI Tool Domains in Radiology

Domain	*Tasks*	*Examples*
Detection and prioritization	Disease detection and flagging of critical findings for prioritization	• Intracranial hemorrhage detection (CT) • Stroke detection (CT/MRI) • Pulmonary embolism detection (CT) • Pneumothorax detection (Chest X-ray) • Fracture detection (X-ray) • Aneurysm detection (CT) • Malpositioned medical devices (Chest X-ray) • Intracranial hemorrhage detection (CT) • Stroke detection (CT/MRI) • Pulmonary embolism detection (CT) • Pneumothorax detection (Chest X-ray) • Fracture detection (X-ray) • Aneurysm detection (CT) • Malpositioned medical devices (Chest X-ray)
Comparative and longitudinal analysis	Disease progression monitoring Treatment response evaluation	• Tracking complex abdominal aneurysm size changes over time (CT) • Monitoring lung nodule growth (CT)
Opportunistic screening	Identifying incidental findings of potential clinical relevance	• Detection of osteopenia or osteoporosis on routine chest or abdominal CT • Coronary artery calcium scoring on non-cardiac chest CT • Fatty liver detection on abdominal imaging • Aortic aneurysm screening on spine CT
Quantitative imaging and measurement	Automatically outlining lesion boundaries and calculating volume or size Providing consistent and precise anatomical measurements	Tumor volumetry in oncology imaging, liver lesion segmentation. Left ventricular ejection fraction calculation on cardiac MRI.
Image classification and characterization	Distinguishing between benign and malignant lesions or characterizing disease subtypes	• Benign vs. malignant liver or renal masses (CT) Identifying and classifying pelvic fractures on CT.

Anatomy Segmentation and Disease State Monitoring: AI-driven segmentation techniques offer a framework for standardizing three-dimensional (3D) anatomical measurements, crucial for accurate disease state monitoring (Monti et al., 2022). In complex abdominal aortic aneurysms (AAA), automated segmentation ensures consistent volumetric assessments across serial imaging, mitigating variability introduced by manual processes and technical factors such as slice selection (Postiglione et al., 2024). By automating the delineation and quantification of aneurysm size and morphology, AI enhances reproducibility, enabling consistent longitudinal evaluations. This

Table 8.2 Non-Interpretive AI Tool Domains in Radiology

Domain	*Tasks*	*Examples*
Image Production and Quality Control	Radiation and Contrast Dose Reduction Scan Time Reduction Automated Image Quality Assessment	AI models generate high-quality images with lower radiation/contrast dose. AI-based reconstruction speeds up MRI and CT scanning. Detects artifacts and suboptimal images for quality control.
Workflow Optimization	Study Protocoling Hanging Protocols Predictive staffing	Automated selection of optimal imaging protocols. AI personalizes image display settings based on user preferences.
Reporting and Communication	Automated extraction of incidental findings Automatically generated radiology report impressions	AI can structure radiology reports, extract findings, and improve communication.
Scheduling and Resource Allocation	Scheduling Optimization Missed Appointment Prediction	AI predicts scanner utilization and optimizes appointment scheduling. Identifies patients likely to miss appointments to optimize scheduling.
Revenue Cycle	Automated medical coding Prior authorization	AI assigns codes to radiology reports and procedures for claim submission.
Education	Personalized and adaptive learning Objective skill assessments Augmented diagnostic training	AI-powered educational platforms can recommend cases to address individual weaknesses and reinforce strength areas.

standardization improves workflow efficiency, significantly reducing the manual effort required for contouring while ensuring accurate disease progression assessment.

AI-driven disease state monitoring extends beyond volumetric analysis, now incorporating multimodal data to enhance predictive accuracy. Advanced models are emerging that can integrate demographic, clinical, and pharmacological information, outperforming conventional AAA rupture risk prediction methods that rely solely on aortic diameter (Skovbo et al., 2025). Machine learning algorithms leverage complex data patterns to stratify patients more accurately, facilitating tailored clinical decision-making. This data-driven approach enables the identification of high-risk patients who may benefit from earlier intervention while avoiding unnecessary procedures in low-risk cases.

As these models continue to evolve with real-world data integration, they are poised to enhance disease surveillance reliability, reduce observer variability, and optimize patient outcomes.

Opportunistic screening: Opportunistic screening in radiology involves utilizing imaging data, originally acquired for unrelated clinical reasons, to identify latent health risks, such as body composition abnormalities, bone mineral density deficits, or atherosclerotic plaque burden. Greater than 400 CT scans per 1,000 patients over the age of 65 are performed annually in the US

(Paderno et al., 2024); this approach capitalizes on this existing imaging resource by applying AI algorithms to extract additional insights beyond the primary purpose of the scan. By leveraging AI, radiologists can detect subclinical conditions, such as early-stage cardiovascular disease or metabolic disorders, which would otherwise remain undiagnosed until later, more symptomatic stages. Opportunistic screening can also potentially close screening gaps in populations that demonstrate low engagement with traditional screening pathways.

An example of AI in opportunistic screening is the automated risk stratification of coronary artery disease through the assessment of coronary calcium burden. AI algorithms can process CT images to rapidly quantify coronary calcium levels and evaluate atherosclerotic plaque burden with high accuracy. This automated analysis enables early identification of high-risk patients, facilitating timely interventions that could mitigate the progression of cardiovascular diseases (Malik et al., 2024).

Unlike traditional organized screening programs, which rely on dedicated exams and patient recruitment, AI-driven opportunistic screening optimizes existing imaging resources without additional patient burden or cost. Although no outcomes of a successfully implemented comprehensive opportunistic screening program have been reported to date, this approach is poised to potentially reduce healthcare costs and close screening gaps by facilitating early, evidence-based clinical decisions (Pickhardt et al., 2023; Söreskog et al., 2025).

8.3.3 Non-Interpretive AI

Communication and reporting: AI is reshaping radiology communication and reporting by automating specific aspects of data extraction, synthesis, and presentation. One recent development in this area is the automated extraction of incidental findings, which leverages natural language processing (NLP) alone or in combination with machine learning to identify and extract incidental findings from radiology reports. Given that 15–30% of all diagnostic imaging studies reveal at least one incidental finding (Oda et al., 2024), implementing robust closed-loop communication systems is essential to ensure appropriate follow-up and prevent clinical oversights.

These automated systems reduce the administrative burden associated with managing incidental findings by streamlining communication and follow-up processes. Integrating failsafe mechanisms within these AI-driven systems further enhances patient safety by ensuring that significant findings are reliably communicated to the appropriate healthcare providers. This not only supports compliance with reporting standards but also helps maintain continuity of care through prompt and consistent follow-up. As the adoption of AI in radiology communication continues to evolve, careful evaluation and continuous monitoring are essential to maintain accuracy and reliability while minimizing the potential for errors in clinical decision-making.

Automated radiology report impression generators for the purposes of improving radiologist efficiency and enhancing clarity of communication are another example of how AI is being incorporated into radiology reporting. These tools learn the radiologist's dictation style through analysis of prior reports and suggest the content of the report impression based on the radiologist's reporting history and by analyzing the content of the radiology report or findings section. The radiologist reviews the AI-generated impression to ensure it accurately reflects all of the relevant diagnostic conclusions and can then accept, reject, or edit the automatically generated impression. Potential challenges of this approach include the ability of AI to capture nuanced clinical judgment or contextual subtleties and the associated potential diminished role of the Radiologist in crafting an individualized, nuanced impression. Additionally, inconsistencies between automated outputs and individual reporting styles may arise, necessitating customization and fine-tuning.

Appropriate imaging recommendations and automated protocoling: A group from UCSF Center for Intelligent Imaging developed an NLP algorithm that matches free-text clinical indications to American College of Radiology (ACR) Appropriateness Criteria, an evidence-based imaging recommendation resource that provides specific imaging guidance for 205 commonly encountered symptom presentations or disease states. This tool decreases the barrier of manual search currently needed to access these guidelines in order for physicians to benefit from this reference resource (Chaudhari et al., 2022). Although not widely used yet, AI systems have also been shown to accurately select imaging protocols based on the patient's clinical history, physician order, and presenting symptoms. This automated protocoling, traditionally performed manually by radiologists, has the potential to reduce the administrative burden on radiologists as well as maintain consistency in imaging practices (Wong et al., 2023).

MRI acceleration and image reconstruction: The application of deep learning-based image reconstruction algorithms to accelerate MRI has allowed the performance of diagnostic-quality MRI to be 50% faster than traditional acceleration methods. In addition to lowering the cost per scan, faster MRIs lead to greater MRI availability and accessibility, improved tolerance, and decreased need for sedation and anesthesia, augmenting throughput and resource utilization (Fritz et al., 2022). These algorithms are now widely commercially available and in clinical use.

CT quality improvement: AI shows potential in monitoring CT quality across multiple scanners, an increasingly important task as most radiology departments now encompass numerous geographically disparate imaging centers and equipment resources, increasing the challenge of ensuring standard quality. A group from the University of California San Diego evaluated the use of a deep learning algorithm to assess the quality of CT pulmonary angiography (CTPA) by measuring central pulmonary artery enhancement over 3,000 CTPA scans, demonstrating high accuracy when compared to manual radiologist measurements. The use of this algorithm revealed that most suboptimal scans originated from a specific scanner, highlighting the algorithm's potential for quality improvement in radiology (Hahn et al., 2022).

Workflow and operational management: AI is being used for scheduling and resource allocation in Radiology. Algorithms can predict patient no-shows or cancellations by analyzing historical data and patient demographics, allowing schedulers to make adjustments proactively. Load leveling, which involves distributing workload evenly among available staff, imaging equipment, and radiologists, is also being enhanced through AI-driven optimization models. This is increasingly important as the radiology footprint within large healthcare institutions continues to expand in terms of geographical location as well as imaging volume. Strategies to ensure that imaging studies are efficiently allocated across the network can minimize delays in care and lead to more cost-effective resource utilization (Richardson et al., 2021) and ensure equitable distribution of work among radiologists.

AI is also proving valuable in pre-authorization, billing, and coding processes. Algorithms can extract relevant diagnostic information from clinical notes and imaging reports, automatically generating accurate billing codes. This reduces the administrative burden on radiology staff and decreases the likelihood of coding errors that could result in claim denials. Furthermore, AI-driven tools assist in pre-authorization by cross-referencing imaging requests with payer guidelines, identifying cases that may require additional documentation, and streamlining the approval process. Through these applications, AI not only enhances operational efficiency but also reduces costs associated with claim rejections.

Video radiology reports—a multimedia approach to patient-centered reporting: Recht et al. piloted a program where patient-centered video radiology reports using understandable language and annotated images were created by radiologists and made available to patients. Patients overwhelmingly preferred a combination of video and radiologist-written reports over written reports alone, commenting that the use of nonmedical terminology and having the radiologist show the pertinent findings on images through video increased their ability to understand their imaging results (Recht et al., 2022). This project did not use AI; however, it highlights the unmet demand for patient-centered reporting in radiology, a potential target for AI implementation through the use of video avatars or AI-generated video content.

8.3.4 Patient Feedback

Although the enthusiasm around the promise of AI in healthcare is palpable in the medical community, patients are still hesitant. A recent Pew Research Center survey found that of 11,004 US adults surveyed, 60% would feel uncomfortable if their own healthcare provider relied on AI to do things like diagnose diseases and recommend treatments, and 57% felt this technology would make the patient-provider relationship worse. Thirty-three percent believe this use of AI would lead to worse outcomes, while 27% feel it would not make much difference. Seventy-five percent were concerned that healthcare providers would move too fast using this technology, before fully understanding the risks for patients (Tyson et al., 2023). Surveys like these provide valuable insights into patient acceptance and perceived value of AI tools, highlighting the importance of engaging patients and patient advocacy groups as health AI tools gain traction in order to foster an environment of trust.

8.4 Challenges and Future Opportunities

8.4.1 Key Challenges in Scaling AI

The scaling of AI in radiology faces several critical challenges, particularly in terms of trust, integration, and the broader healthcare environment. One of the most significant barriers is the lack of trust in AI's performance and its generalizability across diverse clinical settings. Many institutions struggle with outdated workflows and IT infrastructures, which are often incapable of fully harnessing AI's potential. Additionally, many smaller organizations do not possess the internal capability or support needed to manage AI solutions in a sustainable and scalable manner, limiting the ability to implement AI technologies effectively (Makeeva V, 2022).

8.4.1.1 Usefulness and Usability

While AI use cases in radiology have advanced, many remain categorized as "nice to have" rather than indispensable. The integration of AI outputs often results in added steps for radiologists, such as additional clicks or navigational hurdles in accessing results. This can lead to workflow inefficiencies, diminishing the practical value of AI tools in real-world clinical environments. Without streamlined interfaces or user-centric designs, AI applications may not achieve their intended benefits, limiting their widespread adoption.

8.4.1.2 Technical Barriers

AI models in radiology require high-quality, annotated imaging datasets for training, yet challenges arise due to data heterogeneity and data siloing. Variations in imaging protocols, equipment, and patient demographics create inconsistencies that complicate the development of reliable and robust AI algorithms. Additionally, many radiology departments continue to operate on legacy systems that lack the necessary interoperability to support seamless AI integration. This lack of alignment can disrupt established workflows and negate the efficiency improvements that AI promises.

8.4.1.3 Regulatory and Legal Issues

The regulatory framework surrounding AI in healthcare is constantly evolving, with differing guidelines across regions and jurisdictions. Ensuring that AI systems comply with these dynamic regulations is a complex and time-consuming process that poses a significant obstacle to widespread adoption. Moreover, liability and ethical concerns remain pivotal in the implementation of AI-driven decisions. When AI systems make errors, determining accountability becomes a multifaceted issue. Clear and consistent guidelines are essential to navigate the ethical and legal implications of AI, safeguarding both patient care and clinical practice.

8.4.1.4 Financial and Organizational Barriers

The financial burden of adopting AI technologies is a major deterrent for many healthcare institutions. The upfront investment required for acquiring AI solutions, along with the ongoing costs for maintenance and system updates, can be prohibitive. Furthermore, clinicians and staff often display resistance to change, driven by concerns over job security and potential disruptions to well-established workflows. Overcoming this skepticism is vital for achieving successful AI integration. In addition, many questions remain as to who should pay for the cost of AI implementations. Options include: Radiologists' practice (relying on professional revenue), Hospitals (relying on technical revenue), IT Departments or malpractice insurers.

8.4.1.5 Bias, Transparency, and Trust

AI systems are inherently vulnerable to biases in the data they are trained on, which can exacerbate existing healthcare disparities. Ensuring the diversity and representativeness of training datasets is essential to mitigate this risk. Moreover, the "black box" nature of many AI models, which operate without clear explanations for their decision-making processes, can hinder trust and acceptance among clinicians. Developing explainable AI models that provide transparency and clarity is crucial for fostering confidence and ensuring effective integration into clinical workflows.

8.5 Future Opportunities

8.5.1 Large Language and Vision Models/Multimodal Foundation Models

Next-generation AI in radiology promises general-purpose AI applicability to interpret complex medical images and generate coherent, contextually rich narrative reports by leveraging large vision and language models or multimodal foundation models. Additionally, it provides a natural language interface for radiologists or clinicians to interact with imaging datasets (Rao et al., 2025; Linguraru et al., 2024). Unlike existing AI systems that are typically limited to detecting specific pathologies within isolated imaging modalities, this approach aspires to deliver comprehensive, integrative reports by synthesizing data from heterogeneous sources—such as MRI, CT, and other imaging techniques—while concurrently contextualizing findings within the patient's clinical background. These models can be used for more complex tasks, such as classifying medical imaging as normal versus abnormal, rather than the current state of supervised machine learning tasks focused on single abnormality detection (Linguraru et al., 2024). This technology has the potential to alleviate radiology workload and address the shortage of specialized reporting expertise. This capability could be particularly valuable in resource-limited settings, where access to specialty care remains constrained.

8.5.2 Agentic AI

Agentic AI is an emerging technology that combines the above referenced large language models or multimodality foundation models with traditional programming to coordinate the actions of multiple AI agents. These systems are designed to make decisions autonomously, act based on those decisions, and learn from interactions with minimal supervision. They operate probabilistically, relying on pattern recognition and likelihood estimation to make context-aware choices. This adaptability makes them well-suited to dynamic environments and complex tasks, often described as functioning like a "co-pilot" to support human users.

Although agentic AI systems have yet to be widely implemented in radiology workflows, they could potentially address challenges related to real-time decision support. One example use case is during image-guided interventional procedures, where an agentic AI system might provide guidance on lesion targeting or catheter placement. It could analyze patient-specific factors, imaging inputs, and procedural progress to offer real-time recommendations that adjust as the procedure progresses and new data becomes available. There are also potential applications beyond interventional radiology, including multi-agent collaboration, supporting precision medicine pathways, and providing personalized follow-up recommendations.

As with any AI technology, substantial technical and clinical challenges must be addressed to ensure safe and reliable deployment of multimodality foundation models and agentic AI. The absence of standardized evaluation benchmarks further complicates efforts to assess model efficacy across diverse clinical settings and imaging modalities. To bridge this gap, it is imperative to develop open, rigorously validated benchmarks and guidelines that align with regulatory standards, fostering consistent collaboration between AI developers and clinical experts as these technologies advance to the clinical setting in order to maintain patient safety and care quality (Lekadir et al., 2023).

8.5.3 Data Integration with Other Healthcare Systems

Data confined within separate healthcare systems present a major challenge for AI implementation, particularly in the context of multimodal AI models like agentic AI. Medical data are often confined to individual healthcare institutions, limiting the breadth and diversity of datasets available for training AI models. This fragmentation can lead to model bias, as algorithms trained on data from a single institution may not generalize well to broader populations or different clinical settings.

AI models, particularly those that aim to integrate multiple data types, struggle to correlate information from disparate systems. For example, integrating imaging data with lab results and patient history becomes difficult when these data are siloed. The lack of holistic data reduces the AI's ability to generate accurate, comprehensive insights, undermining its potential for real-time decision support.

Furthermore, data silos complicate model validation and benchmarking across diverse healthcare environments. Without access to data from multiple institutions, it is challenging to assess the AI's performance across varied patient demographics and practice conditions. This reduces the reliability and safety of AI systems when deployed outside their original training context (Mongan & Halabi, 2023).

To address these challenges, federated learning offers a solution, allowing AI models to train on decentralized datasets without the need for direct data sharing. However, issues like data heterogeneity and inconsistent data formats still pose significant barriers (Kitamura et al., 2024; Mongan & Halabi, 2023). Overcoming these challenges will require technical advancements alongside policy changes to facilitate secure, standardized data sharing.

8.5.4 Global Health and Accessibility

The potential of AI to mitigate healthcare disparities in resource-limited settings has yet to be fully realized. In regions facing shortages of skilled healthcare professionals, AI can alleviate some of the burden by automating critical tasks, such as medical image analysis, thereby providing local healthcare practitioners with immediate, actionable insights. This reduces dependence on distant specialists and mitigates delays in diagnostic interpretation, which are common barriers to timely intervention. The deployment of existing AI systems capable of analyzing imaging modalities could enable frontline healthcare providers in underserved areas to identify pathologies—such as fractures, infections, or tumors—more efficiently and with greater confidence.

Many healthcare facilities in low-resource environments rely on outdated or basic diagnostic technologies, which limit their diagnostic capabilities. AI has the potential to enhance the accessibility and utility of diagnostic tools in settings with limited resources by optimizing the performance of existing equipment, improving the accuracy and speed of diagnostics without necessitating costly upgrades.

8.6 Conclusion

Current applications of radiology AI span from interpretive diagnostic tools to non-interpretive solutions that enhance workflow and communication. Looking forward, advancements in agentic AI—systems that can autonomously take actions based on learned models—and multimodal generative AI, capable of integrating diverse data sources like imaging, clinical notes, and patient history, could facilitate a more comprehensive approach to clinical decision-making. Despite these promising technologies, significant barriers remain, including patient hesitancy and challenges related to trust, usability, algorithmic transparency, and technical infrastructure that must be addressed for broader implementation.

References

AI Statistics 2024 · AIPRM. (n.d.). Retrieved March 22, 2025, from https://www.aiprm.com/ai-statistics/

Beecy, A. N., Longhurst, C. A., Singh, K., Wachter, R. M., & Murray, S. G. (2024). The chief health AI officer — an emerging role for an emerging technology. *NEJM AI, 1*(7). https://doi.org/10.1056/AIP2400109

Brady, A. P., Allen, B., Chong, J., Kotter, E., Kottler, N., Mongan, J., Oakden-Rayner, L., Pinto dos Santos, D., Tang, A., Wald, C., & Slavotinek, J. (2024). Developing, purchasing, implementing and monitoring AI tools in radiology: Practical considerations. A multi-society statement from the ACR, CAR, ESR, RANZCR & RSNA. *Journal of the American College of Radiology, 21*(8), 1292–1310. https://doi.org/10.1016/j.jacr.2023.12.005

CHAI Responsible AI Guide. (2025). https://chai.org/wp-content/uploads/2025/03/CHAI_Responsible-AI-Guide_Executive-Summary_03212025.pdf

Chaudhari, G. R., Chillakuru, Y. R., Chen, T. L., Pedoia, V., Vu, T. H., Hess, C. P., Seo, Y., & Sohn, J. H. (2022). Clinical language search algorithm from free-text: Facilitating appropriate imaging. *BMC Medical Imaging, 22*(1). https://doi.org/10.1186/S12880-022-00740-6

Chekmeyan, M., Baccei, S. J., & Garwood, E. R. (2023). Cross-check QA: A quality assurance workflow to prevent missed diagnoses by alerting inadvertent discordance between the radiologist and artificial intelligence in the interpretation of high-acuity CT scans. *Journal of the American College of Radiology : JACR, 20*(12), 1225–1230. https://doi.org/10.1016/J.JACR.2023.06.010

Economou-Zavlanos, N. J., Bessias, S., Cary, M. P., Bedoya, A. D., Goldstein, B. A., Jelovsek, J. E., O'Brien, C. L., Walden, N., Elmore, M., Parrish, A. B., Elengold, S., Lytle, K. S., Balu, S., Lipkin, M. E., Shariff, A. I., Gao, M., Leverenz, D., Henao, R., Ming, D. Y., … Poon, E. G. (2024). Translating ethical and quality principles for the effective, safe and fair development, deployment and use of artificial intelligence technologies in healthcare. *Journal of the American Medical Informatics Association, 31*(3), 705–713. https://doi.org/10.1093/jamia/ocad221

Fleisher, L. A., & Economou-Zavlanos, N. J. (2024). Artificial intelligence can be regulated using current patient safety procedures and infrastructure in hospitals. *JAMA Health Forum, 5*(6), e241369. https://doi.org/10.1001/jamahealthforum.2024.1369

Fritz, J., Kijowski, R., & Recht, M. P. (2022). Artificial intelligence in musculoskeletal imaging: a perspective on value propositions, clinical use, and obstacles. *Skeletal Radiology, 51*(2), 239–243. https://doi.org/10.1007/S00256-021-03802-Y

Hahn, L. D., Hall, K., Alebdi, T., Kligerman, S. J., & Hsiao, A. (2022). Automated deep learning analysis for quality improvement of CT pulmonary angiography. *Radiology. Artificial Intelligence, 4*(2). https://doi.org/10.1148/RYAI.210162

Kitamura, F. C., Prevedello, L. M., Colak, E., Halabi, S. S., Lungren, M. P., Ball, R. L., Kalpathy-Cramer, J., Kahn, C. E., Richards, T., Talbott, J. F., Shih, G., Lin, M. H., Andriole, K. P., Vazirabad, M., Erickson, B. J., Flanders, A. E., Mongan, J., & Are Co-Senior, J. M. (2024). Lessons learned in building expertly annotated multi-institution datasets and hosting the RSNA AI challenges content code. *Radiology: Artificial Intelligence, 6*(3). https://doi.org/10.1148/ryai.230227

Kotter, E., Akinci, T. D., Cuocolo, R., Hierath, M., Huisman, M., Klontzas, M. E., Martí-Bonmatí, L., Stefan May, M., Neri, E., Nikolaou, K., Pinto dos Santos, D., Radzina, M., Cheng Shelmerdine, S., Bellemo, A., & Society of Radiology, E. (2025). Guiding AI in radiology: ESR's recommendations for effective implementation of the European AI Act. *Insights into Imaging, 16*(1), 1–11. https://doi.org/10.1186/S13244-025-01905-X

Langlotz, C. P., Allen, B., Erickson, B. J., Kalpathy-Cramer, J., Bigelow, K., Cook, T. S., Flanders, A. E., Lungren, M. P., Mendelson, D. S., Rudie, J. D., Wang, G., & Kandarpa, K. (2019). A roadmap for foundational research on artificial intelligence in medical imaging: From the 2018 NIH/RSNA/ACR/The Academy workshop. *Radiology, 291*(3), 781–791. https://doi.org/10.1148/RADIOL.2019190613

Lekadir, K., Feragen, A., Fofanah, A. J., Frangi, A. F., Buyx, A., Emelie, A., Lara, A., Porras, A. R., Chan, A.-W., Navarro, A., Glocker, B., Botwe, B. O., Khanal, B., Beger, B., Wu, C. C., Cintas, C., Langlotz, C. P., Rueckert, D., Mzurikwao, D., … Starmans, M. P. A. (2023). FUTURE-AI: International consensus guideline for trustworthy and deployable artificial intelligence in healthcare. *BMJ.* https://doi.org/10.1136/bmj-2024-081554

Linguraru, M. G., Bakas, S., Aboian, M., Chang, P. D., Flanders, A. E., Kalpathy-Cramer, J., Kitamura, F. C., Lungren, M. P., Mongan, J., Prevedello, L. M., Summers, R. M., Wu, C. C., Adewole, M., & Kahn, C. E. (2024). Clinical, cultural, computational, and regulatory considerations to deploy AI in radiology: Perspectives of RSNA and MICCAI experts. *Radiology. Artificial Intelligence, 6*(4), e240225. https://doi.org/10.1148/ryai.240225

Makeeva V. (2022). *An essential roadmap for AI in radiology*. https://www.acr.org/Blogs/DSI/2022/An-Essential-Roadmap-for-AI-in-Radiology

Malik, R. F., Sun, K. J., Azadi, J. R., Lau, B. D., Whelton, S., Arbab-Zadeh, A., Wilson, R. F., & Johnson, P. T. (2024). Opportunistic screening for coronary artery disease: An untapped population health resource. *Journal of the American College of Radiology : JACR*, *21*(6), 880–889. https://doi.org/10.1016/J.JACR.2024.02.010

Mongan, J., & Halabi, S. S. (2023). On the centrality of data: Data resources in radiologic artificial intelligence. *Radiology: Artificial Intelligence*, *5*(5). https://doi.org/10.1148/RYAI.230231

Mongan, J., Vagal, A., & Wu, C. C. (2022). Imaging AI in practice: Introducing the special issue. *Radiology: Artificial Intelligence*, *4*(2). https://doi.org/10.1148/RYAI.220039

Monti, C. B., Assen, M. van, Stillman, A. E., Lee, S. J., Hoelzer, P., Fung, G. S. K., Secchi, F., Sardanelli, F., & De Cecco, C. N. (2022). Evaluating the performance of a convolutional neural network algorithm for measuring thoracic aortic diameters in a heterogeneous population. *Radiology. Artificial Intelligence*, *4*(2). https://doi.org/10.1148/RYAI.210196

Oda, S., Chikamoto, A., Khant, Z. A., Uetani, H., Kidoh, M., Nagayama, Y., Nakaura, T., & Hirai, T. (2024). Clinical impact of radiologist's alert system on patient care for high-risk incidental CT findings: A machine learning-based risk factor analysis. *Academic Radiology*, *32*(1), 112–119. https://doi.org/10.1016/j.acra.2024.09.034

Paderno, A., Ataide Gomes, E. J., Gilberg, L., Maerkisch, L., Teodorescu, B., Koç, M., & Meyer, M. (2024). Artificial intelligence-enhanced opportunistic screening of osteoporosis in CT scan: A scoping review. *Osteoporosis International*, *35*(10), 1681–1692. https://doi.org/10.1007/S00198-024-07179-1/TABLES/2

Pencina, M. J., McCall, J., & Economou-Zavlanos, N. J. (2024). A federated registration system for artificial intelligence in health. *JAMA*. https://doi.org/10.1001/jama.2024.14026

Pickhardt, P. J., Summers, R. M., Garrett, J. W., Krishnaraj, A., Agarwal, S., Dreyer, K. J., & Nicola, G. N. (2023). Opportunistic screening: Radiology scientific expert panel. *Radiology*, *307*(5), e222044. https://doi.org/10.1148/RADIOL.222044

Postiglione, T. J., Guillo, E., Heraud, A., Rossillon, A., Bartoli, M., Herpe, G., Adam, C., Fabre, D., Ardon, R., Azarine, A., & Haulon, S. (2024). Multicentric clinical evaluation of a computed tomography-based fully automated deep neural network for aortic maximum diameter and volumetric measurements. *Journal of Vascular Surgery*, *79*(6), 1390-1400.e8. https://doi.org/10.1016/J.JVS.2024.01.214

Rao, V. M., Hla, M., Moor, M., Adithan, S., Kwak, S., Topol, E. J., & Rajpurkar, P. (2025). Multimodal generative AI for medical image interpretation. *Nature*, *639*(8056), 888–896. https://doi.org/10.1038/s41586-025-08675-y

Recht, M. P., Westerhoff, M., Doshi, A. M., Young, M., Ostrow, D., Swahn, D. M., Krueger, S., & Thesen, S. (2022). Video radiology reports: A valuable tool to improve patient-centered radiology. *American Journal of Roentgenology*, *219*(3), 509–519. https://doi.org/10.2214/AJR.22.27512

Richardson, M. L., Garwood, E. R., Lee, Y., Li, M. D., Lo, H. S., Nagaraju, A., Nguyen, X. V., Probyn, L., Rajiah, P., Sin, J., Wasnik, A. P., & Xu, K. (2021). Noninterpretive uses of artificial intelligence in radiology. *Academic Radiology*, *28*(9), 1225–1235. https://doi.org/10.1016/J.ACRA.2020.01.012

Russakovsky, O., Deng, J., Su, H., Krause, J., Satheesh, S., Ma, S., Huang, Z., Karpathy, A., Khosla, A., Bernstein, M., Berg, A. C., & Fei-Fei, L. (2015). ImageNet large scale visual recognition challenge. *International Journal of Computer Vision*, *115*(3), 211–252. https://doi.org/10.1007/S11263-015-0816-Y/FIGURES/16

Skovbo, J. S., Andersen, N. S., Obel, L. M., Laursen, M. S., Riis, A. S., Houlind, K. C., Diederichsen, A. C. P., & Lindholt, J. S. (2025). Individual risk assessment for rupture of abdominal aortic aneurysm using artificial intelligence. *Journal of Vascular Surgery*, *81*(3). https://doi.org/10.1016/J.JVS.2024.11.017

Söreskog, E., Lopez, B., Bean, T., Lewis, P., Ashley, N., Da Palma Lopes, J., Meertens, R., & Ratcliffe, A. (2025). Exploring the potential cost-effectiveness and societal burden implications of screening for fracture risk in a UK general radiography setting. *BMC Musculoskeletal Disorders*, *26*(1), 112. https://doi.org/10.1186/S12891-024-08202-6

Togher, D., Dean, G., Moon, J., Mayola, R., Medina, A., Repec, J., Meheux, M., Mather, S., Storey, M., Rickaby, S., Abubacker, M. Z., & Shelmerdine, S. C. (2025). Evolution of radiology staff perspectives during artificial intelligence (AI) implementation for expedited lung cancer triage. *Clinical Radiology, 81*. https://doi.org/10.1016/J.CRAD.2024.09.010

Tyson, A., Pasquini, G., Spencer, A., & Funk, C. (2023). *60% of Americans would be uncomfortable with provider relying on AI in their own health care* (Vol. 22). www.pewresearch.org

Wong, K. A., Hatef, A., Ryu, J. L., Nguyen, X. V., Makary, M. S., & Prevedello, L. M. (2023). An artificial intelligence tool for clinical decision support and protocol selection for brain MRI. *American Journal of Neuroradiology, 44*(1), 11–16. https://doi.org/10.3174/AJNR.A7736

Chapter 9

The Expanding Role of AI in Life Sciences Innovation

David A. Shoultz, PhD, MBA and Rita Suhuyini Salifu, PhD

9.1 Overview

In this chapter, we explore the transformative potential of artificial intelligence (AI) in life sciences innovation, addressing its strategic application across diverse healthcare domains. We discuss the role of AI in altering traditional research paradigms by leveraging machine learning (ML), deep learning (DL), and other AI tools to accelerate drug discovery, diagnostics, and personalized medicine. We outline a strategic framework following the approach advocated by Rumelt (Rumelt, 2011), emphasizing the diagnosis of challenges in life science innovation, a guiding policy for AI implementation, and coherent actions for successful integration of AI-enabled innovation into real-world practice with patient benefit.

We include illustrative strategies and case studies for the diagnosis of myeloproliferative neoplasms (MPN), digital therapeutics for chronic cough, and screening for peripartum cardiomyopathies (PPCM), particularly in low- and middle-income countries (LMICs). We highlight the importance of quality data, models, and organizational structures, alongside the issues of transparency, reproducibility, ethics, and effectiveness (Vollmer et al., 2020).

Ours is a patient-centric vision, prioritizing AI applications that deliver tangible benefits to patients, healthcare providers, and systems. We stress the importance and necessity of interdisciplinary collaboration and robust data governance. We conclude by acknowledging the challenges and future opportunities, underscoring the potential of AI to bridge healthcare disparities and advance health globally.

9.2 Introduction

The life sciences stand at the precipice of a new era, one defined by the convergence of biological understanding and computational prowess. Artificial intelligence (AI) is no longer a futuristic concept but a tangible force beginning to reshape how we approach fundamental biological questions, discover and develop new diagnostics and therapeutics, and ultimately achieve our aim

DOI: 10.4324/9781003621294-11

of improving human health. This chapter explores this transformative intersection, examining how the use of AI tools accelerates the often lengthy and complex journey from initial research discoveries to tangible benefits for patients. We will delve into the specific applications of these technologies across the life sciences spectrum, from classification of hematopathology images to digital therapeutics for respiratory disease and screening for heart disease in pregnancy in Nigeria.

The traditional model of life sciences innovation, characterized by sequential and often siloed research stages, is being fundamentally disrupted by AI. ML algorithms can now sift through massive datasets of biological information – including genomic data, protein structures, and clinical trial results – to identify patterns and insights that, in many cases, would be impossible for human researchers to discern alone. This ability to accelerate data analysis and generate novel hypotheses has the potential to meaningfully reduce the time required for drug discovery, development, and clinical translation. Furthermore, AI technologies are empowering researchers to move beyond a one-size-fits-all approach to healthcare, paving the way for personalized medicine tailored to individual patient needs and genetic profiles.

This chapter will showcase specific examples of AI-driven innovation in the life sciences, highlighting best practices, discussing common perils and pitfalls, and showcasing several real-world case studies. We will explore how AI is being used to enhance the diagnosis of complex diseases, enable the development of digital therapeutics, and reduce rates of peripartum mortality and morbidity. By examining these practical applications, we aim to provide a comprehensive overview of the transformative potential of AI in the life sciences and its profound implications for the future of healthcare. We will also explore potential risks and ethical considerations associated with the use of AI in life sciences innovation.

AI is not a monolithic technology as applied to life sciences innovation. Rather, it is a set of tools often casually or popularly referred to as "AI" that includes machine learning (ML), deep learning (DL), hidden Markov models (HMMs), neural networks (NNs), generative models (including large language models), molecular dynamics (MD), virtual screening, and structure-activity relationship (SAR) models. It is important to understand the definitions, details, and distinctions of these various tools to be able to discern how they can be most appropriately and productively applied to the discovery, development, and deployment of new life sciences innovations. (Olawade et al., 2024) AI tools frequently used in the context of life sciences innovation are described and detailed in Table 9.1.

Too often, consideration of the use of AI tools in life sciences innovation is exclusively centered around applications in high-income settings. There are numerous and important existing and potential uses of AI tools in life sciences innovation in low- and middle-income settings. For instance, Akingbola et al. recently reviewed applications in oncology in African countries (Akingbola et al., 2024). The authors call attention to the fact that the predominance of AI innovations to date on the African continent has been in the field of diagnostics. They highlight specific technologies, including DataPathology (Casablanca, Morocco), which operates in Morocco, the Democratic Republic of the Congo, and Senegal. The company provides AI-enabled digital pathology services, including for oncology.

We are increasingly familiar with some generative AI methods, including large language models (LLMs), given the proliferation of tools such as ChatGPT (OpenAI, San Francisco, CA), Gemini (Alphabet, Mountain View, CA), and Claude (Anthropic, San Francisco, CA). The reader may already have experience using one or more of these various models for language or graphics-based output in their personal or professional life. In fact, the first draft of this Introduction was written using a structured prompt to the Gemini Advanced Flash 2.0 model (Alphabet, Mountain View, CA). The authors later modified the text to its current format.

Table 9.1 Some of the AI Tools Commonly Used in the Context of Life Science Innovation

AI Tool	*Definition*	*Examples of Innovation Utility*	*Considerations*
Machine learning	ML methods include supervised learning, unsupervised learning, and sequential learning. Existing data are used to train algorithms for pattern recognition and prediction.	• Target ID • Virtual screening • Lead optimization • *In vivo* activity prediction • Clinical trial design • Patient subgroup selection • Medical imaging, including US	• Data quality and diversity • Model selection and cross-validation • Biases in data • Data privacy • Computational requirements • Regulatory
Deep learning	A specialized, more advanced form of ML using multilayered neural networks and larger, more intricate datasets.	• Similar to examples provided for ML • PK modeling • Clinical trial data analysis • Analysis of complex biomedical data • Medical imaging, including US	• Similar to ML
Neural networks	A subset of ML and a key component of deep learning systems. Key features include nodes, input layers, hidden layers, and output layers. Often said to be systems that mimic human cognition.	• QSAR analysis • PK and PD modeling • Drug repurposing • Medical imaging, including US • Digital health applications, including cough recognition	• Data availability, curation, and diversity • Network architecture selection • Network complexity • Interpretability
Generative models	Types of models capable of generating detailed outputs (e.g., protein structures) based on proprietary or publicly available input datasets. Examples include RF Diffusion (Watson et al., 2023), ProteinMPNN (Dauparas et al., 2022), and AlphaFold (Jumper et al., 2021).	• Drug and biomarker discovery • *De novo* design of proteins and other molecules • Compound library expansion • Lead optimization • ADME prediction	• Importance of interdisciplinary collaboration for the successful implementation of models
Hidden Markov models	Statistical models based on the transition probabilities between states, both observed and hidden. May be specifically used in analyses of gene expression or protein-protein interactions.	• Protein structure prediction • Gene prediction and annotation • Motif discovery • Drug resistance analysis • Virtual screening • Target ID	• Definition of hidden states • Assumptions underlying transition probabilities • Model validation • Used with other methods

Askr et al., 2023; Blanco-González et al., 2023; Patel & Shah, 2022; Réda et al., 2020; Turon et al., 2023.

ID = identification; US = ultrasound; QSAR = quantitative structure-activity relationship; PK = pharmacokinetic; PD = pharmacodynamic; ADME = absorption, distribution, metabolism and excretion.

9.3 Strategy and Vision for AI

In considering a strategy and vision for the use of AI tools in life sciences innovation, it is helpful to define what we mean by *strategy* and *vision*. In his excellent book *Good Strategy, Bad Strategy: The Difference and Why It Matters*, Richard Rumelt describes strategy as the act of designing a way to confront an important problem or challenge. (Rumelt, 2011) He defines the *kernel* of a good strategy as consisting of a *diagnosis* that accurately frames the challenge; a *guiding policy* that provides an approach that directs actions to be taken in confronting the challenge; and a set of *coherent actions* by which the guiding policy is carried out. This is the definition of strategy that we'll use in this chapter.

Usefully defining *vision* can be a challenge all its own. Here, we'll define vision as the long-term goals and desired future state that we aim to achieve. There is necessarily an aspirational component to vision statements, and our vision for the use of AI tools in life sciences innovation includes that aspiration while sounding a cautionary note about the sometimes too-fine line between ambition and fantasy. Most of this section will focus on developing a strategy for the use of AI tools in life sciences innovation and will conclude with the articulation of a vision based on this strategy.

A Strategy for the Use of AI Tools in Life Sciences Innovation

Following Rumelt's approach, we will address the *diagnosis* ("what is the challenge in life sciences innovation that we are aiming to solve?"), *guiding policy* ("how is the use of AI tools going to be a solution to this challenge?"), and a set of *coherent actions* ("what specific steps are required to successfully implement the AI tools?"). The use of AI tools in the life sciences in the absence of a good strategy is wasteful in the best-case scenario and dangerous in the worst-case scenario. With that in mind, let's develop a strategy for the use of AI tools for life sciences innovation.

9.3.1 What Are the Challenges That We Are Aiming to Solve?

For our purposes, life sciences innovation is a broad field encompassing drugs and vaccines, biomarkers and diagnostics, digital tools, and medical devices, among a myriad of other activities and products ultimately intended to expand our scientific knowledge base, develop new products, and ultimately diagnose, prevent, treat, or ameliorate conditions or diseases impacting human health. This innovation takes place in many different settings and contexts, including countries and communities across the globe and the income spectrum, institutional and community settings, and spanning for-profit and not-for-profit enterprises. A one-size-fits-all strategy would not suffice for an innovation environment that is this broad or diverse. Nonetheless, there is a recurring set of challenges or problems faced in life sciences innovation, whether one is working for a US-based non-profit, a university in Ghana, or a pharmaceutical company in the UK. These persistent challenges include those outlined below in Table 9.2.

Life sciences innovation is hampered by high and growing resource demands, inherent uncertainty, and low PTRS, the complexities of disease biology and inadequate models, difficulties in identifying meaningful biomarkers, a significant translational research gap, manufacturing and quality control standards for different product types, the need for rapid responses to emerging pathogens, data privacy and governance concerns, challenges in capturing user requirements, low

Table 9.2 Persistent Challenges in Life Sciences Innovation

Challenge
1. Resource requirements (including capital, time, labor, and data)
2. Uncertainty and low PTRS
3. Complex pathobiology and inadequate *in vitro* and *in vivo* models
4. Identification of meaningful biomarkers and surrogate endpoints
5. Translational research gap from preclinical to clinical studies
6. Manufacturing and QC (across different product types)
7. Emerging pathogens and rapid response requirements
8. Data privacy and governance
9. Low signal-to-noise ratios
10. Highburden of regulatory requirements and processes

PTRS = probability of technical and regulatory success; QC = quality control.

STN ratios, and a burdensome regulatory landscape that varies by country. These factors impede progress and delay the delivery of important new technologies, ultimately limiting advancements in human health. In short, *life sciences innovation is complex, resource-intensive, replete with uncertainty, and highly regulated; these inherent attributes reduce and delay individual and societal benefits.*

9.3.2 How Is the Use of AI Tools Going to Be a Solution To These Challenges?

In Table 9.3, we have summarized the rationale for using AI tools alongside the specific challenge to be addressed. Depending on the specific challenge(s), these rationales may include decreasing the labor or time required, increasing the probability of technical and regulatory success (PTRS), or increasing biologic insight. Note that in most cases, these solutions (i.e., to the challenge of resource requirements, uncertainty, or complex pathobiology) are most likely to be *partial* in their nature. *Reducing* uncertainty by using AI tools is not the same as *eliminating* uncertainty.

9.3.3 What Specific Steps Are Required to Successfully Implement AI Tools?

As illustrated in Figure 9.1, we propose a roadmap for the strategic and successful implementation of AI tools in life science innovation. This process starts with the identification of key challenges. Next, the rationale for the use of AI tools specifically in response to the key challenge(s) must be studied and articulated. Once AI tools are confirmed as the best approach, at least five key considerations must be addressed. Only then can a set of coherent actions be prescribed to implement a specific strategy for using AI. Note that any of the five considerations included in Figure 9.1 may, in fact, discourage or block the use of AI tools in a specific case.

Table 9.3 Persistent Challenges and Rationale for the Use of AI Tools in Life Sciences Innovation

Challenge	*Rationale for Using AI Tools*
1. Resource requirements	↓ Labor required ↓ Time required
2. Uncertainty and low PTRS	↓ Uncertainty ↑ PTRS
3. Complex pathobiology and inadequate models	↑ Biologic insight ↑ Data relevance to translation
4. Identification of biomarkers and surrogate endpoints	↑ Regulatory options ↓ Time required for development ↑ Development of new diagnostics ↓ Costs involved
5. Translational research gap	↓ Uncertainty ↑ PTRS ↑ Biologic insight ↑ Data relevance to translation
6. Manufacturing and QC	↓ Labor required ↓ Time required ↓ Uncertainty ↓ Time to problem recognition
7. Emerging pathogens and rapid response requirements	↑ Surveillance capacity ↓ Time to threat identification ↑ Biologic insight ↓ Uncertainty
8. Data privacy and governance	! Use of AI tools will increase data privacy and governance challenges.
9. Low signal-to-noise ratios	↓ Uncertainty ↑ Biologic insight ↑ PTRS ! Use of AI tools may increase STN ratios depending on the amount and quality of data.
10. Burden of regulatory requirements and processes	↓ Labor required? ↓ Time required? ! Use of AI tools may result in an increase in regulatory burden as agencies consider the use of new methods, including for research and development (R&D).

PTRS = probability of technical and regulatory success; STN = signal-to-noise.

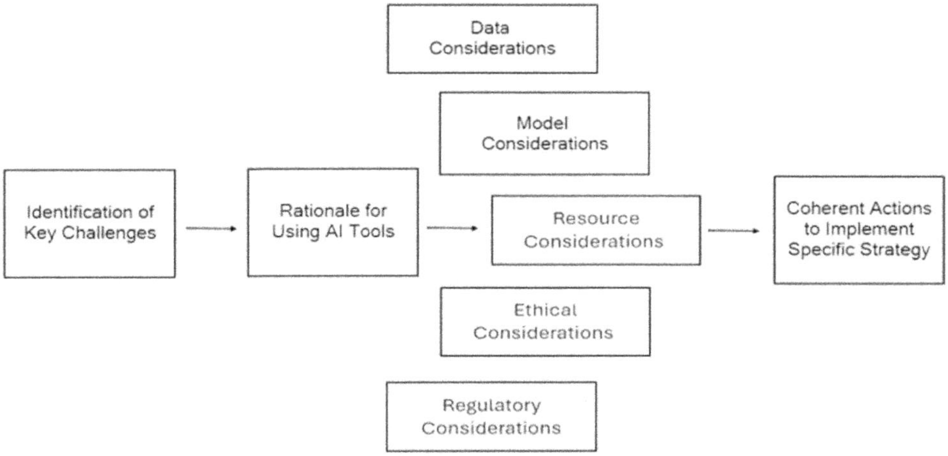

Figure 9.1 Illustration of the key steps in formulating a specific strategy for the use of AI tools in life sciences innovation. Strategies must be fashioned based on the specific challenges and reasons for using AI instead of conventional tools.

9.3.4 Three Examples of Strategy for the Use of AI Tools in Life Sciences Innovation

As generic strategies are of little practical use or value, we will not try to articulate a general strategy for the use of AI tools in life sciences innovation in this chapter. Rather, we will construct specific illustrative strategies for the use of AI tools in life sciences innovation in three specific use cases and will also revisit each of these strategies in a brief case study: clinical decision support for the diagnosis of myeloproliferative neoplasms (MPNs), digital and scalable treatment for cough, and screening for peripartum cardiomyopathies (PPCM) in Nigeria.

9.4 Clinical Decision Support Tool: Diagnosis of MPNs

9.4.1 Background

The MPNs include essential thrombocythemia (ET), polycythemia vera (PV), and myelofibrosis (MF). MF can be classified as either primary (PMF) or secondary (SMF). A recurring challenge faced by clinicians and hematopathologists is the differentiation of ET from a condition referred to as "pre-PMF," despite these two conditions having very different median overall survival times and requiring distinct approaches to treatment and management. Distinguishing between pre-PMF and ET requires considerable expertise on the part of hematopathologists and clinicians, time, and scarce human resources. Such resources may be limited to select academic institutions and tertiary referral centers. (Srisuwananukorn et al., 2023, 2024)

9.4.2 Illustrative Strategy

The clinical and histopathological diagnosis and differentiation of pre-PMF and ET require specialized expertise and resources, which are typically limited to academic institutions and tertiary referral centers. Patients may receive a delayed or incorrect diagnosis as a result. Using an AI-enabled imaging processing clinical decision support tool, hematopathologists can quickly differentiate pre-PMF from ET on consumer-grade hardware and an open-source AI framework with a high level of classification accuracy. This fast, potentially inexpensive approach has a high degree of specificity for the diagnosis of pre-PMF. Implementation of this approach should initially be undertaken as a decision support tool for hematopathologists, with center-specific and multicenter studies to inform and support the evolution of the algorithm and implementation. Clinicians should be engaged at each step of this process to build trust in the value and accuracy of this new AI-enabled clinical decision support tool.

9.5 Digital and Scalable Treatment for Cough

9.5.1 Background

Chronic cough is estimated to affect 5–10% of people worldwide. Causes may include asthma, gastroesophageal reflux disease (GERD), and upper airway cough syndrome (UACS). The condition is a source of frustration for patients, healthcare providers, and family members due to the complex etiology, comorbidities, and lack of definitive treatments for chronic cough. Non-pharmacologic behavioral cough suppression therapy (BCST) has been demonstrated to be effective in reducing cough severity and cough frequency. Depending on the etiology of the condition, this makes BCST much more effective than FDA-approved drugs or drugs in development. However, access to BCST is very limited. In the US, only 200 specialists are available who provide BCST for patients who suffer from chronic cough, including an estimated 12 million people in the US. (Chaccour et al., 2025; Kaplan, 2019; Yi et al., 2024)

9.5.2 Illustrative Strategy

Chronic cough is a prevalent and problematic condition affecting 5–10% of people globally. The effectiveness of pharmaceutical treatment can be quite limited due to multiple factors and may involve undesirable side effects. BCST has been shown to be effective in reducing both the severity and frequency of cough, but requires skilled practitioners trained in BCST methods. Using a digital platform and an AI-enabled cough detection algorithm will provide patients with a physician-prescribed "digital therapeutic" to deliver BCST and cough monitoring in a scalable, inexpensive fashion that is safe and side-effect-free and includes objective monitoring. Implementation of this approach should be undertaken by an established pharmaceutical company in a specific country with a relatively large and homogeneous pharmaceutical market and a national health insurance scheme, such as Japan. Post-marketing studies should be carried out in partnership with the pharmaceutical company to validate real-world evidence (RWE) for effectiveness, safety, and health economics. This validation can then be used to stimulate interest in partnerships with other pharmaceutical companies in larger markets (e.g., UK, Europe, China).

9.6 Screening for PPCMs in Nigeria

9.6.1 Background

Pregnancy is a time of numerous health risks for women. Although not widely appreciated outside of the medical community, these risks include cardiovascular disease (CVD). Worldwide,

1–4% of pregnant women may experience at least one type of CVD, including PPCMs. CVD is the leading cause of maternal mortality behind obstetric causes (e.g., hemorrhage, infection, and labor and delivery complications). While incidence rates of PPCM are high in many African countries, Nigeria leads the continent and the globe with respect to rates of PPCM. It is estimated that approximately 1 in every 100 deliveries may result in PPCM, and that mortality rates may approach 50% at one year of follow-up. Diagnosis of PPCM can be challenging due to many factors, including the difficulty of distinguishing PPCM from physiological effects of pregnancy on the heart and circulatory system. Adverse health outcomes may result from misdiagnoses or diagnoses that are delayed. Both AI-enabled electrocardiograms (ECGs) and digital stethoscopes have shown promise in identifying PPCM, including in LMICs such as Nigeria. (Adedinsewo et al., 2024; Karaye, Ishaq, et al., 2020; Karaye, Sa'idu, et al., 2020; Schaufelberger, 2019).

9.6.2 Illustrative Strategy

Left-sided ventricular dysfunction (LVSD) is an important component of PPCM. Incidence rates of PPCM in Nigeria are the highest in the world, occurring in approximately 1 in every 100 deliveries. Maternal mortality rates at one year of follow-up may reach nearly 50% in this West African country. Appropriate diagnosis is challenging for several important reasons, including the difficulty of differentiating LVSD from the typical physiological changes that occur during pregnancy. The use of AI digital stethoscopes has demonstrated effectiveness in the detection of LVSD, with areas under the curve (AUCs) ranging from 0.976 (95% confidence interval [CI] 0.953–0.998) to 0.985 (95% CI 0.974–0.996), depending on left ventricular ejection fraction (LVEF). The use of AI digital stethoscopes should be prioritized in settings such as Nigeria, where the relative gains in patient benefit are likely to be the largest, including settings with high incidence rates, high rates of morbidity and mortality in the postpartum period, and where access to obstetrical and cardiology expertise is limited. Implementation should include robust training programs for healthcare providers, awareness promotion programs for the importance of PPCM screening, and data on epidemiology, outcomes, and the effectiveness of AI digital stethoscopes should be collected, analyzed, and reported through efforts such as the *Pe*rip*a*rtum *C*ardiomyopathy in Nig*e*ria (PEACE) Registry. (Karaye, Ishaq, et al., 2020)

A Vision for the Use of AI Tools in Life Sciences Innovation

AI is not a monolithic or magical technology. It is a collection of tools whose appropriate use in life sciences innovation has the potential to be truly transformative in the coming one to two decades. The use of AI in this setting requires careful thought, cultivated expertise, a well-informed ethical framework, and the strategic and timely application of the best-fitting tool given the use case.

Our vision for the use of AI tools in life sciences innovation is centered on patient benefit; we assign value and priority to use cases with relevance to patients, healthcare systems, and healthcare providers (HCPs). Finally, as with the well-documented example of leapfrogging and mobile telephony in the African context, the transformative potential of the deliberate use of AI tools in life sciences innovation is especially profound and important in LMIC. Any vision lacking the application of AI tools in this context is a myopic one.

To summarize, our vision for the use of AI tools in life sciences innovation is one in which a strategic approach is centered on patient benefit and the AI tools used are well-suited to the application, whether this be diagnostics, therapeutics, or medical devices. Investing in large, high-quality datasets for training AI models, fostering interdisciplinary collaborations between biologists, clinicians, and data scientists, and developing well-validated, reproducible algorithms are *sine qua nons* of this vision. Ethical considerations, including data privacy and algorithmic fairness, must be integrated throughout the development and deployment process to ensure responsible and equitable innovation. Finally, we recognize the enormous value of the potential for these tools to accelerate life sciences innovation and patient benefit in LMICs and prioritize their use in this setting to help close the longstanding life sciences innovation gap between high-income countries (HICs) and LMICs.

9.7 Implementation Best Practices Focused on Patient Benefit

Makarov et al. (Makarov et al., 2021) articulate 11 best practices for the use of AI tools in biopharmaceutical R&D, including at the data, technology, and organizational levels. Similarly, Vollmer et al. (Vollmer et al., 2020) discuss 20 critical questions to be addressed with respect to the use of ML and AI research for patient benefit, with particular focus on transparency, replicability, ethics, and effectiveness. We see these best practices and critical questions as essential ingredients in the recipe for successful implementation and in fulfilling the truly transformative potential of AI tools in life sciences innovation described above. As highlighted by Makarov and Vollmer, best practices begin with the premise that *data are the foundation of AI* and with the question, *what is the health question relating to patient benefit?*

Based on these works and our own experience, we have distilled five best practices, principles, and critical questions for implementing the use of AI tools in life sciences innovation. As outlined above in the discussion of a proposed vision for the use of AI tools in life sciences innovation, our recommendations for implementation best practices are predicated and centered on patient benefit. We see these best practices and critical questions outlined below as essential ingredients in the recipe for successful use of AI tools in life sciences innovation.

9.7.1 Quality Data

The first usage of the axiom "garbage in, garbage out" may have been employed by US Army mathematicians in the late 1950s and is now used so ubiquitously that it has been acronymized as GIGO. Nonetheless, this bedrock principle underlies the use of AI tools in life sciences innovation and is the root of several best practices in implementing AI tools. Users of AI tools must a) understand the attributes and metadata that comprise data of sufficient quality, b) use only data that meet these standards for sufficient quality and relevance, c) have the domain expertise necessary to make accurate determinations of data quality in specialized areas (e.g., hematopathology, cough sound analysis, digitized heart sounds), and d) be exacting about which and what type of data are used for training AI models.

9.7.2 Quality Models

Whether one is building a simple linear regression model, a Markov chain model, or a convolutional neural network (CNN) model, the resulting construct must be fit-for-purpose, reproducible, and subject to validation. Best practices include a) selecting AI tools that are suitable for the use case, b) implementing a management system for model creation, testing, and versioning, c) including sufficient information pertaining to models and datasets to allow for external validation, and d) the evaluation of trade-offs to be considered in the use of the AI tool versus the standard of care approach.

9.7.3 Quality Organizations

As with any human enterprise involving science and technology, the importance of a coherent and competent organizational framework is often overlooked by those who become mesmerized by a technology (e.g., AI and ML, CRISPR gene editing, mRNA vaccines). Our experience is that the organizational context is at least as important as technology in fulfilling the potential of technologies. This certainly appears to be the case for AI tools and life sciences innovation.

Best practices in this domain include a) expectation management, b) ensuring that the AI tools are complemented by deep biological and human insight, c) including true AI expertise at the uppermost levels of organizational leadership, and d) creating a culture with an experimental approach in which failing (and *failing fast*) is encouraged. This last point is so important that it could be the subject of an entire chapter in this book and still merit additional emphasis and discussion. (Sjödin et al., 2021)

9.7.4 TREE Issues

Vollmer (Vollmer et al., 2020) reminds us that *just because we can, it does not mean we should*, and this ethos applies to the critical questions that need to be asked about the TREE issues, including transparency, reproducibility, ethics, and effectiveness. The use of AI tools in life sciences innovation does not occur in a vacuum or somehow beyond the reach of these considerations. The best practice for their use includes pausing to address these questions at multiple points in the innovation process; neither expediency nor procrastination should be allowed to derail the essential value that asking and answering these questions provides.

9.7.5 Patient Benefit

Our vision for the use of AI tools in life sciences innovation is one that is centered on patient benefit, and our recommendations for implementation of best practices are focused on this same premise. Not only should the implementation be relevant to at least one aspect of patient benefit (e.g., patients, healthcare providers, healthcare systems), but the use of AI tools should provide a demonstrable set of benefits greater than conventional (e.g., non-AI) methods. Finally, the maxim "first, do no harm" (*primum non nocere*) must be ever-present in the minds and work of AI users: early, consistent, and priority consideration is to be given to issues of ethics, data privacy, and equity, including when building training, validation, and test datasets.

9.8 Initial Results and Case Studies

A growing body of evidence points to the utility of the use of AI tools in life science innovation. As the three case studies below help to illustrate, promising results are emerging in diagnostics, therapeutics, and medical devices. Importantly, these initial results include the application of AI tools in LMICs and help to demonstrate the value for patients, healthcare providers, and health systems (e.g., patient benefit).

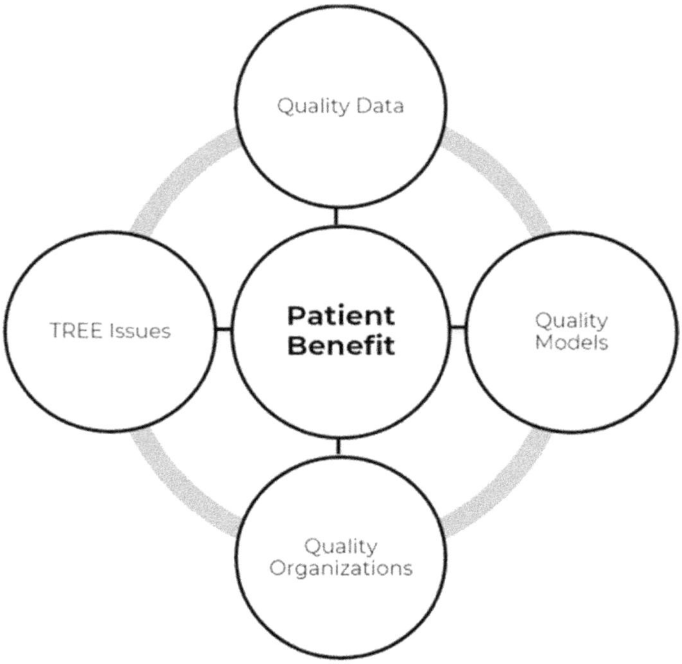

Figure 9.2 Representation of implementation best practices for AI tools in life sciences innovation that is centered on patient benefit and includes best practices in the domains of quality data, quality models, quality organizations, and takes into account TREE considerations, including transparency, reproducibility, ethics, and effectiveness. Adapted from Makarov and Vollmer (Makarov et al., 2021; Vollmer et al., 2020).

In Case Study A, Srisuwananukorn et al. (Srisuwananukorn et al., 2023) develop and validate an AI tool for the analysis of whole-slide images (WSIs) and demonstrate a high degree of classification accuracy of hematopathology samples for the diagnosis of pre-PMF. Case Study B focuses on the partnership between Hyfe (an AI respiratory care company) and Kyorin (a pharmaceutical company) dedicated to bringing a digital therapeutic for chronic cough to the Japanese market (Chaccour et al., 2025). Finally, in Case Study C, Adedinsewo et al. (Adedinsewo et al., 2024) demonstrate the value of AI-enabled digital stethoscopes in screening for PPCM in Nigeria.

CASE STUDY A: A CLINICAL DECISION SUPPORT TOOL FOR DIAGNOSIS OF MPNS.

At the 2023 American Society of Hematology (ASH) Annual Meeting, Dr Andrew Srisuwananukorn and his colleagues presented the results of their study titled "Interpretable AI Differentiates Pre-PMF from ET: A Multicenter Study of a New Clinical Decision Support Tool." Dr Srisuwananukorn et al. (a hematologist-oncologist and assistant professor of medicine at The Ohio State University Comprehensive Cancer Center) developed and validated a model using a neural network, RetCCL.[ref], and custom scripts written using *Slideflow*, an open-source AI framework for digital histopathology. RetCCL was pretrained on 32,000 WSIs before the researchers employed a training cohort of 200 patients (100 pre-PMF, 100 ET) from Florence, Italy, and an external test cohort comprised of 26 patients (6 pre-PMF, 20 ET) from Tampa, Florida. Bone marrow WSIs were tessellated into representative image tiles for training, and then a prediction for individual patient WSIs was calculated based on a method known as attention-based multiple-instance learning. The final version of the model produced an AUC of 0.90 and a classification accuracy of >92%, including a sensitivity of 67% and a specificity of 100% for the diagnosis of pre-PMF. Using consumer-grade hardware, the evaluation time was ~6 seconds for each image.

◀▶

> We imagine that a potential high-speed, low-cost algorithm may reliably distinguish pre-PMF from ET patients with high specificity which can be democratized to the MPN clinical community in routine practice and drive clinical trial accrual for biologically rational novel therapeutics.

CASE STUDY B: A DIGITAL AND SCALABLE TREATMENT FOR CHRONIC COUGH.

Hyfe is a private company focused on developing tools for AI-enabled respiratory care, and its product suite includes cough monitoring hardware and software, a wellness-focused app for cough management, and digital therapeutics for cough treatment. In early 2025, Hyfe announced a partnership with the Japanese pharmaceutical company Kyorin. The two companies intend to develop a digital therapeutic based on BCST for the Japanese market. Hyfe originally deployed a free smartphone app that allowed it to ethically collect a huge number of explosive, cough-like sounds from around the world and in hundreds of different settings. To date, the company has collected more than 1 billion sounds, of which hundreds of millions are cough-like sounds. The company conducted human annotation of more than ten million sounds. These were then used as data to train a convolutional neural network. Once the performance of the algorithm reached the desired level of accuracy, it was locked down to allow for the development of the company's different products.

◀▶

> Given the system's high accuracy, usability, and scalability, it has the potential to greatly improve clinical care, drug development and regulatory efforts, particularly among subjects with a high cough burden.

CASE STUDY C: SCREENING FOR PPCMS IN NIGERIA.

In September 2024, Adedinsewo et al. published the results of a multicenter, open-label randomized clinical trial (RCT) conducted among more than 1,200 women who were pregnant or within 12 months postpartum and receiving obstetrical care. The trial was undertaken in collaboration with and partly funded by the Mayo Clinic (Rochester, Minnesota). The study was designed to assess the use of AI-enabled screening methods (including ECG with asynchronous AI predictions and digital stethoscope recordings with point-of-care (POC) AI predictions). These methods were compared to usual care, and diagnoses of LVSD were confirmed with echocardiography. The researchers reported that using the AI-enabled digital stethoscope resulted in the identification of 24/587 (4.1%) patients with LVSD versus 12/608 (2.0%) patients with LVSD assessed using only usual care methods. Importantly, the study authors reported that there were no adverse effects related to study participation and concluded that screening using AI-enabled digital stethoscopy improved the diagnosis of PPCM in Nigeria, an LMIC.

◀▶

...AI-guided screening with the use of a digital stethoscope was associated with an increase in the diagnosis of cardiomyopathy associated with LVSD compared to usual care. This intervention has the potential to improve cardio-obstetric care by reducing delays in the diagnosis of a life-threatening but treatable condition.

9.9 Challenges and Future Opportunities

There are many reasons to be cautiously optimistic about the use of AI tools in life sciences innovation. As illustrated in the three case studies above, appropriate implementation and ethical application of AI tools are already yielding early and important advances in diverse use cases. Nonetheless, this cautious optimism is built on the premise that the best practices and critical questions described above will be seriously considered and addressed.

There is no shortage of challenges to be surmounted in the use of AI tools in life sciences innovation. These largely fall into the domains outlined above and include challenges related to data, models, organizations, and the TREE issues: *transparency, reproducibility, ethics, and effectiveness*. Use of an approach focused on patient benefit is necessary but not sufficient to overcome these and other critical hurdles.

The future of AI in life sciences innovation holds immense promise, offering opportunities to transform healthcare globally. By focusing on patient benefit and ethical implementation, AI can be used to accelerate drug discovery, enhance diagnostic accuracy, and offer more personalized treatments to patients. Investment in high-quality, diverse datasets will be crucial for developing robust models. Interdisciplinary collaboration between biologists, clinicians, and data scientists is the engine that will drive patient-centric innovation. AI-enabled advances can help to bridge healthcare disparities, particularly in LMICs, by enabling scalable, cost-effective innovation. The TREE issues (transparency, reproducibility, ethics, and effectiveness) are critical guideposts for those using AI tools from bench to bedside and beyond.

References

Adedinsewo, D. A., Morales-Lara, A. C., Afolabi, B. B., Kushimo, O. A., Mbakwem, A. C., Ibiyemi, K. F., Ogunmodede, J. A., Raji, H. O., Ringim, S. H., Habib, A. A., Hamza, S. M., Ogah, O. S., Obajimi, G., Saanu, O. O., Jagun, O. E., Inofomoh, F. O., Adeolu, T., Karaye, K. M., Gaya, S. A., ... SPEC-AI Nigeria Investigators. (2024). Artificial intelligence guided screening for cardiomyopathies in an obstetric population: A pragmatic randomized clinical trial. *Nature Medicine*, *30*(10), 2897–2906. https://doi.org/10.1038/s41591-024-03243-9

Akingbola, A., Adegbesan, A., Ojo, O., Otumara, J. U., & Alao, U. H. (2024). Artificial intelligence and cancer care in Africa. *Journal of Medicine, Surgery, and Public Health, 3*, 100132. https://doi.org/10.1016/j.glmedi.2024.100132

Askr, H., Elgeldawi, E., Aboul Ella, H., Elshaier, Y. A. M. M., Gomaa, M. M., & Hassanien, A. E. (2023). Deep learning in drug discovery: An integrative review and future challenges. *Artificial Intelligence Review, 56*(7), 5975–6037. https://doi.org/10.1007/s10462-022-10306-1

Blanco-González, A., Cabezón, A., Seco-González, A., Conde-Torres, D., Antelo-Riveiro, P., Piñeiro, Á., & Garcia-Fandino, R. (2023). The role of AI in drug discovery: Challenges, opportunities, and strategies. *Pharmaceuticals, 16*(6), Article 6. https://doi.org/10.3390/ph16060891

Chaccour, C., Sánchez-Olivieri, I., Siegel, S., Megson, G., Winthrop, K. L., Botella, J. B., de-Torres, J. P., Jover, L., Brew, J., Kafentzis, G., Galvosas, M., Rudd, M., & Small, P. (2025). Validation and accuracy of the Hyfe cough monitoring system: A multicenter clinical study. *Scientific Reports, 15*, 880. https://doi.org/10.1038/s41598-025-85341-3

Dauparas, J., Anishchenko, I., Bennett, N., Bai, H., Ragotte, R. J., Milles, L. F., Wicky, B. I. M., Courbet, A., de Haas, R. J., Bethel, N., Leung, P. J. Y., Huddy, T. F., Pellock, S., Tischer, D., Chan, F., Koepnick, B., Nguyen, H., Kang, A., Sankaran, B., … Baker, D. (2022). Robust deep learning–based protein sequence design using ProteinMPNN. *Science, 378*(6615), 49–56. https://doi.org/10.1126/science.add2187

Jumper, J., Evans, R., Pritzel, A., Green, T., Figurnov, M., Ronneberger, O., Tunyasuvunakool, K., Bates, R., Žídek, A., Potapenko, A., Bridgland, A., Meyer, C., Kohl, S. A. A., Ballard, A. J., Cowie, A., Romera-Paredes, B., Nikolov, S., Jain, R., Adler, J., … Hassabis, D. (2021). Highly accurate protein structure prediction with AlphaFold. *Nature, 596*(7873), 583–589. https://doi.org/10.1038/s41586-021-03819-2

Kaplan, A. G. (2019). Chronic cough in adults: Make the diagnosis and make a difference. *Pulmonary Therapy, 5*(1), 11–21. https://doi.org/10.1007/s41030-019-0089-7

Karaye, K. M., Ishaq, N. A., Sa'idu, H., Balarabe, S. A., Talle, M. A., Isa, M. S., Adamu, U. G., Umar, H., Okolie, H. I., Shehu, M. N., Mohammed, I. Y., Sanni, B., Ogah, O. S., Oboirien, I., Umuerri, E. M., Mankwe, A. C., Shidali, V. Y., Njoku, P., Dodiyi-Manuel, S., … Isezuo, S. A. (2020). Incidence, clinical characteristics, and risk factors of peripartum cardiomyopathy in Nigeria: Results from the PEACE registry. *ESC Heart Failure, 7*(1), 235–243. https://doi.org/10.1002/ehf2.12562

Karaye, K. M., Sa'idu, H., Balarabe, S. A., Ishaq, N. A., Adamu, U. G., Mohammed, I. Y., Oboirien, I., Umuerri, E. M., Mankwe, A. C., Shidali, V. Y., Njoku, P., Dodiyi-Manuel, S., Olunuga, T., Josephs, V., Mbakwem, A. C., Okolie, H., Talle, M. A., Isa, M. S., Ogah, O. S., & Stewart, S. (2020). Clinical features and outcomes of peripartum cardiomyopathy in Nigeria. *Journal of the American College of Cardiology, 76*(20), 2352–2364. https://doi.org/10.1016/j.jacc.2020.09.540

Makarov, V. A., Stouch, T., Allgood, B., Willis, C. D., & Lynch, N. (2021). Best practices for artificial intelligence in life sciences research. *Drug Discovery Today, 26*(5), 1107–1110. https://doi.org/10.1016/j.drudis.2021.01.017

Olawade, D. B., Teke, J., Fapohunda, O., Weerasinghe, K., Usman, S. O., Ige, A. O., & Clement David-Olawade, A. (2024). Leveraging artificial intelligence in vaccine development: A narrative review. *Journal of Microbiological Methods, 224*, 106998. https://doi.org/10.1016/j.mimet.2024.106998

Patel, V., & Shah, M. (2022). Artificial intelligence and machine learning in drug discovery and development. *Intelligent Medicine, 2*(3), 134–140. https://doi.org/10.1016/j.imed.2021.10.001

Réda, C., Kaufmann, E., & Delahaye-Duriez, A. (2020). Machine learning applications in drug development. *Computational and Structural Biotechnology Journal, 18*, 241–252. https://doi.org/10.1016/j.csbj.2019.12.006

Rumelt, R. (2011). *Good Strategy Bad Strategy: The difference and why it matters*. Crown Business.

Schaufelberger, M. (2019). Cardiomyopathy and pregnancy. *Heart, 105*(20), 1543–1551. https://doi.org/10.1136/heartjnl-2018-313476

Sjödin, D., Parida, V., Palmié, M., & Wincent, J. (2021). How AI capabilities enable business model innovation: Scaling AI through co-evolutionary processes and feedback loops. *Journal of Business Research, 134*, 574–587. https://doi.org/10.1016/j.jbusres.2021.05.009

Srisuwananukorn, A., Krull ,Jordan E., Ma ,Qin, Zhang ,Ping, Pearson ,Alexander T., & and Hoffman, R. (2024). Applications of artificial intelligence to myeloproliferative neoplasms: A narrative review. *Expert Review of Hematology*, *17*(10), 669–677. https://doi.org/10.1080/17474086.2024.2389997

Srisuwananukorn, A., Loscocco, G. G., Kuykendall, A. T., Dolezal, J. M., Santi, R., Zhang, L., Singh, A. M., Guglielmelli, P., Vannucchi, A. M., Tremblay, D., Pearson, A. T., Salama, M. E., & Hoffman, R. (2023). Interpretable Artificial Intelligence (AI) Differentiates Prefibrotic Primary Myelofibrosis (pre-PMF) from Essential Thrombocythemia (ET): A Multi-Center Study of a New Clinical Decision Support Tool. *Blood*, *142*, 901. https://doi.org/10.1182/blood-2023-173877

Turon, G., Hlozek, J., Woodland, J. G., Kumar, A., Chibale, K., & Duran-Frigola, M. (2023). First fully-automated AI/ML virtual screening cascade implemented at a drug discovery centre in Africa. *Nature Communications*, *14*(1), 5736. https://doi.org/10.1038/s41467-023-41512-2

Vollmer, S., Mateen, B. A., Bohner, G., Király, F. J., Ghani, R., Jonsson, P., Cumbers, S., Jonas, A., McAllister, K. S. L., Myles, P., Grainger, D., Birse, M., Branson, R., Moons, K. G. M., Collins, G. S., Ioannidis, J. P. A., Holmes, C., & Hemingway, H. (2020). Machine learning and artificial intelligence research for patient benefit: 20 critical questions on transparency, replicability, ethics, and effectiveness. *BMJ*, *368*, l6927. https://doi.org/10.1136/bmj.l6927

Watson, J. L., Juergens, D., Bennett, N. R., Trippe, B. L., Yim, J., Eisenach, H. E., Ahern, W., Borst, A. J., Ragotte, R. J., Milles, L. F., Wicky, B. I. M., Hanikel, N., Pellock, S. J., Courbet, A., Sheffler, W., Wang, J., Venkatesh, P., Sappington, I., Torres, S. V., … Baker, D. (2023). De novo design of protein structure and function with RFdiffusion. *Nature*, *620*(7976), 1089–1100. https://doi.org/10.1038/s41586-023-06415-8

Yi, B., Wang, S., Xu, X., & Yu, L. (2024). Efficacy of behavioral cough suppression therapy for refractory chronic cough or unexplained chronic cough: A meta-analysis of randomized controlled trials. *Therapeutic Advances in Respiratory Disease*, *18*, 17534666241305952. https://doi.org/10.1177/17534666241305952

3 AI FOR SMARTER HEALTHCARE OPERATIONS

AI will not replace humans, but those who use AI will replace those who don't.

Ginni Rometty, Former CEO of IBM

DOI: 10.4324/9781003621294-12

Chapter 10

Artificial Intelligence-Driven Innovations in Healthcare Finance

Zahid Lalani, DDS, MBA, PhD and Sarah Lalani

10.1 Overview

The use of artificial intelligence (AI) in its various iterations and forms can be utilized in healthcare finance to improve efficiency and reduce administrative costs for healthcare organizations. This would allow for the allocation of resources to the mission and goal of most healthcare organizations, which is the delivery of healthcare. The success of AI-driven innovations in healthcare finance is predicated upon organizations having robust systems in place that provide an array of data to answer questions or improve processes and systems. The diversity of data from the organization and other sources, which may be regional, national, or international, are critical to obtaining AI-generated outcomes that take nuances and differences in populations into account. The role of AI is to help sort through a large swath of accurate data and provide analytics to humans, who can use critical thinking and the broad picture of the organization's goals and mission to improve processes and change systems to make them more efficient, allowing for better allocation of resources and strategic decisions that will improve the delivery of healthcare and outcomes for the population it serves. It is important to develop and build best practices for the use of AI in healthcare finance and establish ethical guardrails around its use. Constant updates to data driving AI-based recommendations to systems and processes, as well as regulatory compliance, are critical to ensure that the outcomes are valid and trusted. Quality and transparency of data being utilized, along with its storage, are also key components to ensure the success of AI-driven solutions in healthcare finance.

DOI: 10.4324/9781003621294-13

10.2 Introduction

Healthcare finance involves the processes and strategies for generating, allocating, and utilizing financial resources within a healthcare system. The importance of healthcare finance lies in utilizing its component pieces to optimize the allocation of resources with the goal of improving the quality and efficiency of healthcare delivery and allowing for equitable access to healthcare. The goal of healthcare finance for any organization is to effectively generate and manage funds and mitigate risks in order to achieve its mission and goals.

The components of healthcare finance may vary between organizations. However, common functions include:

1. Financial evaluation and planning,
2. Budgeting and forecasting,
3. Revenue cycle management and compliance,
4. Inventory and supply chain management,
5. Cash flow management,
6. Working capital management,
7. Investment decisions and recommendations,
8. Financing decisions,
9. Fraud detection,
10. Lease negotiations and contract management, and
11. Financial analytics specific to the organization.

Financial management in healthcare organizations is similar to that in organizations from different industries. However, there are a number of industry-specific nuances and challenges since the healthcare industry has to consistently prioritize patient safety and confidentiality while carrying out operations. Payment systems for healthcare vary in different countries, from single-payer systems to combinations of government, commercial, and self-payment for services provided (Jowett et al., 2020; WHO, 2021, 2022, 2023). Government mandates and guidelines for the delivery of care, personnel supply and demand, competition for personnel and between organizations in the same geographic area, electronic medical record systems – implementation and maintenance, the need for capital-intensive medical equipment, rapidly changing technology and its adaptation for healthcare delivery, and reimbursement rates are a few of the many factors that play a significant role in the financial management and success of healthcare organizations (Kutzin, 2013).

Healthcare organizations have been shifting focus from volume-based, specialty-focused care and fee-for-service care models to quality of care and outcomes-based metrics, though this varies widely across the world (Jowett et al., 2020; WHO, 2021, 2023). This shift has been prompted by three main forces:

1. A shift in governmental policy due to increasing healthcare spending as the population ages,
2. A changing attitude amongst patients for successful outcomes and evidence-based treatment recommendations, and
3. A change in reimbursement rates due to the aforementioned shifts in the government and patients' focus.

This trend will continue as policymakers, insurance companies, and patients gain increased access to data that shows them what to expect for disease processes, the evidence-based treatment recommendations for various ailments, and the probabilities for optimal outcomes (Bajwa et al., 2021; McIntyre & Kutzin, 2016; WHO, 2023). The dissemination and use of this information will be amplified with the increasing use of artificial intelligence (AI) in healthcare (Mrazek & O'Neill, 2020; Panesar & Panesar, 2021; Pujari et al., 2023; WHO, 2022).

Managed care models, Accountable Care Organizations, and global coverage for repeat admissions and complications occurring within a specified period for medical procedures in the US have shifted financial risk to healthcare organizations and physicians. These changes in the post-COVID era, where input costs for healthcare staff, equipment, and supplies have risen substantially, have put significant pressure on the operating margins of healthcare organizations. This has led to an increasing reliance on healthcare accounting and finance teams to help organizations navigate this changing landscape competitively and strategically.

10.3 AI Technologies and Their Applications

Artificial intelligence encompasses various technologies (Gaffari et al., 2024), each with unique applications in healthcare finance:

1. **Machine Learning (ML)**: ML algorithms can analyze vast datasets to identify patterns and predict outcomes. In healthcare finance, ML can forecast patient admission rates, optimize staffing levels, and predict financial performance. For example, ML can analyze historical patient data to predict future admission rates, allowing hospitals to allocate resources more effectively.
2. **Deep Learning**: Deep learning models, such as neural networks, can process complex data like medical images and electronic health records. These models can enhance fraud detection by identifying anomalies in billing patterns. For instance, deep learning can detect unusual billing patterns that may indicate fraudulent activity, helping healthcare organizations save millions in potential losses.
3. **Natural Language Processing (NLP)**: NLP can automate the extraction of relevant information from clinical notes and patient records, improving coding accuracy and speeding up the billing process. NLP can also be used to analyze patient feedback and identify areas for improvement in health care services.
4. **Artificial Neural Networks (ANNs)**: ANNs can be used for predictive analytics, helping healthcare organizations anticipate financial trends and make informed investment decisions. For example, ANNs can predict the financial impact of new healthcare policies or changes in reimbursement rates.
5. **Convolutional Neural Networks (CNNs)**: CNNs are particularly useful in analyzing medical images for diagnostic purposes, which can indirectly impact healthcare finance by improving patient outcomes and reducing unnecessary tests. For instance, CNNs can help radiologists identify early signs of diseases, leading to timely interventions and cost savings.

10.4 Strategy and Vision for AI in Healthcare Finance

AI-based improvements to current systems controlled by humans should be based on the following primary question:

Which tasks and processes can be easily automated, do not require human creativity, and can be completed more effectively by a machine that has copious data at its fingertips for decision-making?

To have these tasks and processes carried out by AI, relevant and nuanced data has to be available and mined. There are a number of iterations and foundational bases of AI – machine learning, deep learning, natural language processing, artificial neural networks, convolutional neural networks, genetic algorithms, and many more (Gibson, 2024). Each of these uses of AI has specific roles and advantages based on the process one wants them to address (Gaffari et al., 2024; Ho et al., 2020; Nilsson, 2021; OECD, 2022; WHO, 2022).

In the realm of healthcare finance, one can state that the goal of AI would be to improve access to healthcare and optimize the allocation of resources (Mathauer & Oranje, 2024; WHO, 2021, 2022, 2023). Resources should be allocated in a way that improves the quality and efficiency of healthcare delivery and achieves the mission and goals of the organization. This can be done in many ways.

1. *Evaluation of the population being served*:
   Data is needed on the demographics, healthcare needs, socio-economic stratification, key insurance providers, typical reimbursement rates for various diagnosis-related groups (DRGs) and procedural codes. This data is important to have and analyze to come up with a plan for what service lines are needed, staffing needs, revenue forecasting and budgeting, and capital expenditure needs. This data would need to be constantly updated and input into the system such that it is available for analysis using AI. The common ailments afflicting different populations, with variations attributed to geography, socio-economic status, diet, cultural beliefs, genetic traits, living in areas with access to ingredients for preparing food versus food deserts, habits like smoking, alcohol, tobacco use, and substance abuse, environmental pollution, and exercise versus a sedentary lifestyle can also be effectively analyzed by AI based on existing data from government, healthcare insurance carriers, pharmaceutical companies, and publications to evaluate the medical and healthcare needs of the population. AI can be further used to analyze both data sets described above and look at the competition in the area, the volume of patients that form the pool for each service line, and the input costs to help the leadership team make decisions regarding resource allocations for their organizations.
2. *Revenue cycle management*:
   a) What is the average census for various service lines? This data can then be used to compare the organizational data to local, regional, and national metrics, and AI can be used to analyze this to understand if there are areas of concern, areas where there are opportunities to improve and enhance efficiencies, or enact changes in processes or innovate to improve outcome measures.
   b) What is the average time from delivery of service to receiving reimbursement? The answer to this question is critical and can show if there are issues with coding and billing for services provided, the reasons for delays in submitting claims, if any, the ratio of clean claims to those returned due to errors, types of claim errors, and the time lapse from submission of clean claims to receipt of reimbursement from commercial carriers and government agencies like Medicare and Medicaid. The data obtained from asking these questions and evaluating the answers utilizing AI can identify areas where problems are occurring in the workflow and processes. AI can subsequently be utilized to

change or design processes to remove the barriers to effective and efficient submission of clean claims and shorten the time for reimbursement.

c) What are the cost of the service and the amount of reimbursement for it? The answer to this question gives the team the reimbursement percentage to billed charges (i.e., collected revenue) for Medicare, Medicaid, and different commercial carriers. This is critical data for negotiation with commercial carriers and also with Medicaid based on the service lines, patient population, and the number of organizations and providers in the geographic area available to provide the service. These are tasks that can be easily done by AI and repeated on a scheduled basis – every quarter, semi-annual, or annual. This information can then be utilized by the leadership team to negotiate rates with various organizations.
d) What is the denial rate for claims? AI can sift through the denials and analyze the trends and reasons given in the denial letter using machine learning. This can then lead to an understanding of the criteria for approval for specific services and reduce the time and revenue lost when claims are denied, as well as the negative aspects of informing patients that their service claim was denied and they might be liable for the billed amount.
e) What is the average time for appealing denials and receiving reimbursement? The answer to this question, which can be easily analyzed using AI, shows the efficiency of the processes in place in the organization. The value of improving the processes and making them more efficient using AI has tremendous value in cash flow management for the organization and the time and money saved in terms of human hours spent by preventing denials. Generative AI can also write appeal letters for denied claims using past data and rationale for successful appeals.
f) Generative and machine learning AI technology can generate letters of predetermination for services that are needed based on clinical notes and standardized templates.

The data for all these questions is already available to the organization. AI can look at the data relating to each individual question and then combine it and look at trends and analytics to better derive a composite picture for the organization. This picture can then be utilized to make changes to service lines, operations, coding and billing, and staffing to improve efficiency across the organization. Once the systems are designed and fine-tuned to look at the data and analytics described above, the process could potentially be automated to a large extent using AI to minimize human errors and make the system more efficient and cost-effective, such that more resources can be spent on delivering healthcare rather than administering it.

3. *Budgeting and forecasting*:
   a) What percentage of the local population is likely to receive care at the organization, and the daily, weekly, and monthly census figures for those patients across different service lines? What are the organization's staffing needs based on this patient census data? Patient safety and delivery of care are dependent upon appropriate and adequate staffing. Staffing is also one of the largest cost centers for an organization. Analyzing patient census data that may have seasonal trends for various service lines for an organization is very important to develop an appropriate level of staffing at different times of the week, month, and year.
   b) Is there an adequate supply of individuals who have the training and credentials to perform those functions in the community, and what are the supply and demand characteristics for staffing? Human capital is critical to any organization, and even more so for healthcare organizations where attrition after the COVID-19 pandemic has been

significant. A significant number of healthcare organizations competing with each other and vying for a finite group of individuals also creates uncertainty with regard to staffing that forms the backbone of delivering care to patients. Analyzing staffing needs across various service lines and the competition for that group of individuals is a key factor in strategy development for healthcare organizations. Information gleaned from these kinds of analytics that can be done by AI using available data would allow organizations to develop local programs to increase the pool of available talent to satisfy the healthcare staffing needs of the community.

c) What is the cost of inventory? Inventory forms another large cost center for healthcare organizations. Having an adequate inventory of the vast number of supplies required for patient care in a healthcare organization, tracking its use, billing for its use, replenishing it in a timely manner, keeping abreast of cost changes, and minimizing its expiration can have a significant impact on the overall cost.

d) Is the supply chain such that there are multiple vendors for the products being purchased? Sourcing inventory and supplies needed by healthcare organizations from multiple vendors, analyzing the trends, and communicating with them on a regular basis is key to ensuring that supply chain issues do not affect the delivery of healthcare. Having AI look at multiple sources for inventory and supplies with price comparisons and locations of suppliers is a valuable tool to have to spread the risk and negotiate the best prices for comparable products of high quality.

e) What are the competitive strategies and barriers to them for various service lines, and what is the capital expenditure needed for the organization in order to stay competitive? These questions need to be looked at, reviewed, and discussed by the leadership team of the healthcare organization. The data that AI can sift through, analyze, and report on, as discussed above, provides a strong and broad basis for the organization to develop and build a competitive strategy and allocate resources to different service lines via expansion, staffing, capital expenditure, and marketing. AI can then follow up on these decisions, and based on data going forward after the execution of their strategy, allow the organization to evaluate the success or failure of its strategies and guide changes to it as deemed necessary.

4. *Inventory and supply chain management*:

a) What are the inventory needs for medical devices, medical supplies, and medications for various service lines over different times of the year? AI-based technology can be used for inventory management. A number of vendors of medical supplies and devices now provide software programs that have details of the stock supplied, reference and lot numbers of these supplies, and embedded technology to bill the vendor when supplies are used by the organization, as well as a mechanism to inform the vendor to restock the supplies when the stock reaches a certain level. Most healthcare organizations have systems in place that track the patients for whom supplies are used, along with reference and lot numbers, and bill the patients or their insurance providers for the same when the patient is discharged or treatment is complete. An AI-generated system can merge both these functions such that ordering from vendors, assessing the cost after comparing similar quality supplies, making recommendations for cost per unit, assessing expiration dates of existing supplies, utilizing supplies so that no product has to be discarded due to expiration, assessing utilization of supplies every 30 days, issuing instructions for payment to vendors, ordering restocking of inventory based on seasonal trends and census, and billing patients for supplies used is performed without human intervention. AI systems can also be designed to check the work described above and ensure that there are no errors, waste, or fraud in inventory management and billing.

b) Are there multiple vendors who can supply the products needed? It is important for healthcare organizations to source supplies from multiple vendors who source their products both locally, nationally, and internationally as supply chain disruptions can cause severe problems if all products are sourced from one vendor. Utilizing AI to identify vendors with these and other specific and nuanced requirements while maintaining quality requirements and cost parity can be done more efficiently than using human resources.

c) Can price negotiations occur based on the volume of products used? Human powers of negotiation can be used to generate contracts based on volume pricing from different vendors. Statistical learning AI methods can then be used to create ideal volume ordering from different vendors to optimize discounts for the organization.

d) Is there an opportunity to consolidate supplies across service lines? This process can be easily solved by AI that can look at the ordering of supplies and inventory across various service lines utilizing the organization's data and then consolidating ordering and managing supplies based on utilization data across service lines while keeping the broad vendor selection, diversification, volume cost structure, payment system, and billing under the larger organization structure. AI can also be used to detect waste in different service lines, and it can also help plot a cost versus reimbursement analysis for each service line.

e) Are medications utilized based on evidence-based criteria? AI can help sift through peer-reviewed publications and help the organization develop best practices that are evidence-based for prescribing medications and appropriate dosages for various clinical applications. These can then be reviewed and evaluated by a panel of physicians and pharmacists at the organization, and formularies developed. Patient safety algorithms can also be embedded into the organization's electronic medical records utilizing AI with regard to medications and their interactions with each other.

f) What is the reimbursement rate for various products used in the organization by the major insurance providers in the region? Medical devices are an expensive line item for a healthcare organization. Knowledge regarding the reimbursement rates of the wide array of medical devices used in a healthcare organization and negotiating cost structures with vendors and payment methods based on utilization as compared to stocking inventory can be very important in revenue cycle management. Billing and receiving reimbursement for these devices as a separate item rather than being bundled in the procedural reimbursement is also a key component of negotiation with commercial health insurance carriers, Medicare and Medicaid.

g) What time period do vendors allow for payment? How does that compare to receiving reimbursement for services provided that include the use of medical devices, medical supplies, and medications for patient care? It is important to know what the revenue cycle and process from the utilization of supplies to billing and receiving reimbursement for the healthcare organization is for commercial health insurance carriers, Medicare and Medicaid; denial rates, time for appeals; and their resolution. All these factors can be analyzed by AI across different carriers to get an average time for reimbursement. This data can then be used by the healthcare organization to negotiate payment duration with vendors, which can typically range from 30 to 90 days.

5. *Financial analytics*:
   a) What is the average census for the organization for inpatient and outpatient visits, emergency department visits, operating room procedures, outpatient procedures, and ancillary services like radiology, laboratory services, and pharmacy? This data that can be collected by AI from the hospital database can be quickly analyzed, and seasonal and annual trends identified. These data points are critical to look at areas of opportunity, the need for expansion, and the costs associated with it, the competitive landscape in the local geographical environment, and resource allocation for capital expenditure and human capital.
   b) What is the average number of inpatient admission days for various services, cash on hand for operations, accounts receivable, accounts payable, and the number of days of inventory supplies for various services? These analytics change daily, and AI can gather the data and perform analytics done automatically on a daily basis to ensure smooth operations, examine changes in current and historical trends, and provide the operations and leadership team with a broad and dynamic overview of the healthcare organization, allowing them the flexibility to develop strategies for the future and create plans for contingencies and emergencies.

These questions seek to ascertain just a few of many metrics that may be relevant to a particular organization. All of the above metrics are based on past data, changing demographics of the community, and competition from other organizations in the community. Predictive analysis of this information is likely done more efficiently and effectively by AI (Ho et al., 2020; Mathauer & Oranje, 2024). Processes such as these are better evaluated by AI, as the trends and outliers will likely be better identified (Mathauer & Oranje, 2024). Natural language processing, for example, can be utilized for coding various aspects of hospital stays, treatments, and use of medical devices from operative and procedure notes and via the electronic medical record. Utilization of medications, supplies, medical devices, and other products in a facility can be tracked for charges, payment to vendors, and restocking based on bar code utilization across the facility. Utilization of staff based on staff versus patient census in different service lines at different times of the day, week, month, and year can be tracked, allowing for more efficient utilization of staffing and ultimately lower costs.

What AI likely cannot do better than humans is deciding what the competitive advantages of purchasing certain capital-intensive equipment are, what marketing efforts should focus on, what financial and investment decisions are best suited for the organization, lease negotiations and contract management, and payment incentives for staff and physicians for retention purposes. AI learns from past data and looks at emerging trends to predict what would be best for the future. However, shocks to the system may stump AI, thus necessitating human intervention in those situations. AI and human interventions in healthcare finance can be synergistic to make the system more efficient and productive, thereby improving the chances of success for the organization in achieving its mission and goals.

10.5 Synopsis of Utilization of AI in Healthcare Finance Based on Our Discussion

Predictive Analytics in Revenue Cycle Management: AI can streamline revenue cycle management by automating tasks such as eligibility verification, patient intake, and prior authorization. AI systems can instantly verify insurance coverage, reducing the waiting time for both patients and providers (Nilsson, 2021; Panesar & Panesar, 2021; WHO, 2023). Automated billing systems can process claims faster and more accurately, reducing errors and speeding up reimbursement.

Predictive Analytics for Financial Planning: AI can forecast financial trends, helping healthcare organizations plan budgets and allocate resources more effectively (Grover et al., 2019; Ho et al., 2020; WHO, 2021, 2022). For instance, predictive models can anticipate seasonal variations in inpatient admissions and adjust staffing levels accordingly. Healthcare organizations can use AI to improve financial planning and decision-making (Jödicke et al., 2019).

Fraud Detection: AI can enhance fraud detection by analyzing billing patterns and identifying anomalies (Hassan & Abraham, 2013; Ortega et al., 2006; Sowah et al., 2019). AI systems can detect unusual billing activities and flag suspicious transactions, helping healthcare organizations prevent fraud and reduce financial losses (Hassan & Abraham, 2013; Ortega et al., 2006; Sowah et al., 2019).

Resource Allocation: AI can optimize resource allocation by analyzing demographic data, healthcare needs, and socio-economic factors. For example, AI can identify areas with high rates of chronic diseases and recommend targeted interventions, ensuring resources are allocated where they are needed most. AI can also analyze patient data to predict future healthcare needs and allocate resources accordingly (WHO, 2021, 2022, 2023).

Budgeting and Forecasting: AI can enhance budgeting and forecasting by analyzing historical data and predicting future trends (Mathauer & Oranje, 2024). For example, AI can forecast patient admission rates, staffing needs, and revenue, helping healthcare organizations plan budgets more effectively. AI can also identify seasonal trends and adjust staffing levels accordingly, ensuring optimal resource allocation.

Inventory and Supply Chain Management: AI can improve inventory and supply chain management by analyzing usage patterns and predicting future needs. AI systems can track inventory levels, order supplies automatically, and negotiate prices with vendors. AI can also identify potential supply chain disruptions and recommend alternative suppliers, ensuring continuous availability of essential supplies (Bajwa et al., 2021; Jödicke et al., 2019). Healthcare organizations can use AI to ensure continuous availability of essential supplies.

Financial Analytics: AI can enhance financial analytics by analyzing large datasets and identifying trends and patterns (Mathauer & Oranje, 2024; Thesmar et al., 2019). AI systems can track key financial metrics such as revenue, expenses, and cash flow, providing real-time insights into financial performance. AI can also predict future financial trends and recommend strategies to improve financial health.

Automated Billing: AI-powered billing systems can automate data entry, reducing errors and speeding up the reimbursement process. This leads to faster claim approvals and improved cash flow. Healthcare organizations can use AI to streamline billing processes and reduce administrative burdens (Hassan & Abraham 2013; Ho et al., 2020; Pague & Alcantara, 2021; Pujari et al., 2023; Sowah et al., 2019; Thesmar et al., 2019; WHO, 2023).

10.6 Best Practices in Utilization of AI in Healthcare Finance

Best practices need to be developed, tested, and established for the use of AI in healthcare finance (Ho et al., 2020; Mathauer & Oranje, 2024; Panch et al., 2019; Pujari et al., 2023; Steinzor, 2024). Some of the areas that need to be considered while developing the best practices in this area include:

1. Develop and use datasets that include a diverse group of the population that will be served, as each will have nuances to them that are unique.
2. Conduct an ongoing audit of the dataset and update it so that there is a dynamic process from which AI can learn as its utilization creates an impact.
3. Identify specific problems in healthcare finance where the utilization of AI has the potential to improve processes that can then be measured.
4. Prioritize areas where AI has the potential to deliver measurable maximum impact in improving processes and analytics.
5. Set realistic expectations with regard to what AI can deliver for the organization.
6. Engage key stakeholders who will be involved in the process of developing and updating the data sets that AI will use at the outset.
7. Provide education, support, and training to help the stakeholders understand the potential for the use of AI in the organization.
8. Create a framework in which the role of AI is to augment processes and workflow to augment human capabilities and educate the stakeholders in the organization on this core concept.
9. Establish clear ethical guidelines that include fairness, transparency, and accountability that AI must use in every decision node.
10. Choose AI models that provide insight and explain the processes through which they arrive at their decisions.
11. Continuous monitoring of the solutions offered by AI is critical to identify areas where improvements can be made and input adjustments may be warranted.
12. Evaluation and validation should be carried out continuously to ensure that the AI models and tools address the questions or processes that they were intended to solve in an accurate, measurable manner.
13. Establish a post-hoc surveillance mechanism to monitor potential adverse outcomes or events after AI solutions are deployed.

The use of AI in healthcare finance needs to be balanced with patient data privacy and with a moral obligation to look at the big picture of what the mission and goals of the organization are and the needs of the population it serves. Allowing AI to make recommendations on its own may lead to decisions being made solely on a financial or mathematical basis (Mathauer & Oranje, 2024). The input from a human perspective on the role of healthcare to serve a population and community is critical.

10.7 Challenges of Utilizing AI in Healthcare Finance

1. Data Privacy: Ensuring patient data is protected is paramount. AI systems must comply with regulations like GDPR and HIPAA to safeguard sensitive information. Healthcare organizations must implement robust data security measures to prevent unauthorized access and data breaches (AIDA, 2023; Möllmann et al., 2021; OECD, 2022; Pujari et al., 2023; WHO, 2021, 2023).
2. Bias, Fairness and Ethics: AI systems must be designed to make fair and unbiased decisions (Ho et al., 2020; Panch et al., 2019; UNESCO, 2021). Consequently, AI models must be trained on diverse datasets to avoid biases that could lead to unfair treatment or financial decisions. Healthcare organizations should regularly audit AI systems to ensure they

are making fair and unbiased decisions and implement ethical guidelines to govern AI use across the enterprise.

3. Transparency: Healthcare organizations should be transparent about how AI systems make decisions, allowing stakeholders to understand and trust the technology. Organizations should provide clear explanations of AI algorithms and decision-making processes (Ho et al., 2020; Oala et al., 2021).
4. Data Collection: Collecting high-quality, relevant data is the first step. This includes patient records, billing information, and demographic data. Healthcare organizations should implement standardized data collection processes to ensure data accuracy and consistency (Ho et al., 2020; Oala et al., 2021; Panch et al., 2019).
5. Data Quality: AI systems rely on high-quality data. Inaccurate or incomplete data can lead to incorrect predictions and decisions. Healthcare organizations must implement robust data collection and validation processes to ensure data quality (Ho et al., 2020; Oala et al., 2021; Panch et al., 2019).
6. Data Analysis: AI tools can analyze data to identify trends, predict outcomes, and optimize processes. Regular audits and updates ensure the data remains accurate and useful (Ho et al., 2020; Oala et al., 2021; Panch et al., 2019). Healthcare organizations should implement data governance frameworks to manage data effectively.
7. Data Storage: Secure storage solutions, such as cloud-based systems, ensure data is accessible and protected (AIDA, 2023; WHO, 2023; Mathauer & Oranje, 2024; Möllmann et al., 2021; Pujari et al., 2023). Healthcare organizations should use encryption and access controls to safeguard data.
8. Integration: Integrating AI into existing systems can be complex and costly. Healthcare organizations must invest in infrastructure and training to ensure successful implementation. Organizations should develop integration strategies to minimize disruptions and maximize benefits.
9. Regulatory Compliance: Navigating regulations like GDPR and HIPAA can be challenging. AI systems must be designed to comply with these regulations to protect patient data (AIDA, 2023; WHO, 2023; Mathauer & Oranje, 2024; Möllmann et al., 2021; Pujari et al., 2023). Healthcare organizations should implement compliance frameworks to ensure regulatory adherence.

The success of AI depends on constantly inputting and updating data, since the machine's success is based on looking at past trends. The need for data to be updated is critical to the ability of AI to morph its recommendations. The input of new data can also be outsourced to machines, but human checks and balances must be put in place to ensure that the data and assumptions are correct. Errors in data input will lead to errors in recommendations given by AI. Ultimately, AI can have a significant impact in automating and linking a number of inputs from a healthcare organization in order to improve the delivery and quality of care while reducing resulting costs.

10.8 Future Opportunities Utilizing AI in Healthcare Finance

1. **Predictive Analytics**: AI can enhance predictive analytics, allowing healthcare organizations to forecast financial trends and make informed decisions. For example, AI can predict patient admission rates, helping hospitals optimize staffing and resource allocation.

Predictive analytics can also help organizations anticipate changes in reimbursement rates and adjust financial strategies accordingly.

2. **Personalized Medicine**: AI can support personalized medicine by analyzing patient data to recommend tailored treatments. This can improve patient outcomes and reduce healthcare costs. Healthcare organizations can use AI to develop personalized treatment plans and improve patient care.
3. **Blockchain Technology**: Blockchain can enhance data security and transparency in healthcare finance. By providing a secure, decentralized ledger, blockchain can prevent fraud and ensure accurate record-keeping. Healthcare organizations can use blockchain to improve data integrity and trust.
4. **Telemedicine**: AI can support telemedicine by analyzing patient data and providing real-time recommendations. This can improve access to care and reduce costs associated with in-person visits. Healthcare organizations can use AI to enhance telemedicine services and improve patient outcomes.
5. **AI-Driven Decision Support**: AI can provide decision support by analyzing data and recommending strategies. Healthcare organizations can use AI to improve financial planning, resource allocation, and operational efficiency. AI-driven decision support can help organizations navigate complex financial landscapes and achieve their goals.
6. **Automated Financial Reporting**: AI can automate financial reporting, reducing errors and improving accuracy. Healthcare organizations can use AI to generate real-time financial reports and gain insights into financial performance. Automated reporting can enhance decision-making and improve financial transparency.

10.9 Conclusion

The use of AI models to solve problems, improve processes, and increase efficiency in healthcare finance is significant. Automation of many processes can augment and improve decision-making processes for humans in healthcare organizations. The cost savings that can accrue using AI models in healthcare finance can be allocated to areas that are critical to the mission of all healthcare organizations – delivery of high-quality healthcare to the populations they serve.

Developing accurate data sets and updating them on a continuous and dynamic basis is key to the successful utilization of AI. Having ethical frameworks in place and developing, implementing, evaluating, and modifying best practices as necessary for the utilization of AI in healthcare finance are also essential to its success.

References

Bajwa, J., Munir, U., Nori, A., & Williams, B. (2021, July). Artificial intelligence in healthcare: Transforming the practice of medicine. Future Healthcare Journal, 8(2), e188–e194. https://doi.org/10.7861/fhj.2021-0095

Gaffari, M., Zhu, Y., & Shrestha, A. (2024). A review of advancements of artificial intelligence in dentistry. Dentistry Review, 4, 1–13. https://doi.org/10.1016/j.dentre.2024.100081

Gibson, K. (2024). Building an AI business strategy: A beginner's guide. HBS Online Business Insights.

Government of Canada. (2023). The Artificial Intelligence and Data Act (AIDA) – Companion document. Government of Canada. Retrieved May 24, 2023, from https://ised-isde.canada.ca/site/innovation-better-canada/en/ artificial-intelligence-and-data-act-aida-companion-document

Grover, D., Bauhoff, S., & Friedman, J. (2019, January 29). Using supervised learning to select audit targets in performance-based financing in health: An example from Zambia. PLoS ONE, 14(1), e0211262. http://dx.doi.org/10.1371/journal.pone.0211262

Hassan, A. K. I., & Abraham, A. (2013). Computational intelligence models for insurance fraud detection: A review of a decade of research. Journal of Network and Computer Applications, 1, 341–347. Retrieved October 16, 2023, from https:// isda04.softcomputing .net/jnic3.pdf

Ho, C. W. L., Ali, J., & Caals, K. (2020, April 1). Ensuring trustworthy use of artificial intelligence and big data analytics in health insurance. Bulletin of the World Health Organization, 98(4), 263–269. http://dx.doi.org/10.2471/BLT.19.234732

Jödicke, A. M., Zellweger, U., Tomka, I. T., Neuer, T., Curkovic, I., Roos, M., et al. (2019, December 11). Prediction of health care expenditure increase: How does pharmacotherapy contribute? BMC Health Services Research, 19, 953. http://dx.doi.org/10.1186/s12913-019-4616-x

Jowett, M., Kutzin, J., Kwon, S., Hsu, J., Sallaku, J., & Solano, J. G. (2020). Assessing country health financing systems: The health financing progress matrix. World Health Organization. Retrieved October 13, 2023, from https:// iris.who.int/bitstream/handle/10665/337938/9789240017405-eng .pdf

Kutzin, J. (2013, August 1). Health financing for universal coverage and health system performance: Concepts and implications for policy. Bulletin of the World Health Organization, 91(8), 602–611. http://dx.doi.org/10.2471/BLT.12.113985

Mathauer, I., & Oranje, M. (2024). Machine learning in health financing: Benefits, risks and regulatory needs. Bulletin of the World Health Organization, 102(3), 216–224. https://doi.org/10.2471/BLT.23 .290333

McIntyre, D., & Kutzin, J. (2016). Health financing country diagnostic: A foundation for national strategy development. World Health Organization. Retrieved January 13, 2023, from https:// iris.who.int/ handle/ 10665/ 204283

Möllmann, N. R. J., Mirbabaie, M., & Stieglitz, S. (2021, October–December). Is it alright to use artificial intelligence in digital health? A systematic literature review on ethical considerations. Health Informatics Journal, 27(4). http://dx.doi.org/10.1177/14604582211052391

Mrazek, M., & O'Neill, F. (2020). Artificial intelligence and healthcare in emerging markets. The World Bank. Retrieved July 8, 2022, from https://openknowledge.worldbank.org/ handle/10986/34855

Nilsson, E. (2021). 4 strategies for AI-driven approach to improve revenue cycle. Healthcare Financial Management Association. https://www.hfma.org/revenue-cycle/4-strategies-for-ai-driven-approach -to-improve-revenue-cycle/

Oala, L., Murchison, A. G., Balachandran, P., Choudhary, S., Fehr, J., Leite, A. W., et al. (2021). Machine learning for health: Algorithm auditing & quality control. Journal of Medical Systems, 45(12), 105. http://dx.doi.org/10.1007/s10916-021-01783-y

Organization for Economic Co-operation and Development. (2022). Recommendation of the Council on Artificial Intelligence. OECD. Retrieved May 31, 2023, from https://legalinstruments.oecd.org/en/ instruments/OECD-LEGAL-0449

Ortega, P., Figueroa, C., & Ruz, G. (2006, June 26–29). A medical claim fraud/abuse detection system based on data mining: A case study in Chile. In Proceedings of the 2006 international conference on data mining. *ResearchGate GmbH.* Retrieved October 16, 2023, from https://www.researchgate .net/publication/220704891_A_Medical_Claim_FraudAbuse_Detection_System_based_on_Data _Mining_A_Case_Study_in_Chile

Pague, B., & Alcantara, A. C. (2021, July 12–15). Claims management using artificial intelligence: Experiences from PhilHealth in the Philippines. In 2021 World congress on health economics. International Health Economics Association. Retrieved December 4, 2023, from https://www.healtheconomics.org/wp-content/uploads/2022/ 07/ihea_2021_ - _full _program _boo .pdf

Panch, T., Mattie, H., & Atun, R. (2019, December). Artificial intelligence and algorithmic bias: Implications for health systems. Journal of Global Health, 9(2), 010318. http://dx.doi.org/10.7189/ jogh.09.020318

Panesar, A., & Panesar, H. (2021). Artificial intelligence and machine learning in global healthcare. In R. Haring, I. Kickbusch, D. Ganten, & M. Moeti (Eds.), Handbook of global health (pp. 1–39). Springer International Publishing. http://dx.doi.org/10.1007/978-1-4842-6537-6

Pujari, S., Reis, A., Zhao, Y., Alsalamah, S., Serhan, F., Reeder, J. C., et al. (2023, June 1). Artificial intelligence for global health: Cautious optimism with safeguards. Bulletin of the World Health Organization, 101(6), 364–364A. http:// dx.doi.org/10.2471/BLT.23.290215

Sowah, R. A., Kuuboore, M., Ofoli, A., Kwofie, S., Asiedu, L., Koumadi, K. M., et al. (2019). Decision support system (DSS) for fraud detection in health insurance claims using genetic support vector machines (GSVMs). Journal of Engineering, 2019, 1–19. http://dx.doi.org/10.1155/2019/1432597

Steinzor, P. (2024). Best practices for implementing AI into value-based care. American Journal of Managed Care.

Thesmar, D., Sraer, D., Pinheiro, L., Dadson, N., Veliche, R., & Greenberg, P. (2019, June). Combining the power of artificial intelligence with the richness of healthcare claims data: Opportunities and challenges. PharmacoEconomics, 37(6), 745–752. http://dx.doi.org/10.1007/s40273-019-00777-6

United Nations Educational, Scientific and Cultural Organization. (2021). Recommendation on the ethics of artificial intelligence. UNESCO. Retrieved October 13, 2023, from https://unesdoc.unesco.org/ark:/ 48223/pf0000381137

World Health Organization. (2021a). Digital technologies for health financing: What are the benefits and risks for UHC? Some initial reflections. WHO. Retrieved October 13, 2023, from https://iris.who.int /handle/10665/343505

World Health Organization. (2021b). Ethics and governance of artificial intelligence for health: WHO guidance. WHO. Retrieved January 13, 2023, from https://iris.who.int/handle/10665/341996

World Health Organization. (2021c). Global strategy on digital health 2020–2025. WHO. Retrieved May 22, 2023, from https://iris.who.int/handle/10665/344249

World Health Organization. (2022). The implications of artificial intelligence and machine learning in health financing for achieving universal health coverage: Findings from a rapid literature review. WHO. Retrieved October 13, 2023, from https://iris.who.int/handle/10665/365483

World Health Organization. (2023a). Assessing the effects of digital technologies on health financing and universal health coverage objectives: A guide with key questions. WHO. Retrieved October 13, 2023, from https://iris.who.int/handle/10665/372456

World Health Organization. (2023b). Regulatory considerations on artificial intelligence for health. WHO. Retrieved November 10, 2023, from https://iris.who.int/handle/10665/ 373421

World Health Organization. (2023c). The role of digital claims management for Estonia's health insurance: A leverage for making healthcare purchasing more strategic. WHO. Retrieved March 3, 2023, from https://iris.who.int/handle/10665/366053

Chapter 11

The Role of AI in Mitigating Healthcare Fraud

James R. Langabeer, PhD

11.1 Introduction

Healthcare fraud remains a significant issue globally, potentially draining billions from healthcare systems annually. According to the National Health Care Anti-Fraud Association (NHCAA), the financial losses due to healthcare fraud in the United States alone are estimated at over $68 billion annually (NHCAA, 2022). The U.S. Department of Justice estimates that fraud, waste, or abuse consumes up to 10% of all healthcare expenditures. There is no question that fraud occurs across organizations, payers, and vendors, but the bigger question is how to identify and prevent fraud before it happens. The more traditional detection methods, which rely on manual audits of small samples or outliers, lack the speed and adaptability to detect widespread, sophisticated fraud. Artificial intelligence (AI), with its ability to process massive datasets and uncover hidden patterns, is emerging as a powerful tool to address these limitations.

11.2 Fraud

The Association of Certified Fraud Examiners defines fraud as "any activity that relies on deception to achieve a gain" (ACFE, 2025). Fraud can manifest in various forms, including billing for services not performed (phantom billing), charging higher prices or additional services at rates higher than allowed (upcoding), and kickbacks. Traditional detection methods—largely reliant on manual audits—lack the speed and adaptability to detect sophisticated fraud. One bright spot for significantly improving the ability to act on fraud more quickly is artificial intelligence (AI). AI has a tremendous ability to process massive datasets and uncover hidden patterns and is emerging as a powerful tool to address these limitations.

It is helpful to understand why actors of all sorts commit fraudulent acts. Fraud is usually found where people have the *opportunity* to create some type of gain that they may not otherwise be able to capture legitimately. Often, these individuals are under some sort of *pressure*, financially

DOI: 10.4324/9781003621294-14

or otherwise, that causes them to look beyond reasonable and acceptable legal measures to achieve their goals. They can also justify or *rationalize* it to themselves in some distorted fashion (e.g., "that organization owed it to me for all the time I gave them as an employee"). These three factors comprise the occupational fraud triangle (Tickner & Button, 2021).

Who has the opportunity, pressure, and ability to rationalize deceptive practices in healthcare? Indeed, vendors might create invoices for items that weren't delivered. Some providers are also very susceptible to committing fraud. They could double-bill the patient and an insurance company for the same services or send multiple invoices for the same procedures. Or, they could bill for patients who aren't real or whom they haven't seen. Employees of hospitals or health systems could also commit fraud for various personal or organizational reasons. Fraud can also be committed at an individual or organizational level, both within and outside that organization. Fraud can come from anywhere.

11.3 Common Types of Healthcare Fraud

The most worrisome form of fraud is performed deliberately or intentionally. Accidental or friendly fraud is typically due to an employee's lack of training or awareness rather than malicious intent. The consequences can be just as significant; however, intentional fraud is more common.

In the healthcare industry, there are three major categories of potential fraud: 1) deception from medical providers, typically in the form of billing fraud; 2) internal deception within the organization; and 3) vendor or procurement fraud. The first category is medical fraud, which most people think of first. Billions of healthcare claims and invoices are paid each year. Keeping track of these is complex. Healthcare fraud includes fraudulent billing, falsifying records, and providing unnecessary services. Key types of fraud include:

- **Phantom Billing**: Charging for services not rendered.
- **Prescription fraud**: Prescriptions are either illegally written, acquired fraudulently, or they're misused. Forging scripts is one example, as well as the diversion of medical scripts for illicit purposes.
- **Double Billing**: Sending multiple invoices for procedures, goods, or services.
- **Upcoding or Overbilling**: Billing for more expensive services than those performed.
- **Unbundling**: Billing for services separately that should be billed together.
- **Inflated invoices**: An inflated invoice is one that exceeds the actual value of what a customer or patient received.
- **Kickbacks**: Financial incentives for patient referrals or service utilization.
- **Medical Identity Theft**: Using another person's credentials for treatment or claims.

Equally as consequential are those fraudulent activities performed by employees. These include asset misappropriation, such as theft of inventory or supplies, and payroll manipulation. Fictitious employees are sometimes created and paid, diverting those funds to the fraudster. Then there is vendor or procurement fraud, such as rigging procurement bids or creating fictitious organizations that bill for items they never provide. Fraud can come in many forms. For this chapter, we'll deal with billing fraud. Identifying and preventing these activities requires scalable, intelligent systems, something AI is well-suited to provide.

11.4 Payment Integrity

Payment integrity is the term used in medical billing to ensure the integrity and authenticity of payments made. Payment integrity helps to ensure the accuracy of bills and payments and prevents improper payments from being made (CMS, 2023). Various processes are contained within payment integrity, such as the review of coding practices, compliance with contracts, claims review and editing, and coordination of benefits between insurers. All of these are quite complex and involve multiple pieces of data, making it ideal for data mining and machine learning. Artificial intelligence supports payment integrity in a number of different ways we'll explore below.

11.5 Audit Techniques for Fraud Detection

Before you can address fraud, you must be able to detect it. Discovery is a challenge in healthcare, largely due to high volumes as well as a separation between the actual consumer and the payer in many cases. Traditionally, fraud has been kept low using robust internal controls, policies, and procedures that govern how an organization or individual will receive payment for goods and services. Training employees is also very useful, informing them of the risks of fraud and their role in preventing it. Creating an ethical culture also helps, as does letting employees know that they are being monitored and are always subject to review. These methods work well for internal fraud but do little to address fraud coming from outside the organization.

To focus on fraud more broadly, the use of internal or external audits is common. An audit is simply an inspection of the details of accounts, performed by professional, independent people outside the process. Typically, audits collect physical and electronic supporting documentation to match what was invoiced or billed. One way is to calculate financial ratios to look for outliers or abnormalities. Another way is to select a random sample, a percentage of claims or invoices, for detailed review to see if any unusual activity exists. Auditors can also conduct interviews to root out potential issues. A control assessment can also be used. This is the process of evaluating how effectively controls are implemented and functioning within an organization or information system, ensuring they are correctly applied, operating as expected, and meeting relevant security or privacy requirements. All of these traditional methods can be effective, but they are time-intensive and work better with small samples and populations. That is where AI comes in.

There are three main steps to managing fraud, as outlined in Figure 11.1.

Artificial intelligence can help with the first of these two steps: identifying and quantifying the risks and impact of fraud at a detailed level. The third step, mitigation, involves reducing the future risk and addressing the risks that were detected.

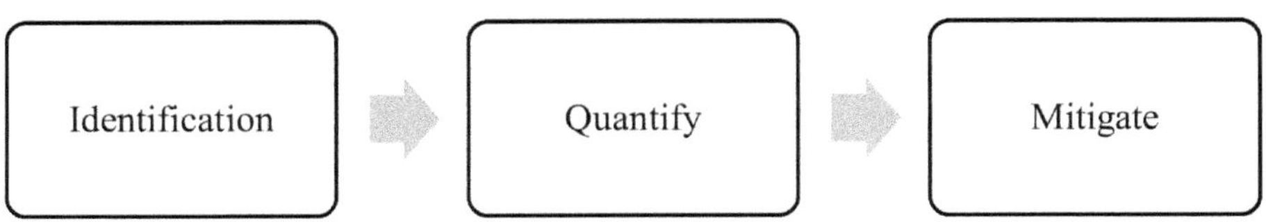

Figure 11.1 Managing healthcare fraud.

11.6 Artificial Intelligence Techniques

Artificial intelligence (AI) offers a range of techniques that are highly effective in identifying and combating healthcare fraud. One of the most promising approaches is machine learning (ML), which detects fraudulent activity by uncovering patterns in large datasets. Supervised ML models, such as decision trees and neural networks, learn from historical data labeled as "fraudulent" or "legitimate". In contrast, unsupervised methods like clustering and anomaly detection identify irregularities without predefined labels (Bauder et al., 2017).

Natural language processing (NLP) is another valuable AI tool that analyzes textual data, including clinical notes and diagnostic reports, to identify inconsistencies between reported and billed services. NLP uses the written text in billing, rather than the structured codes and numbers, to look for key terms that could be inconsistent with the billing information provided. This allows auditors to detect discrepancies often missed by traditional review methods (Chen et al., 2019).

Predictive analytics also plays a key role, using statistical models to assess the likelihood of fraud in claims data. These models prioritize investigations by ranking providers or claims based on risk scores (Kumar et al., 2020). Similarly, anomaly detection techniques flag behavior that significantly deviates from typical patterns, such as providers billing for an unusually high number of procedures compared to their peers (Omar et al., 2013).

11.7 Applications of AI in Healthcare Fraud Detection

For example, if we used a large dataset where each row of data represents a patient's billing information, our goal would be to predict whether a claim is fraudulent based on specific features. Those features or components would need to be based on the specific type of diagnosis, but let's assume we start with the basics as columns:

- Total charges
- Number of procedures
- Number of diagnoses
- Visit time or inpatient length of stay
- Patient age

Then, we could apply a machine learning model, such as a regression or decision tree, to classify fraudulent vs. non-fraudulent claims and visualize them. The analytical engine would determine which of these five factors influences a positive prediction score most, measured by a metric relevant to that model. A common one is called the area under the curve (AUC). AUC would measure how well your model classifies or discriminates between the data in binary categories, such as either fraud or non-fraud. How would we know? Well, we'd "feed" (or provide data for training purposes) the model with knowledge based on fraudulent and non-fraudulent data with these same factors. Once trained, the system could work on all data available, and the system could create principal factors that simplify the model and speed up processing by identifying a smaller set of factors responsible for at least 95% of the variance. We'd end up with a visual like this (Figure 11.2).

In this simplified visual example, each point on the graph shows a different billing case. The model simplified the analyses into two primary factors using principal component analysis. Then, the points are color-coded to differentiate between fraudulent (in white squares) and those not fraudulent (in black circles). The decision boundary between the two outcomes is shown using a

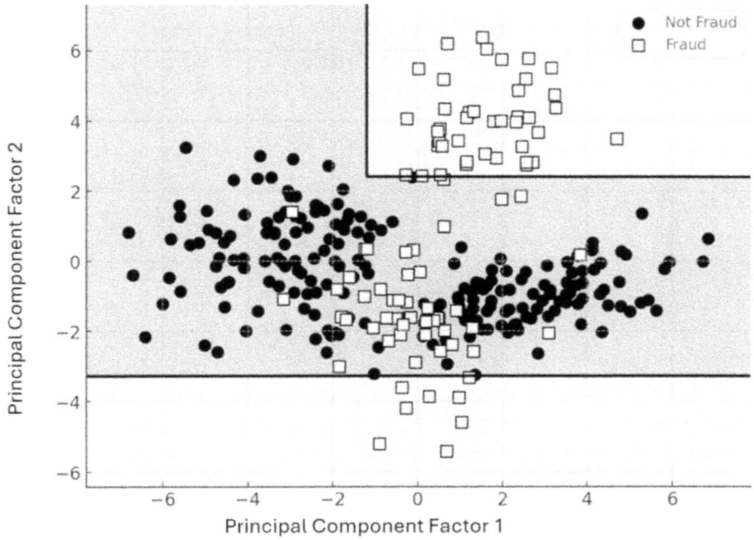

Figure 11.2 Machine learning model for fraud detection.

line, in this case from a decision tree model, but it could be from logistic regression or random forest models, which are both commonly used.

In real-life practice, large companies have integrated AI into various stages of fraud detection and prevention. In claims screening, AI systems evaluate incoming insurance claims in real-time, helping to assess fraud risk and prevent improper payments. For example, the largest health insurance companies analyze hundreds of millions of claims annually using AI, saving billions in potential losses. Provider profiling uses AI to monitor billing practices, identifying outliers through comparisons with industry benchmarks. Unusual patterns—like excessive use of costly procedures—are flagged for further scrutiny (Figueiredo et al., 2022). In retrospective audits, AI analyzes historical data to uncover long-standing fraud schemes or patterns that may have gone undetected. Machine learning also helps combat medical identity theft by detecting inconsistencies in patient histories, such as sudden changes in demographics or medical profiles, which could indicate misuse of patient identities (Sharma et al., 2018). Additionally, network analysis leverages graph-based algorithms to examine relationships between patients, providers, and services, exposing collusion or referral fraud rings (Sulaiman et al., 2021).

11.8 Building an AI Model

Creating an AI or machine learning model is a multi-step process that begins with gathering and preparing relevant data. This initial phase involves collecting raw information, checking for accuracy through data cleansing, and transforming it into a format suitable for analysis. Once the data is ready, the next step is to choose an appropriate algorithm based on the problem at hand—classification, regression, clustering, or another type of task.

After selecting the algorithm, it's essential to adjust and fine-tune its parameters through a process known as hyperparameter optimization. This ensures the model learns effectively and can generalize well to new data. Models that work only on limited data sets are of no practical value. Once the model has been trained, its performance must be rigorously evaluated using various

Figure 11.3 Steps in building an AI learning model.

metrics, such as error rates or R-squared measures, and validation techniques to ensure accuracy, reliability, and robustness.

After all this, a well-performing model is deployed into a production environment, where it can make real-time predictions and support data-driven decisions. By following this structured approach, we improve the model's predictive capabilities and create practical solutions that can address real-world challenges in payment integrity. Figure 11.3 presents the steps in building an AI learning model.

11.9 The Benefits of AI

AI dramatically increases efficiency by allowing for the analysis of millions of claims at a speed and scale impossible for human reviewers. Imagine where each claim or bill must be manually reviewed before payment for authenticity and legitimacy. That is still the case in many places, but systems have automated payments using simple checks. Advanced AI tools will help augment this and enable near real-time fraud detection and intervention (Bauder et al., 2017). It should also enhance accuracy by reducing false positives and false negatives, helping to ensure that resources are directed toward genuinely suspicious cases (Chen et al., 2019).

Financially, AI offers significant cost savings by identifying and preventing fraudulent claims before payments are made. Moreover, these systems continually improve through adaptive learning, updating their models based on new fraud tactics (Kumar et al., 2020). AI further supports decision-making by providing auditors and compliance officers with prioritized case lists and actionable insights (Figueiredo et al., 2022).

These are just some of the benefits of AI in fraud detection.

1. **Efficiency and Scale.** AI will enable the analysis of millions of claims rapidly, far beyond human capacity. It enables scalable real-time detection and intervention (Bauder et al., 2017).
2. **Improved Payment Integrity and Accuracy.** Machine learning systems will ensure payments to the right providers, that bills accurately reflect the services provided, and that

payments are consistent with the existing contracts. AI will also help reduce false positives and negatives, ensuring that investigations focus on genuinely suspicious activity.
3. **Cost Reduction.** By preventing fraudulent payments before they occur, AI can save payers and governments significant resources.
4. **Adaptive Learning.** AI systems improve over time. They are considered learning models that adapt with new data to better identify fraud tactics by adjusting detection criteria dynamically. Adaptive learning improves fraud detection since new schemes can be incorporated into the system, and new fraud patterns can be detected more rapidly.
5. **Decision Support.** AI can assist auditors and compliance officers by providing actionable insights, prioritizing high-risk cases, and offering supporting data (Figueiredo et al., 2022).

11.10 Challenges and Limitations

Despite its upside potential, AI in healthcare fraud detection faces several challenges. Although there are large amounts of data in healthcare (or "big data"), the data are often disparate, which makes learning models challenging. If the systems are not connected, you would have to create multiple models, which is complex. Poor data quality is also a significant hurdle. Healthcare information systems are known to have issues with completeness and accuracy. Finally, systems are often not integrated well, and many healthcare information systems still operate in silos, making it challenging to gather and standardize information (Bauder et al., 2017). Electronic health record systems (EHRs) might be suitable for a large portion of data, but they are often not the only data source. Laboratory information systems, revenue cycle tools, pharmacy, and radiology systems are usually all distinct systems that frequently don't communicate with each other and use different types of structured and unstructured data. Many AI models also struggle with interpretability, making it hard for auditors and regulators to understand the rationale behind certain flags (Rudin, 2019).

A bigger problem comes in the form of systematic bias. We have bias in training for any number of reasons, and these can lead to unfair outcomes, particularly if specific populations are underrepresented in historical fraud investigations (Obermeyer et al., 2019). Privacy is another key concern in all areas of medicine. Since healthcare data is highly sensitive and protected, AI tools must comply with regulations like HIPAA and GDPR (Sharma et al., 2018). Lastly, false positives still occur and require human investigation, potentially increasing operational burdens.

11.11 Ethical and Regulatory Considerations

This book has a separate chapter on the ethics surrounding artificial intelligence. However, regarding the ethical use of AI in fraud detection, some key concerns need to be addressed in the application of AI.

- **Transparency**: Ensuring AI decisions are interpretable, particularly in high-stakes areas like fraud detection.
- **Accountability**: Assigning responsibility for errors in fraud classification.
- **Informed Consent**: Clarifying how patient data is used in AI systems.
- **Compliance**: Aligning AI use with data protection laws such as the Health Insurance Portability and Accountability Act (HIPAA).

11.12 Outlook

The future of AI in healthcare fraud detection will be shaped by how well the models can be built and interpreted. Some of these AI models are very complex, and although analytical methods have been used, they are not easily understood or interpreted by users. To help rectify this, many people are talking about something referred to as Explainable AI, or XAI. XAI helps make decision-making transparent and understandable to consumers, users, regulators, and auditors. There will also have to be substantially improved interoperability. The future of AI in healthcare will primarily be built on:

1. Improved Interoperability: Initiatives like the Fast Healthcare Interoperability Resources (FHIR) can help integrate datasets and standardize healthcare data formats, making AI models more effective.
2. Blockchain Integration: Combining AI with blockchain (a record of transactions between computers) could create better record-keeping and transparent records that might deter fraud.
3. Collaborative Network and Ecosystems: We don't see enough evidence of all parties in the healthcare system working together. Payers, providers, and regulatory agencies need to do a much better job of collectively sharing data, AI tools, and insights to combat fraud.

11.13 Conclusion

As the healthcare industry continues to grow and scale, fraud management needs to keep up with the digitization of so many pieces of information. AI offers a scalable, efficient, and self-learning solution to the growing problem of healthcare fraud. By leveraging machine learning, NLP, and predictive analytics, healthcare organizations can detect and prevent fraud quickly and more accurately than ever. While challenges around bias, interpretability, and privacy persist, ongoing technological advancements and regulatory frameworks promise to refine AI's role in safeguarding healthcare systems. With the proper implementation and oversight, AI will undoubtedly play a central role in fraud detection and prevention in the future.

References

ACFE. (2025). *What is fraud?* https://www.acfe.com/fraud-resources/fraud-101-what-is-fraud

Bauder, R. A., Khoshgoftaar, T. M., & Seliya, N. (2017). A survey on the state of healthcare upcoding fraud analysis and detection. *Health Information Science and Systems*, *5*(1), 1–16.

Centers for Medicare and Medicaid Services (CMS). (2023). *Medicare and Medicaid Payment Integrity. Annual Report to Congress, 2021*. U.S. Department of Health and Human Services, Centers for Medicare and Medicaid Services.

Chen, J. H., Alagappan, M., Goldstein, M. K., Asch, S. M., & Altman, R. B. (2019). Decaying relevance of clinical data towards future decisions in data-driven inpatient clinical order sets. *International Journal of Medical Informatics*, *125*, 1–7.

Figueiredo, A., Costa, C., & Portugal, I. (2022). Healthcare fraud detection using supervised learning: A systematic literature review. *Journal of Biomedical Informatics*, *132*, 104122.

Kumar, A., Pareek, R., & Singh, P. (2020). AI-based fraud detection in healthcare: Trends and challenges. *Procedia Computer Science*, *173*, 415–422.

National Health Care Anti-Fraud Association (NHCAA). (2022). *The challenge of healthcare fraud*. https://www.nhcaa.org
Obermeyer, Z., Powers, B., Vogeli, C., & Mullainathan, S. (2019). Dissecting racial bias in an algorithm used to manage the health of populations. *Science*, *366*(6464), 447–453.
Omar, N., Ngadi, M. A., & Ahmad, R. B. (2013). Machine learning techniques for anomaly detection: An overview. *International Journal of Computer Applications*, *79*(2), 33–41.
Rudin, C. (2019). Stop explaining black box machine learning models for high-stakes decisions and use interpretable models instead. *Nature Machine Intelligence*, *1*(5), 206–215.
Sharma, D. C., Gupta, S., & Singh, A. (2018). Privacy and security issues in e-healthcare systems. *Procedia Computer Science*, *132*, 1033–1040.
Sulaiman, R., Basri, S., & Khalid, R. (2021). Application of graph analytics for fraud detection in healthcare claim data. *Journal of Big Data*, *8*(1), 1–21.
Tickner, P., & Button, M. (2021). Deconstructing the origins of Cressey's Fraud Triangle. *Journal of Financial Crime*, *28*(3), 722–731.

Chapter 12

AI and the Health Information Workforce

David T. Marc, PhD and Kerryn Butler-Henderson, PhD, FAIDH

12.1 Introduction

Artificial intelligence (AI) is transforming healthcare by automating tasks, improving decision-making, and enhancing operational efficiency. This technological evolution presents both challenges and opportunities for the health information workforce, a sector central to managing, safeguarding, and optimizing healthcare data. As AI technologies continue to advance, health information professionals must adapt by acquiring new competencies in data management, AI governance, and the ethical deployment of these technologies. This article explores the emerging impact of AI on the health information workforce, addressing critical areas of workforce development, training, and ethical considerations. It emphasizes the need for updated curricula, regulatory frameworks, and collaborative efforts between industry stakeholders to ensure a future-proof workforce capable of navigating the complexities of AI adoption. By embracing AI responsibly, the health information workforce can enhance healthcare delivery while safeguarding patient care, privacy, and overall data integrity.

12.2 Strategy and Vision for AI for the Health Information Workforce

In the rapidly evolving landscape of healthcare, technological advancements are fundamentally reshaping how care is delivered and managed. Among the most transformative innovations is artificial intelligence (AI), which holds the potential to revolutionize healthcare practices, from patient care to administrative functions. However, the integration of AI presents a unique challenge to the health information workforce, a group that has historically been at the forefront of driving digital transformation. As AI continues to reshape job roles and operational workflows, it is crucial for health information professionals to embrace the future, ensuring they possess the skills and knowledge to leverage AI's potential effectively and ethically.

DOI: 10.4324/9781003621294-15

AI is fundamentally altering job roles and the tasks performed within healthcare professions. The rapid evolution of AI applications has created a shift that requires healthcare professionals to adapt quickly, ensuring they remain at the forefront of industry standards and technological integration.

Healthcare professionals fulfill diverse roles within the sector, ranging from direct patient care to the management of systems that ensure accurate and secure data collection and utilization. AI is poised to impact all healthcare professionals, either directly through automation and decision support or indirectly by reshaping operational workflows. This disruption extends beyond simple efficiency gains, influencing decision-making processes, operational priorities, and the overall healthcare delivery model. At the heart of these changes lies the health information workforce, whose essential skills and competencies are continually evolving to meet new challenges.

Health information professionals refer to those responsible for the management, analysis, and security of health data within healthcare organizations. This workforce plays a critical role in ensuring that health information is accurate, accessible, secure, and used efficiently to improve patient care, support clinical decision-making, and ensure regulatory compliance. It includes a variety of roles, such as:

- **Health Information Technicians**: Manage medical records and ensure their accuracy and accessibility.
- **Health Informatics Specialists**: Apply data analysis techniques and information technology to improve healthcare processes and outcomes.
- **Health Data Analysts**: Analyze health data to generate insights for improving healthcare delivery, policy-making, and research.
- **Clinical Coders**: Assign standardized codes to medical diagnoses, treatments, and procedures for billing and regulatory purposes.
- **Chief Information Officers (CIOs)** and **Health IT Managers**: Oversee the implementation and management of health IT systems and infrastructure.

As healthcare increasingly relies on digital systems and artificial intelligence, the health information workforce is evolving to include skills in data analytics, cybersecurity, machine learning, and AI integration. These professionals are crucial in ensuring the safe, efficient, and ethical use of health information technology, and their skills are shifting to meet the evolving needs of the healthcare industry globally.

A historical example of how the health information workforce has adapted to technological shifts is the widespread adoption of Electronic Health Records (EHRs). In the face of this digital transformation, health information professionals played a key role in reengineering workflows and redefining data management principles to ensure the successful integration of EHR systems. AI, however, presents a challenge of even greater magnitude. It necessitates that the profession prepares healthcare settings for AI adoption while simultaneously adapting their own roles to accommodate this seismic shift. The goal is to ensure that AI adoption does not introduce new barriers to patient care but instead enhances the efficiency, accuracy, and accessibility of health information.

In 2021, Butler-Henderson, Day, and Gray introduced the concept of the HIDDIN workforce, which comprises professionals responsible for specialized functions in Health Informatics, Digital, Data, Information, and kNowledge (HIDDIN) (Butler-Henderson et al., 2021). Reddy and Cooper (2021) outlined several key ways AI will influence this workforce, including automating administrative tasks (Stanfill & Marc, 2019), creating a demand for new competencies in data management and analytics, and introducing complex ethical and governance challenges. To address these transformations, structured education, regulatory adjustments, and strategic workforce development will be essential. The scope of these transformations will require collaboration between industry leaders, policymakers, educators, and frontline workers to ensure a balanced and equitable approach to AI integration.

As AI gains prominence through increased adoption of large language models (LLMs) and other digital tools, the health information profession is actively preparing for these inevitable changes. This preparation is primarily focused on the following key areas:

- **Integration of AI in Healthcare Workflows**: AI is increasingly applied in diagnostics, clinical decision support, and automation of routine healthcare tasks. The workforce must be prepared to collaborate with AI systems and integrate them into existing workflows seamlessly. AI-driven automation can reduce clinician burnout, minimize errors, and improve patient outcomes when implemented effectively.
- **Development of AI Training and Education**: Despite AI's growing role in healthcare, there remains a gap in formal AI training for health professionals. Future healthcare education will need to incorporate fundamental AI concepts, algorithms, and data science principles. Medical and health informatics curricula will need to be redesigned to equip professionals with AI competencies that align with industry needs and ethical considerations.
- **Shifting Roles and Responsibilities**: AI adoption will transform traditional job functions, necessitating new skills in data interpretation, AI model validation, and decision-making in collaboration with AI systems. Practitioners will leverage AI-driven capabilities, including machine learning analytics, computer vision, and natural language processing, in their daily work. Additionally, the rise of AI-assisted diagnostics and robotic process automation will require interdisciplinary collaboration to ensure seamless workflow integration.
- **Ethical and Regulatory Challenges**: AI introduces significant ethical and regulatory considerations, including bias, privacy concerns, and liability issues. The workforce must be equipped to manage these risks and ensure responsible AI deployment. Ensuring transparency in AI decision-making and mitigating algorithmic biases will be crucial for maintaining public trust and compliance with evolving legal frameworks.
- **Digital Literacy and AI Adoption**: Successful AI implementation depends on improved digital literacy and the willingness of professionals to adopt new technologies. Healthcare organizations must invest in training and policy development to facilitate this transition. Digital transformation strategies should emphasize change management, user-friendly AI interfaces, and continuous learning opportunities to ensure seamless AI adoption.
- **Future Training Needs**: While some professionals will require advanced AI expertise to serve as advisors and specialists, others will focus on integrating AI into routine healthcare practices. A dedicated subset of professionals will also be responsible for developing and delivering AI education to the broader workforce. Establishing AI competency frameworks and certification programs will help standardize AI knowledge across healthcare roles.
- **Governance as a Priority**: To address ethical, regulatory, and compliance concerns, AI data governance frameworks will be essential. These frameworks will oversee AI technologies throughout their lifecycle, from development and deployment to long-term use and eventual decommissioning. Standardized governance models will ensure accountability, data security, and ethical AI usage across healthcare settings.

Health information roles are largely in the tertiary care sector; however, roles in primary care are evolving rapidly with the integration of AI. Health information professionals play a crucial role in supporting the use of AI to enhance patient care, streamline operations, and improve outcomes. One of the primary roles is managing EHRs and ensuring data quality. Given that AI relies heavily on accurate and comprehensive data to function effectively, health information professionals will be increasingly critical in the primary care sector for maintaining the integrity of patient records, ensuring that data is complete, accurate, and up-to-date. This involves regular audits, data validation, and implementing best practices for data entry and management. By using AI-powered tools to analyze large datasets and extract meaningful insights, the health information workforce can support value-based healthcare. These insights can help primary care providers identify trends, predict health outcomes, and make informed decisions about care and planning. For example, predictive analytics can be used to identify patients at high risk of developing chronic conditions, allowing for early intervention and preventive care. Health information professionals must be skilled in using these tools and interpreting the results to support clinical decision-making. The health information workforce is involved in developing and implementing policies and procedures to ensure the ethical use of AI in primary care. This includes addressing issues related to data privacy, security, and consent. Health information professionals must ensure that AI applications comply with relevant regulations and standards and that patient data is protected at all times. By establishing robust governance frameworks, health information professionals can help build trust in AI technologies and ensure their responsible use in primary care settings.

They also play a key role in training and educating clinical staff on the use of AI technologies. This includes providing training on how to use AI tools, understanding the limitations and potential biases of AI, and ensuring that staff are comfortable and confident in using these technologies. By fostering a culture of continuous learning and innovation, health information professionals can help clinicians stay up-to-date with the latest advancements in AI and healthcare technology.

As AI continues to evolve, so too must the health information workforce. By embracing continuous learning, fostering collaboration between AI and human expertise, and implementing robust governance measures, healthcare professionals can ensure that AI enhances, rather than replaces, the essential work they perform in advancing healthcare outcomes. The future of AI in healthcare will be defined by how well the workforce adapts, ensuring that technology serves as a tool for innovation, efficiency, and improved patient care rather than a disruptive force that displaces essential human expertise.

12.3 Research and Initial Results

Over the past decade, research on the evolving health information workforce has consistently emphasized the growing need for technical expertise, particularly in informatics, analytics, and information governance. The initial findings in 2014 highlighted the workforce's minimal engagement in informatics and analytics roles, setting the stage for subsequent studies that documented a gradual but definitive shift toward these technical domains (Sandefer et al., 2014). Surveys conducted in 2015 (Sandefer et al., 2015) and a job analysis in 2017 (Marc et al., 2017) reinforced the increasing demand for professionals with analytical and leadership skills, while traditional roles such as medical coding showed signs of decline. The trajectory of research revealed a critical gap between workforce needs and educational preparedness, emphasizing the need for targeted curricula and credentialing initiatives to equip health information professionals for the rapidly evolving healthcare landscape.

The necessity for a well-rounded technical skill set became more apparent in 2016 when an evaluation of biomedical and health informatics training programs exposed a disconnect between educational content and real-world workforce demands (Khairat et al., 2016). While these programs improved employability, concerns emerged regarding graduates' readiness to handle the complexities of healthcare data and IT infrastructure. Further research in 2019 identified global trends in health information jobs, with roles increasingly aligning with health IT, leadership, research, and compliance (Marc et al., 2019; Marc et al., 2021). Countries with advanced digital health adoption demonstrated a higher prevalence of health IT positions, whereas compliance-related roles were dominant in the U.S., further emphasizing the need for workforce development tailored to specific regional demands.

A pivotal moment in this research came in 2019 when the implications of artificial intelligence on the health information workforce were explored (Stanfill & Marc, 2019). The findings underscored AI's potential to disrupt roles in medical coding, data management, privacy, and education, with automation replacing certain functions at a faster pace than initially anticipated. This accelerated adoption of AI-driven processes has heightened the urgency for health information professionals to acquire advanced technical skills in data analytics, AI governance, and system implementation. However, despite these pressing needs, occupational classification systems remain outdated, failing to comprehensively reflect the diverse and evolving roles within the profession. While modifications were made in the 2018 update of the U.S. Standard Occupational Classification system, international classifications have yet to catch up.

The culmination of this decade-long research affirms that the health information profession is at a critical crossroads. The workforce must be equipped with data analysis, leadership, and technology implementation skills to meet the growing clinical, financial, and operational demands of healthcare organizations. However, research from 2022 revealed that accredited curricula for health information programs still lack alignment with industry job postings, with particularly weak coverage in revenue cycle and analytics (Fenton et al., 2022). The 2023 review emphasized the urgent need to modernize educational programs, upskill current professionals, and advocate for more accurate occupational classifications (Nordgren et al., 2023). As artificial intelligence continues to reshape the healthcare landscape, the imperative for a highly skilled, technically proficient health information workforce has never been greater.

In a recent study, Butler-Henderson et al. (2024) examined the challenges in classifying and tracking the health informatics and information management workforce on an international scale. The research highlighted the inadequacies of current occupational classification systems, which often fail to accurately represent the diverse roles within the profession. This misalignment hampers effective workforce planning and the development of targeted educational programs. As AI-driven technologies reshape data management, clinical decision support, and administrative processes, the demand for specialized skills in health informatics, data analytics, and AI governance is surging. However, the inadequacies of current occupational classification systems obscure the visibility of these emerging roles, making it difficult to assess workforce readiness and develop policies that ensure an AI-prepared workforce. Without accurate classification, workforce planning and educational curricula may continue to lag behind industry needs, leaving healthcare organizations struggling to find professionals equipped to manage AI-driven innovations. This highlights the urgency of updating classification frameworks to recognize AI-related competencies and facilitate targeted training initiatives that support the integration of AI into healthcare.

12.4 Implementation Best Practices

AI governance plays a critical role in ensuring that artificial intelligence is implemented ethically, securely, and effectively within healthcare settings. As AI adoption accelerates, health information professionals must be equipped to oversee data quality, bias mitigation, privacy protection, and regulatory compliance. Without a workforce skilled in AI governance, healthcare organizations risk deploying AI solutions that lack transparency, fairness, or adherence to evolving legal and ethical standards. This reinforces the necessity for training programs that specifically address AI governance within health informatics curricula, preparing professionals to manage AI-driven decision-making processes responsibly.

One of the primary training needs for the health information management (HIM) workforce is understanding how AI can be applied to automate and improve the coding processes. AI algorithms can analyze vast amounts of clinical data to identify patterns and generate accurate codes for diagnoses and procedures. This automation can significantly reduce the time and effort required for manual coding, allowing the health information workforce to focus on more complex tasks. However, to effectively use these AI tools, the health information workforce needs to be trained in the basics of AI and machine learning, as well as how to interpret and validate the results generated by these systems. Another critical area of training is data management and governance. AI systems rely on large datasets to function effectively, and the health information workforce must ensure that the data used is accurate, complete, and compliant with privacy regulations. This requires a deep understanding of data governance principles, including data quality, data security, and data privacy. The health information workforce needs to be trained in how to manage and curate datasets for AI applications, as well as how to monitor and maintain the integrity of these datasets over time. Additionally, they must be aware of the ethical considerations surrounding AI to safely and responsibly use AI technology, such as bias in algorithms and the potential for misuse of patient data.

The adoption of AI in healthcare also necessitates a shift in the roles and responsibilities of the health information workforce. As we increase the adoption of AI for health information tasks, the health information workforce will need to develop new skills to stay relevant in the workforce. This includes training in advanced data analysis techniques, such as predictive analytics and natural language processing, which can help the health information workforce extract valuable insights from healthcare data. Furthermore, the health information workforce should be encouraged to pursue continuous learning and professional development opportunities to keep up with the rapidly evolving AI landscape.

To bridge the gap between workforce skills and industry needs, collaboration with employers is essential. Health information professionals must be continuously upskilled through employer-driven training programs that align with real-world AI applications in healthcare. They should provide access to training programs and resources that focus on AI and its applications in healthcare. This can include online courses, workshops, and webinars. Partnerships between academic institutions, healthcare organizations, and technology vendors can facilitate targeted upskilling initiatives, ensuring that professionals are not only proficient in AI tools but also capable of guiding their ethical and strategic deployment. Employers should also foster a culture of continuous learning and innovation, encouraging HIM professionals to stay updated on the latest AI advancements and best practices. As AI continues to reshape healthcare operations, the industry must prioritize structured, competency-based training that integrates AI governance principles, equipping health information professionals to lead in an increasingly digital and automated landscape.

Upskilling health information professionals in AI-related competencies is essential for fostering greater preparedness in managing artificial intelligence through the development and implementation of AI governance. As AI systems become integral to healthcare operations—ranging from clinical decision support to revenue cycle management—health information professionals must acquire technical expertise in data stewardship, algorithmic transparency, and regulatory compliance. Without these skills, organizations risk deploying AI without proper oversight, leading to potential issues such as biased decision-making, data privacy violations, or misalignment with healthcare standards. By integrating AI governance training into professional development, health information professionals can proactively address these challenges, ensuring AI technologies are used ethically and effectively.

Furthermore, AI governance relies on the ability to interpret AI outputs, assess risks, and establish policies that align with both industry regulations and patient safety priorities. Upskilling initiatives, such as specialized certifications, hands-on training programs, and employer-driven workshops, can help professionals develop these critical capabilities. When health information professionals are equipped with governance frameworks, they can lead efforts to monitor AI system performance, advocate for transparency in AI decision-making, and implement safeguards that prevent unintended consequences. Ultimately, a well-trained workforce that understands AI governance will not only enhance healthcare organizations' ability to leverage AI responsibly but also strengthen public trust in AI-driven healthcare innovations.

12.5 Challenges and Future Opportunities

The rapid rise of AI in healthcare presents an opportunity to invigorate the health information profession, positioning professionals at the forefront of AI governance, data management, and ethical implementation. AI has the potential to enhance clinical workflows (Tierney et al., 2024), optimize revenue cycle processes (Kilanko, 2023), and drive data-driven decision-making (Bandi et al., 2024). However, realizing this vision requires a clear strategy that aligns with both healthcare priorities and workforce development.

One of the biggest challenges in advancing AI governance within the health information profession is determining where to start. Numerous AI governance frameworks and ethical guidelines have been published, each offering different perspectives on responsible AI use.

Changing the culture in the health information profession to adopt AI requires a multifaceted approach that addresses both the technical and human aspects of this transformation. The successful integration of AI into health information tasks hinges on fostering a culture that is open to innovation, continuous learning, and collaboration. Education and training are paramount to changing this culture. The health information workforce needs to be equipped with the knowledge and skills to understand and utilize AI technologies effectively, safely, and responsibly. This involves not only technical training on how to use AI tools but also education on the potential benefits and limitations of AI in healthcare. By providing comprehensive training programs, healthcare organizations can demystify AI and reduce the fear of the unknown. Additionally, incorporating AI-related topics into the curriculum of health information educational programs can ensure that new graduates are well-prepared to work with these technologies from the outset.

Leadership plays a crucial role in driving cultural change. Leaders within healthcare organizations must champion the adoption of AI and set a positive example for their teams. This involves not only advocating for the use of AI but also demonstrating a commitment to continuous learning and improvement. Leaders should encourage open communication and provide opportunities for staff to voice their concerns and suggestions regarding AI implementation. By fostering a supportive and inclusive environment, leaders can help build trust and buy-in from their teams. Another important aspect is addressing the ethical and regulatory considerations associated with AI in healthcare. The health information workforce must be aware of the ethical implications of using AI, such as issues related to data privacy, bias, and accountability. Organizations should establish clear guidelines and policies to ensure that AI is used responsibly and ethically. This includes implementing robust data governance practices and ensuring compliance with relevant regulations. By addressing these concerns proactively, organizations can build trust and confidence in AI technologies among HIM professionals.

Collaboration and interdisciplinary teamwork are also essential for successful AI adoption and a cultural change in the health information workforce. The workforce should work closely with data scientists, information technology specialists, and clinicians to develop and implement AI solutions that meet the needs of the healthcare organization. This collaborative approach can help ensure that AI tools are user-friendly and effective, and that they complement rather than replace the expertise of HIM professionals. Regular interdisciplinary meetings and workshops can facilitate knowledge sharing and foster a culture of collaboration. Lastly, to achieve cultural change, it is important to celebrate successes and learn from failures. Recognizing and rewarding the efforts of HIM professionals who successfully integrate AI into their workflows can help reinforce positive behaviors and encourage others to follow suit. Similarly, analyzing and learning from any challenges or setbacks encountered during AI implementation can provide valuable insights and help improve future efforts. By fostering a culture of continuous improvement and resilience, healthcare organizations can ensure that the adoption of AI is a positive and sustainable process.

An example of proposed frameworks includes the Governance Model for AI in Healthcare (GMAIH) proposed by Reddy, Allan, Coghlan, and Cooper (2020). This model aims to address ethical, regulatory, and safety concerns associated with AI applications in clinical settings. It is built on four key principles: fairness, transparency, trustworthiness, and accountability. The model advocates for data governance panels to mitigate bias, explainable AI techniques to enhance transparency, education for both clinicians and patients to build trust, and regulatory oversight to ensure safety and legal clarity. Additionally, it proposes a structured approach for AI approval, introduction, and deployment, emphasizing continuous monitoring, audits, and patient-informed consent. By integrating AI governance within clinical workflows, the framework seeks to balance innovation with ethical and legal responsibilities, ensuring AI's safe and effective adoption in healthcare.

Another example is the "AI Governance Framework" published by Hassan, Borycki, and Kushniruk (2025) which focuses on overcoming challenges in AI adoption by ensuring trust, oversight, and structured implementation. It emphasizes transparency, ethics, bias mitigation, data governance, and safety while facilitating AI integration through a structured oversight process. The framework provides guidelines for regulatory compliance, legal accountability, algorithm development, and continuous monitoring. By embedding assessment tools and expert reviews throughout the AI lifecycle—from ideation to sustainability—it aims to ensure responsible and trustworthy AI adoption in healthcare settings.

A final example is the framework proposed by Wirtz et al. (2022), which is not specific to healthcare, but can be generally applied across industries. The proposed AI governance framework is a risk and guideline-based integrative model designed to address AI-related risks in the public sector. It categorizes risks into six areas—technological, informational, economic, social, ethical, and legal—and aligns them with corresponding guidelines to mitigate their impact. The framework consists of four layers: AI risks, AI risk management and guidance, AI guidelines, and AI governance, which together create a structured process for risk assessment, regulation, and ongoing oversight. By incorporating transparency, accountability, and ethical considerations, the framework aims to ensure responsible AI deployment while balancing innovation and risk mitigation.

While these frameworks provide essential guardrails, the sheer volume of recommendations has created confusion about which standards to follow and struggles with where to start in adopting an AI governance framework, making it difficult for organizations and professionals to take decisive action.

Compounding this challenge is the current state of training programs and workforce readiness. While AI and informatics training programs exist, many institutions are experiencing enrollment challenges (Copley & Douthett, 2020), limiting the pipeline of new health information professionals entering the field with AI competencies. At the same time, the healthcare industry urgently needs a technically skilled workforce to implement and oversee AI systems. Delays in workforce development risk slowing the profession's ability to adapt to the AI era, potentially leaving critical gaps in AI governance, compliance, and integration. If the health information workforce is not prepared to engage with AI, healthcare organizations may struggle to implement AI safely and effectively, increasing the risk of unintended consequences such as biased algorithms, data mismanagement, and ethical lapses.

Despite these challenges, there is ample opportunity for health information professionals to engage with AI technologies and proactively upskill in this evolving landscape. Professionals can seek out specialized training in AI governance, participate in interdisciplinary collaborations with data scientists and clinicians, and advocate for the responsible deployment of AI solutions. Additionally, the health information profession is uniquely positioned to play a central role in shaping AI adoption in healthcare by ensuring that AI systems meet regulatory, ethical, and operational standards. By working collaboratively to develop practical, industry-aligned approaches to AI governance, the health information workforce can help healthcare organizations build and deploy AI technologies that not only address pressing workforce shortages but also improve the quality, efficiency, and accessibility of care. Now is the time for health information professionals to take an active role in leading AI initiatives, ensuring that the profession remains a driving force in the future of healthcare innovation.

As AI continues to make its mark on healthcare, it is clear that the success of its integration hinges on the preparedness of the health information workforce. By investing in AI governance, ensuring robust training and education, and addressing ethical and regulatory concerns, health information professionals will play a central role in shaping the future of AI in healthcare. With continuous learning and collaboration across disciplines, the health information workforce can ensure that AI enhances—not disrupts—their essential work in advancing healthcare outcomes. The next phase of healthcare innovation is upon us, and health information professionals are uniquely positioned to play a pivotal role in guiding the way.

References

Bandi, M., Masimukku, A. K., Vemula, R., & Vallu, S. (2024). Predictive analytics in healthcare: Enhancing patient outcomes through data-driven forecasting and decision-making. *International Numeric Journal of Machine Learning and Robots*, *8*(8), 1–20.

Butler-Henderson K., Day, K., & Gray, K. (Eds.). (2021). *The health information workforce: Current and future developments: Health informatics*. Springer.

Butler-Henderson, K., Fenton, S. H., Lalani, K., & Marc, D. T. (2024). Analysis of the international classification of occupations for the health informatics and information management workforce. *Health Information and Libraries Journal.* https://doi.org/10.1111/hir.12556

Copley, P., & Douthett, E. (2020). The enrollment cliff, mega-universities, COVID-19, and the changing landscape of US colleges. *The CPA Journal, 90*(9), 22–27.

Fenton, S. H., Marc, D. T., Kennedy, A., Hamada, D., Hoyt, R., Lalani, K., ... Reynolds, R. B. (2022). Aligning the American health information management association entry-level curricula competencies and career map with industry job postings: Cross-sectional study. *JMIR Medical Education, 8*(3), e38004.

Hassan, M., Borycki, E. M., & Kushniruk, A. W. (2024, October). Artificial intelligence governance framework for healthcare. In *Healthcare management forum*. SAGE Publications.https://doi.org/10.1177/08404704241291226.

Khairat, S., Sandefer, R., Marc, D., & Pyles, L. (2016). A review of biomedical and health informatics education: A workforce training framework. *Journal of Hospital Administration, 5*(5), 10–20.

Kilanko, V. (2023). Leveraging artificial intelligence for enhanced revenue cycle management in the United States. *International Journal of Scientific Advances, 4*(4), 505–514.

Marc, D., Butler-Henderson, K., Dua, P., Lalani, K., & Fenton, S. H. (2019). Global workforce trends in health informatics & information management. In *MEDINFO 2019: Health and wellbeing e-networks for all* (pp. 1273–1277). IOS Press.

Marc, D. T., Dua, P., Fenton, S. H., Lalani, K., & Butler-Henderson, K. (2021). Occupational classifications in the health information disciplines. In K. Butler-Henderson, K. Day, & K. Gray (Eds.), The health information workforce: Current and future developments (pp. 71–78). Springer.

Marc, D. T., Robertson, J., Gordon, L., Green-Lawson, Z. D., Gibbs, D., Dover, K., & Dougherty, M. (2017). What the data say about HIM professional trends. *Journal of AHIMA, 88*(5), 25–31.

Nordgren, E., Kerr, K., & Marc, D. T. (2023). In an evolving industry, HI professionals must also grow and change. *Journal of AHIMA.* https://journal.ahima.org/page/in-an-evolving-industry-hi-professionals-must-also-grow-and-change

Reddy, S., Allan, S., Coghlan, S., & Cooper, P. (2020). A governance model for the application of AI in health care. *Journal of the American Medical Informatics Association, 27*(3), 491–497.

Reddy, S., & Cooper, P. (2021). Health workforce learning in response to artificial intelligence. In K. Butler-Henderson, K. Day, & K. Gray (Eds.), *The health information workforce: Current and future developments: Health informatics.* Springer.

Sandefer, R., DeAlmeida, D. R., Dougherty, M., Mancilla, D., & Marc, D. (2014). Keeping current in the electronic era: data age transforming him's mandatory workforce competencies. *Journal of AHIMA, 85*(11), 38–44.

Sandefer, R., Marc, D., Mancilla, D., & Hamada, D. (2015). Survey predicts future HIM workforce shifts: HIM industry estimates the job roles, skills needed in the near future. *Journal of AHIMA, 86*(7), 32–35.

Stanfill, M. H., & Marc, D. T. (2019). Health information management: Implications of artificial intelligence on healthcare data and information management. *Yearbook of Medical Informatics, 28*(01), 56–64.

Tierney, A. A., Gayre, G., Hoberman, B., Mattern, B., Ballesca, M., Kipnis, P., ... Lee, K. (2024). Ambient artificial intelligence scribes to alleviate the burden of clinical documentation. *NEJM Catalyst Innovations in Care Delivery, 5*(3), CAT-23.

Wirtz, B. W., Weyerer, J. C., & Kehl, I. (2022). Governance of artificial intelligence: A risk and guideline-based integrative framework. *Government Information Quarterly*, 39(4), 101685.

Chapter 13

Building AI Readiness across the Health Workforce

Kathleen Gray, PhD, FAIDH, OAM and
Kerryn Butler-Henderson, PhD, FAIDH

13.1 Introduction

Clinical health professionals, health service users, and people who fulfil many other roles in the health system all must develop new knowledge, skills, and attitudes to engage safely and responsibly with artificial intelligence (AI). Because AI in healthcare is both shaping and being shaped by a diverse workforce and influencing the health sector on many levels, it is important to undertake relevant workforce capability development as an interprofessional, whole-of-health-system project. This chapter recommends three components of such a project: a nationally coherent framework for learning and development to equip clinical health professionals to use AI safely and responsibly; a nationally accessible programme of learning and development to empower patients and consumers to use AI safely and responsibly; and a national cross-sector learning and development community to enable planners, managers, researchers, and developers to use AI safely and responsibly in health. Concerted efforts are needed in all three areas to prepare the workforce to engage appropriately with AI to achieve shared social goals for health care.

13.2 Strategy and Vision for AI

There are expectations that artificial intelligence (AI) in health will contribute to achieving quintuple aims for individual care, population health, system sustainability, equitable care, and meaningful work. People who are able to engage safely and responsibly throughout AI design, development, implementation, scale-up, and evaluation are crucial to this ambition. Clinical health professionals, health service users, and people who fulfil many other roles in the health system all must develop new knowledge, skills, and attitudes for this work. Countries need a coordinated national programme of learning and development for people across the health sector to become capable of working responsibly with the transformations that AI is bringing. This

DOI: 10.4324/9781003621294-16

programme can leverage existing platforms where possible and must support new initiatives where gaps exist.

To be able to trust AI-powered clinical tools, and to be trusted to use them, the clinician of the future will require training to develop new kinds of clinical judgement. Nations will develop a consensus on foundational clinical competencies, scopes of professional practice, and codes of professional conduct related to using AI in healthcare, to provide a basis for patient safety, service quality, and practitioner credentialing across the many different clinical professions that provide patient care. Health service users must be informed and engaged in decisions about the use of AI and its implications for them, to foster public confidence and willingness to invest in AI in health. Involving patients, caregivers, consumers, and citizens in co-designing AI applications and service innovations in healthcare, and advising on ongoing management, requires them to reach a level of literacy that is inaccessible to most people at present.

Further, AI in healthcare is being shaped by a diverse health workforce that is distributed across many organizations. This includes health service administrators, public health workers, business managers and investors, and science and technology researchers and developers. People with cross-cutting interests in the health sector and the tech industry need a community for personal and organizational learning, where mutual exchanges can strengthen national workforce connections, influence contextually appropriate decisions, and keep healthcare at the leading edge of AI innovation and implementation globally.

This chapter explores the changes required to develop a healthcare workforce that can use AI safely and responsibly. It does this through the lens of three recommendations, which are aimed to: achieve curriculum coherence at the level of a national health system; engage service users and citizens as partners in learning and development; and encourage open knowledge and consensus-building within the socio-technical system where AI in healthcare is maturing.

13.3 Implementation Best Practices

This section explores the implementation best practices required to develop a healthcare workforce that can use AI safely and responsibly. It will do this through the lens of three recommendations.

13.3.1 Implementing a Nationally Coherent Framework for Learning and Development to Equip Clinical Health Professionals to Use AI Safely and Responsibly

Healthcare leaders may perceive many ways that AI will be useful for the clinical workforce (Petersson et al., 2023) – but it cannot be assumed that clinical health professionals will embrace the use of AI. They may have either valid criticisms or misconceptions about the impact of AI on the healthcare system generally and on specific diagnosis and treatment practices. They may hold negative views, for example, about: AI replacing human workers, impacts of AI on procedures such as history-taking and physical examination, accuracy of the algorithms, multinational IT companies' motives in the health sector, or legal liability for using AI in treating patients (Nitiéma, 2023). Internationally, expert consensus is emerging about what all health professionals need to know to be able to use AI responsibly. One study has identified 27 competency statements (Çalışkan et al., 2022), reproduced in Table 13.1.

Table 13.1 AI in healthcare competency statements (Caliskan et al., 2022)

Competency Item
Strong Consensus
1. Uses health data in accordance with legal and ethical norms.
2. Acts in accordance with ethical principles while using AI technologies.
3. Uses artificial intelligence applications in accordance with its purpose.
4. Keeps the healthcare records in accordance with AI can process.
5. Uses information based on AI applications in combination with professional knowledge.
6. Values the use of AI for education, service, and research purposes.
7. Explains how AI applications in healthcare offer a solution to which problem.
8. Organises workflow in accordance with the working logic of AI.
9. Uses AI technologies effectively and efficiently in healthcare delivery.
10. Defines the basic concepts of data science.
11. Follows the current developments and the literature regarding the use of AI technologies in healthcare.
12. Works as a team member with field experts in the development process of AI applications.
13. Accesses, evaluates, uses, shares information, and creates new information by using information and communication technologies.
14. Follows the legal regulations regarding the use of AI technologies in healthcare.
15. Expresses the importance of data collection, analysis, evaluation, and safety for the development of AI applications in healthcare.
16. Foresees the opportunities and threats that AI technology can create.
17. Differentiates between the functions and features of AI-related tools and applications.
18. Properly analyses the data obtained by AI in healthcare.
19. Defines the basic concepts and terminology of AI.
20. Defines the basic concepts of statistics.
21. Decides the use of AI technologies in healthcare.
22. Explains how physician knowledge and experience can be used in the development of AI applications.
23. Chooses the proper AI application for the problem encountered in healthcare.
Weak Consensus
1. Explains how AI systems are trained.
2. Explains the limitations of AI technology.
3. Explains the strengths and weaknesses of AI technology.
4. Explains the AI applications used in healthcare services to the patient.

Another study has categorised similar competencies into six major domains (Russell et al., 2022):

(1) Basic knowledge: explain what AI is and describe its healthcare applications;
(2) Social and ethical implications: explain how social, economic, and political systems influence AI-based tools and how these relationships impact justice, equity, and ethics;
(3) Clinical encounters: carry out AI-enhanced clinical encounters that integrate diverse sources of information in creating patient-centred care plans;
(4) Evidence-based evaluation of tools: evaluate the quality, accuracy, safety, contextual appropriateness, and biases of AI-based tools and their underlying data sets in providing care to patients and populations;
(5) Workflow analysis: analyse and adapt to changes in teams, roles, responsibilities, and workflows resulting from the implementation of AI-based tools;
(6) Practice-based learning and improvement: participate in continuing professional development and practice-based improvement activities related to the use of AI tools in healthcare.

In Australia, a national survey has canvassed health education experts' views on AI education for the health workforce in terms of educational strategies, subject matter priorities, meaningful learning activities, desired attitudes, and skills (AAAIH, 2023). Respondents highlighted the importance of education about ethical implications; suitability of large data sets for use in AI clinical applications, principles of machine learning, specific diagnoses, and treatment applications of AI, alterations to cognitive load during clinical work, and interactions between humans and machines in clinical settings. However, the response rate and the responses themselves indicate that educators in most health professions are not well-positioned to provide the learning and assessment that the current and future workforce needs. Respondents outlined barriers to implementing education and training, such as a lack of structures and processes, resource constraints, and cultural adjustments (Gray et al., 2022).

Some nationally contextualised learning resources have been created by the Australian EHealth Research Centre (AEHRC, 2020). However, with no coordination of curriculum or assessment standards among clinical professions at present, education and training providers and accreditors are working independently. Examples include the Royal Australian and New Zealand College of Radiologists curriculum (RANZCR, 2023), and short courses or one-off professional development events designed by universities or private providers, which may emphasise computational, translational, or governance aspects of AI (Reddy & Cooper, 2021). The partnership between the Australian Health Practitioner Regulation Agency, the National Boards of 15 registered health professions, and their respective accreditation authorities potentially offers an avenue to a nationally coherent approach to ensure that current and future clinical health practitioners have the skills and qualifications to use AI responsibly in each profession.

The most developed example of a national approach at present is the collaboration between the UK's National Health Service AI Lab and Health Education England to develop healthcare workers' confidence in AI, as part of HEE's Digital, AI, and Robotics Technologies in Education. They initially looked at what influences confidence in AI among healthcare workers. Recently, they have identified five archetypes of AI-related workforce responsibilities – shapers, drivers, creators, embedders, and users. They note that these will align more with individuals' roles in the development, implementation, and use of AI technologies in healthcare settings than with traditional professional groups, specialisations, or seniority levels. They describe foundational educational and training needs for all professionals, advanced needs for specific roles, and pathways to meet these needs (NHS AI Lab & HEE, 2022).

In the US, the National Academy of Medicine in 2019 released a special publication focusing on the need for healthcare workers to understand the basic concepts, current state of the art, and future implications of the revolution in AI and machine learning. This was followed by a call to action to the health professional education community, which made it clear that "Educators must act now to incorporate training in AI across health professions or risk creating a health workforce unprepared to leverage the promise of AI or navigate its potential perils." (Lomis et al., 2021) Among various responses, a not-for-profit alliance of clinical experts and industry partners has formed to offer clinical professionals peer-reviewed educational content at introductory and advanced levels, and associated credentialing examinations. Its eventual aim is to become the recognised certification board for an AI sub-specialty in various professions (ABAIM, 2023).

China aims to become a global leader in AI by 2030, with significant investments in AI research and development. The Chinese government has implemented policies to integrate AI into healthcare, including the development of AI training programmes for healthcare professionals. These programmes focus on building technical skills and understanding the ethical implications of AI use in healthcare. Additionally, China is leveraging its large population and vast amounts of health data to train AI algorithms and improve healthcare outcomes. Canada is investing heavily in AI research and education, particularly in the healthcare sector, with the Canadian government investing over $400 million over ten years in AI research and training, with a focus on healthcare applications (Government of Canada, 2024). Canadian institutions, such as the Vector Institute for Artificial Intelligence, are developing training programmes and resources to help healthcare professionals understand and utilise AI technologies. And France is investing $1.8 billion in AI technologies, including in healthcare. The French government is promoting the use of AI in healthcare by encouraging private enterprises to share data and collaborate on AI projects. Educational programmes are being developed to train healthcare professionals in AI competencies, with a focus on data privacy, ethical considerations, and the practical applications of AI in clinical settings.

Secondary to the responsible use of AI in clinical care, there is growing interest in how health profession educators might proceed not only to teach about the use of AI in healthcare settings but also to teach a range of clinical concepts by using AI as an educational tool for learning. AI-enabled simulated patients, large language models in clinical communication and documentation, and robotic clinical tutors have the potential to improve the training of health professionals in many domains if educators are enabled to construct learning experiences that are appropriate (Masters, 2023; Paranjape et al., 2019). A rapid scoping review of artificial intelligence in medical education, with broader relevance for health professions education, notes that scholarly reports to date span different educational stages, specialties, purposes, and use cases. As research into practice in this field matures, it is important for educators to be clear about the category of AI, the use case, the educational context and format, the actual software, and whether integrating AI aims to substitute, augment, modify, or redefine aspects of the learning experience (Gordon et al., 2024).

13.3.2 Providing a Nationally Accessible Programme of Learning and Development to Empower Patients and Consumers to Use AI Safely and Responsibly

As AI continues to advance and permeate healthcare, it is crucial to educate citizens, patients, and their unpaid caregivers on the safe and responsible use of AI. AI holds immense potential to transform healthcare, revolutionising diagnostics, treatment, and patient care. However, its adoption must be accompanied by a comprehensive understanding of the ethical, social, and legal implications it entails, by not only healthcare workers but also the patients, their unpaid caregivers, and the broader citizen population. Whilst there is a generally supportive attitude towards AI among consumers, many believe the benefits outweigh the risks in its use; trust in AI is not perceived as highly in healthcare as in other sectors, and there is a lack of understanding about how it is used in healthcare (Aggarwal et al., 2021; Gaczek et al., 2023; Morley, 2023). Comprehension of AI in healthcare is rated as mediocre at best (Fritsch et al., 2022). It is recommended that a nationally accessible programme of learning and development be developed to empower patients and consumers on the safe and responsible use of AI in healthcare, highlighting the importance of ethical considerations, data privacy, bias mitigation, and the development of algorithmic literacy.

The integration of AI in healthcare raises important ethical considerations. AI algorithms are trained on vast amounts of health data, potentially compromising privacy and confidentiality. Educating consumers about the ethical implications of AI is essential to promote the safe and responsible use of data, including ethical guidelines for AI use, AI and privacy and autonomy, and ethical considerations in the development and deployment of AI in healthcare (Calvillo-Gamez, 2019; Wu et al., 2023). Consumers report they are generally accepting of their data being used for AI training, so long as the resultant tool is used to support care decisions, not replace care decisions, indicating a need for ethical considerations for how AI is used in care planning (Mikkelsen et al., 2023). Further, AI applications in healthcare require access to large volumes of sensitive patient data. Education plays a crucial role in promoting awareness of data storage, security, safety, and privacy regulations and compliance, to both understand how the data is used and how to use and safely secure themselves (Morley, 2023). By providing patients and consumers with greater access to their data to use AI for personalised insights, it empowers them to have greater control of their own care (Beets et al., 2023; Morley & Floridi, 2020).

AI algorithms are vulnerable to inheriting biases from the data on which they are trained, potentially leading to discriminatory outcomes. The education of consumers plays a critical role in raising awareness about the presence of bias in AI systems and the need for bias mitigation strategies. Consumers' understanding of the challenges of bias in AI algorithms can help them critically evaluate AI outputs and address disparities. This will alleviate the fear of uniqueness neglect that can lead to resistance from consumers (Longoni et al., 2019). By promoting diversity and inclusivity in AI development, education can foster the development of more robust, fair, and unbiased AI systems (Oronce, 2020).

Further, there needs to be consumer trust in AI for it to be accepted in healthcare. There is an inverse relationship between perceived risk and perceived benefits by consumers; where consumers perceive the risks of AI to be high, the benefits are perceived to be low (and vice versa) (Esmaeilzadeh, 2020). To improve trust in consumers and, in turn, improve acceptance, their AI literacy, or algorithmic literacy, needs to be improved (Wu et al., 2023). Six areas that could potentially be the focus of algorithmic literacy for patients and consumers include AI concepts, AI acceptability, the AI relationship with humans, AI development and implementation, AI strengths and benefits, and AI weaknesses and risks (Young et al., 2021).

One approach to developing AI health literacy to empower patients and consumers to use AI safely and responsibly involves using AI-powered virtual assistants to provide personalised health information and answer consumer queries, thereby enhancing their understanding of AI applications in healthcare. AI chatbots can offer real-time support and education on managing chronic conditions, medication adherence, and preventive care (Cordina, 2024). Similarly, integrating AI into smart health monitoring devices, which can track vital signs and provide users with insights into their health status, fosters a better understanding of AI's role in health management. Health education platforms are leveraging AI to create tailored educational content that addresses individual learning needs and preferences, making complex AI concepts more accessible to consumers (Mandl, 2025). Consumers' comprehension of transparency, explainability, and accountability of AI empowers them to navigate the complex social and ethical dilemmas associated with AI in healthcare effectively (Chen & Szolovits, 2020). As AI technologies become increasingly integrated into healthcare, it is imperative to understand the safe and responsible use of AI. By fostering a comprehensive understanding of AI's ethical, social, and legal implications, consumers can harness the potential of AI while upholding patient rights, privacy, and fairness in healthcare.

13.3.3 Coordinating a National Cross-Sector Learning and Development Community to Enable Planners, Managers, Researchers, and Developers to Use AI Safely and Responsibly in Health

Healthcare is supported by a diverse workforce that is distributed across a variety of organizations and functions and influenced by global trends. Administrators and funders undertake long-term planning, policy-making, and service regulation in localised and centralised settings. Officers and advocates in public health promotion and monitoring organizations analyse and publish information on health system performance, health conditions, and health issues. Business managers and skilled workers in manufacturing and distribution maintain the health supply chain of medicines, medical devices, and myriad consumables. Technology developers and vendors interact in a digital health ecosystem. Biomedical scientists and health services researchers generate new knowledge to improve practice across this spectrum.

This diverse workforce demand for foundational learning about AI is recognised widely and episodically already – in primers, webinars, short courses, and individually tailored staff development (for example, Catania, 2020; AI4PH, 2023; AIHS, 2023; Jäntti, 2021). However, the safe and responsible use of AI at scale in healthcare must engage this workforce in a scaled-up, joined-up learning health system, in which synergies among science, technology, economic incentives, and organizational cultures enable people in many roles to create and share new knowledge continuously, as an integral by-product of service delivery and as a reliable basis for service innovation (Menear et al., 2019).

13.4 Initial Results

The need for continuous, distributed, whole-system learning was illustrated in the COVID-19 pandemic. AI scientists in the multinational technology company Baidu made available to scientific and medical teams an algorithm that reduced the overall time from 55 minutes to 27 seconds to analyse the secondary structure of COVID-19's RNA sequence. Other tech giants IBM, Amazon, Google, and Microsoft provided the computational power of their servers for analysing datasets in epidemiology, bioinformatics, and molecular modelling. People with AI expertise were mobilised to work on multiple problems in local settings, such as care facility capacity, health data security, medical supply bottlenecks, and geographic and demographic infection hotspots (Radanliev et al., 2021). They generated AI-enabled solutions in many places, and others elsewhere scrambled to understand and apply these, often without the benefit of timely coordinated knowledge sharing.

The need is growing exponentially for collaborative learning across the broader health workforce about the who, where, when, why, and how of safe and responsible AI use, as well as about the most current national and international information on developments in AI. This need is driven by the persistent population health repercussions of the pandemic and by other major health system stressors, such as an ageing population, chronic disease, and climate change. The existing research workforce, trained in conventional research methods and research ethics, needs updated learning and development to grasp the ways in which AI is transforming research design, data collection, interpretation, and dissemination (e.g. Mazza et al., 2023; Samuel et al., 2021; Wen & Wang, 2023). In practice, well-designed project- and work-based activities can foster workforce development of this kind. Examples include applying international standards and communication protocols for large-scale data sharing initiatives, staff workplace exchanges across industry sectors and jurisdictions, and working with open platforms and new models for near real-time information dissemination.

13.5 Challenges and Future Opportunities

The integration of AI into the healthcare sector presents a myriad of challenges for the clinical workforce. One of the primary issues is the shortage of healthcare professionals. Many countries face a significant deficit in doctors, nurses, and other healthcare workers, leading to increased workloads and burnout. This shortage is exacerbated by the uneven distribution of healthcare resources, particularly in rural and underserved areas, which struggle to attract and retain qualified professionals. Another challenge is the rising cost of healthcare. As expenses continue to climb, there is mounting pressure on the workforce to become more efficient and productive. AI has the potential to alleviate some of this burden by automating administrative tasks, such as data entry, appointment scheduling, and clinical coding. However, the implementation of these AI-powered tools can disrupt existing workflows, requiring healthcare professionals to adapt to new ways of working.

Bias and data quality are also significant concerns. AI systems rely on large datasets to function effectively, but these datasets can be biased or incomplete, leading to disparities in treatment and outcomes. Ensuring that AI tools are trained on diverse and high-quality data is crucial to their success, and ensuring the clinical workforce understands the impact of their documentation on training data for AI is of critical importance. Additionally, the lack of transparency in AI algorithms can make it difficult for healthcare professionals to trust and adopt these technologies. Privacy and security issues further complicate the adoption of AI in healthcare, with both impacting the trust of the clinical workforce. The use of AI involves the collection and analysis of vast amounts of sensitive health data, raising concerns about data breaches and unauthorised access. Healthcare organizations must implement robust security measures to protect patient information and comply with regulatory requirements. Lastly, there is the challenge of workforce disruption, as the introduction of AI can lead to changes in job roles and responsibilities, with some functions becoming automated. This shift requires healthcare professionals to acquire new skills and adapt to evolving job requirements. Continuous education and training programmes are essential to help the workforce stay current with technological advancements and maintain their competencies.

Despite these challenges, AI offers numerous opportunities to enhance workforce capabilities and improve healthcare delivery. One of the most promising areas is the enhancement of diagnostic accuracy. AI algorithms can analyse medical images, such as X-rays and computerized tomography (CT) scans, to assist in the early detection and diagnosis of diseases. This can reduce the workload of health professionals and improve health outcomes. AI also has the potential to personalise treatment plans. By analysing the clinical history, genetic information, and other relevant data, AI can help healthcare providers develop tailored treatment plans that are more effective and efficient. This personalised approach can lead to better health outcomes and increased satisfaction. AI-powered chatbots and virtual assistants can triage, provide basic health information, and assist in remote consultations. This can increase access to healthcare in underserved areas and reduce the burden on healthcare facilities.

AI can also impact the workforce responsible for administrative or operational tasks. By automating routine tasks, AI can free up healthcare professionals to focus more on the tasks that require human intervention. This can lead to increased job satisfaction and reduced burnout among the workforce. AI also offers opportunities for continuous learning and professional development, providing real-time recommendations, guidance, and feedback, helping them stay current with the latest advancements and best practices. This can enhance their skills and competencies, ultimately leading to better patient care.

13.6 Conclusion

There is a critical need to develop AI capabilities across the diverse stakeholders who comprise the health workforce, so that humans and AI work together towards the fundamental aims of the health system. The chapter describes three recommendations for achieving this. The need for new clinical competencies, professional practice scopes, and codes of conduct to ensure patient safety and service quality is evident. Engaging health service users in AI-related decisions is essential to build public confidence and willingness to invest in AI technologies. Given the global reach and impact of AI, every nation's health system needs a coordinated approach to equip health professionals, other health sector workers, and health service users with the necessary knowledge, skills, and attitudes not only to use AI but also to critique its use as appropriate. Clear approaches at this level can provide the basis for international consensus on good practice. They can also provide ethics and standards guidance for the ongoing work of AI researchers and developers in health sciences and technology fields – roles not to be overlooked among the stakeholders in this workforce.

As AI continues to become more capable than humans – in some ways that increase safety and quality of care and also in other ways that do not – the future of health and care work will be very different from the experiences for which the current workforce has been trained. In scenarios that most people presently in the workforce cannot imagine, AI is likely to support, strengthen, substitute, and supersede familiar aspects of health and care work variously (Moulds & Horton, 2023). Concerted efforts are needed on many fronts to build the capability of the workforce to adapt to operating in well-governed partnerships with AI to achieve shared social goals for health care.

References

AAAIH Australian Alliance for AI in Healthcare. (2023). *Website*. https://aihealthalliance.org/

Aggarwal, R., Farag, S., Martin, G., Ashrafian, H., & Darzi, A. (2021). Patient perceptions on data sharing and applying artificial intelligence to health care data: Cross-sectional survey. Journal of Medical Internet Research, 23(8), e26162.

AI4PH Artificial Intelligence for Public Health. (2023). *Short courses*. https://ai4ph-hrtp.ca/short-courses/

AIHS Australian Institute of Health & Safety. (2023). *Webinar: Artificial intelligence vision and its use in health and safety*. https://www.aihs.org.au/events/webinar-artificial-intelligence-vision-and-its-use-in-health-and-safety

American Board of Artificial Intelligence in Medicine. (2023). https://abaim.org/

Australian e-Health Research Centre. (2020). https://aehrc.csiro.au/ai/

Beets, B., Newman, T. P., Howell, E. L., Bao, L., & Yang, S. (2023, April 4). Surveying public perceptions of artificial intelligence in health care in the United States: Systematic review. Journal of Medical Internet Research, 25, e40337. https://www.jmir.org/2023/1/e40337/

Çalışkan, S. A., Demir, K., & Karaca, O. (2022). Artificial intelligence in medical education curriculum: An e-Delphi study for competencies. PLoS One, 17(7), e0271872. https://doi.org/10.1371/journal.pone.0271872

Calvillo-Gamez, E., et al. (2019). Ethical challenges of artificial intelligence in health. Revista de Calidad Asistencial, 34(3), 160–164.

Catania, L. J. (2020). Foundations of artificial intelligence in healthcare and bioscience: A user friendly guide for IT professionals, healthcare providers, researchers, and clinicians. Academic Press.

Chen, I. Y., & Szolovits, P. (2020). Ethical challenges of AI in health care: Preventing corruption, bias, and negligence. SSRN Electronic Journal. https://doi.org/10.2139/ssrn.3540631.

Cordina, J. (2024). *Harnessing AI to reshape consumer experiences in healthcare.* McKinsey & Company. https://www.mckinsey.com/industries/healthcare/our-insights/harnessing-ai-to-reshape-consumer-experiences-in-healthcare

Esmaeilzadeh, P. (2020). Use of AI-based tools for healthcare purposes: A survey study from consumers' perspectives. BMC Medical Informatics and Decision Making, 20(1), 170.

Fritsch, S. J., Blankenheim, A., Wahl, A., Hetfeld, P., Maassen, O., Deffge, S., Kunze, J., Rossaint, R., Riedel, M., Marx, G., & Bickenbach, J. (2022). Attitudes and perception of artificial intelligence in healthcare: A cross-sectional survey among patients. Digital Health, 8. https://doi.org/10.1177/20552076221116772

Gaczek, P., Pozharliev, R., Leszczyński, G., & Zieliński, M. (2023). Overcoming consumer resistance to AI in general health care. Journal of Interactive Marketing, 58(2–3), 321–338. https://doi.org/10.1177/10949968221151061

Gordon, M., Daniel, M., Ajiboye, A., Uraiby, H., Xu, N. Y., Bartlett, R., ... Thammasitboon, S. (2024). A scoping review of artificial intelligence in medical education: BEME Guide No. 84. Medical Teacher, 46(4), 446–470.

Government of Canada. (2024). Securing Canada's AI advantage: A foundational blueprint. https://ised-isde.canada.ca/site/ised/en/public-consultations/securing-canadas-ai-advantage-foundational-blueprint

Gray, K., Slavotinek, J., Dimaguila, G. L., & Choo, D. (2022). Artificial intelligence education for the health workforce: Expert survey of approaches and needs. JMIR Medical Education, 8(2), e35223. https://doi.org/10.2196/35223

Jäntti, M. (2021). *Studying digital literacy and AI adoption in software engineering & technology companies.* Proceedings of ICSEA 2021, 16th International Conference on Software Engineering Advances, p. 65.

Lomis, K., Jeffries, P., Palatta, A., Sage, M., Sheikh, J., Sheperis, C., & Whelan, A. (2021). Artificial intelligence for health professions educators. NAM Perspectives. https://doi.org/10.31478/202109a

Longoni, C., Bonezzi, A., & Morewedge, C. K. (2019). Resistance to medical artificial intelligence. Journal of Consumer Research, 46(4), 629–650.

Mandl, K. D. (2025). How AI could reshape health care—Rise in direct-to-consumer models. JAMA. https://doi.org/10.1001/jama.2025.0946

Masters, K. (2023). Ethical use of artificial intelligence in health professions education: AMEE Guide No. 158. Medical Teacher, 1. https://doi.org/10.1080/0142159X.2023.2186203

Mazza, L. C., Wallace, J., & Morita, P. (2023). Exploring data visualizations as a tool to make AI more accessible for qualitative researchers in the healthcare field. Population Medicine, 5(Supplement).

Menear, M., Blanchette, M. A., Demers-Payette, O., & Roy, D. (2019). A framework for value-creating learning health systems. Health Research Policy and Systems, 17(1), 1–13.

Mikkelsen, J. G., Sorensen, N. L., Merrild, C. H., Jensen, M. B., & Thomsen, J. L. (2023). Patient perspectives on data sharing regarding implementing and using artificial intelligence in general practice – A qualitative study. BMC Health Services Research, 23(1), 335.

Morley, J. (2023). Thinking critically about AI in healthcare. Oxford Internet Institute, University of Exford.

Morley, J., & Floridi, L. (2020). The limits of empowerment: How to reframe the role of mHealth tools in the healthcare ecosystem. Science and Engineering Ethics, 26(3), 1159–1183.

Moulds, A., & Horton, T. (2023, November). What do technology and AI mean for the future of work in health care? [Online report]. The Health Foundation. https://www.health.org.uk/reports-and-analysis/briefings/what-do-technology-and-ai-mean-for-the-future-of-work-in-health-care

NHS AI Lab & HEE. (2022). Developing healthcare workers' confidence in AI. https://digital-transformation.hee.nhs.uk/building-a-digital-workforce/dart-ed/horizon-scanning/developing-healthcare-workers-confidence-in-ai

Nitiéma, P. (2023). Artificial intelligence in medicine: Text mining of health care workers' opinions. Journal of Medical Internet Research, 25, e41138. https://doi.org/10.2196/41138

Oronce, C. I., Nakagawa, K., Soohoo, M., & Mangurian, C. (2020). Addressing bias in artificial intelligence in health care. JAMA Network Open, 3(10), e2023404.

Paranjape, K., Schinkel, M., Panday, R. N., Car, J., & Nanayakkara, P. (2019). Introducing artificial intelligence training in medical education. JMIR Medical Education, 5(2), e16048. https://doi.org/10.2196/16048

Petersson, L., Svedberg, P., Nygren, J. M., & Larsson, I. (2023). *Healthcare leaders' perceptions of the usefulness of AI applications in clinical work*. Proceedings of European Federation for Medical Informatics Annual Conference, p. 678. https://ebooks.iospress.nl/pdf/doi/10.3233/SHTI230235

Radanliev, P., De Roure, D., Maple, C., & Ani, U. (2021). Methodology for integrating artificial intelligence in healthcare systems: Learning from COVID-19 to prepare for Disease X. AI and Ethics, 1–8.

RANZCR. (2023). Clinical radiology training program handbook (Version 2.1). https://www.ranzcr.com/

Reddy, S., & Cooper, P. (2021). Health workforce learning in response to artificial intelligence. In J. Murphy, W. Goossen, & C. Weber (Eds.), The health information workforce: Current and future developments (pp. 129–137). Springer. https://link.springer.com/chapter/10.1007/978-3-030-81850-0_8

Russell, R. G., Novak, L. L., Patel, M., Garvey, K. V., Craig, K. J., Jackson, G. P., Moore, D., & Miller, B. M. (2022). Competencies for the use of artificial intelligence-based tools by health care professionals. Academic Medicine, 10–97. https://doi.org/10.1097/ACM.0000000000004963

Samuel, G., Chubb, J., & Derrick, G. (2021). Boundaries between research ethics and ethical research use in artificial intelligence health research. Journal of Empirical Research on Human Research Ethics, 16(3), 325–337.

Wen, J., & Wang, W. (2023). The future of ChatGPT in academic research and publishing: A commentary for clinical and translational medicine. Clinical and Translational Medicine, 13(3), e1209.

Wu, C., Xu, H., Bai, D., Chen, X., Gao, J., & Jiang, X. (2023). Public perceptions on the application of artificial intelligence in healthcare: A qualitative meta-synthesis. BMJ Open, 13(1), e066322.

Young, A. T., Amara, D., Bhattacharya, A., & Wei, M. L. (2021). Patient and general public attitudes towards clinical artificial intelligence: A mixed methods systematic review. The Lancet Digital Health, 3(9), e599–e611. https://doi.org/10.1016/S2589-7500(21)00132-1

Appendix A: Key Terminology

Algorithm: Step-by-step procedure or set of rules or procedural calculations that a computer follows to solve a problem or make a decision. AI algorithms are designed to allow machines to learn from data, identify patterns, and make predictions or decisions with minimal human intervention.

AI Agent: An autonomous entity that perceives its environment, processes information, and takes actions to achieve specific goals (e.g., ChatGPT, Google Gemini).

Artificial Intelligence: Any application, machine, or system that can perform human-like intelligence in terms of behaving, sensing, learning, reasoning, and decision-making. More specifically, AI brings together computers and humans to collaborate to improve functions and outcomes, and most applications focus on automation, data processing, personalization, and analytics.

BioBERT: Bidirectional Encoder Representations from Transformers for Biomedical Text Mining, is a pre-trained biomedical language representation model designed to improve performance on biomedical natural language processing tasks.

Change Management: A structured approach used to transition individuals, teams, and organizations from a current state to a desired future state. It involves preparing for, implementing, and reinforcing changes to processes, systems, structures, or behaviors in a way that minimizes resistance and maximizes engagement, effectiveness, and adoption. Planning, training, and communication are key components.

ClinicalBERT: Bidirectional Encoder Representations from Transformers for Clinical Text, is a domain-specific BERT model pre-trained on clinical notes from the MIMIC-III dataset.

Cloud: Due to the enormous size of data, clouds are a network of remote servers hosted on the internet that provide scalable computing resources, data storage, and services that support the development, training, deployment, and operation of AI models.

Deep Fake: Digitally altered images or videos that create disinformation and mislead people into thinking they are real and authentic.

Deep Learning: A type of machine learning that uses multiple layers of neural networks to learn complex patterns in large amounts of data, often used in image and speech recognition.

Deployment: The process of making a trained AI model available for use in a real-world environment where it can generate predictions or perform tasks based on new, incoming data.

Fine-Tune: The process of taking a pre-trained AI model, usually a large general-purpose model, and continuing its training on a specific dataset by adjusting parameters and adapting it to improve results.

Generative AI: An AI model that can create text, images, audio, and video in response to a user prompt

Large Language Model: A type of artificial intelligence model designed to understand, generate, and work with human language. It is called "large" because it is trained on massive amounts of text data, as well as the parameters or internal settings used to adapt and learn patterns.

Machine Learning: A branch of artificial intelligence (AI) that focuses on developing algorithms and models that allow computers to learn from data and make predictions or decisions without being explicitly programmed for every task.

Model: A mathematical representation or structure that has been trained to recognize patterns, make predictions, or perform tasks based on data.

Natural Language Processing (NLP): It is a field of artificial intelligence (AI) that focuses on the interaction between computers and human language. It enables machines to read, understand, interpret, and generate human language in a meaningful way. It allows machines to process and analyze large amounts of natural language data, like speech or text.

Responsible AI: The practice of designing, developing, and deploying AI with values such as being ethical, private, and transparent.

SimCMF: Simple Cross-modal Fine-tuning is a framework designed to adapt vision foundation models, originally trained on natural RGB images, to other imaging modalities with different physical properties (e.g., polarization).

Supervised Learning: A type of machine learning where the model is trained on categorized data with known inputs and outputs.

Training Dataset: The set of data used to train an AI system.

Unsupervised Learning: A machine learning approach where the model identifies patterns or groupings in data without labeled outputs.

Validation: Term used in modeling to ensure that the model fully reflects reality.

Index

For Product Safety Concerns and Information please contact our EU
representative GPSR@taylorandfrancis.com
Taylor & Francis Verlag GmbH, Kaufingerstraße 24, 80331 München, Germany

www.ingramcontent.com/pod-product-compliance
Ingram Content Group UK Ltd.
Pitfield, Milton Keynes, MK11 3LW, UK
UKHW050058200926
475702UK00019B/2902
9781041028888